BAPTIZED IN BLOOD

CHARLES REAGAN WILSON

BAPTIZED
IN
BLOOD

The Religion of the
Lost Cause
1865–1920

THE UNIVERSITY *of* GEORGIA PRESS
Athens

Copyright © 1980 by the University of Georgia Press
Athens, Georgia 30602

Set in 11 on 13 point Goudy Old Style type
Printed in the United States of America

Library of Congress Cataloging in Publication Data

Wilson, Charles Reagan.
  Baptized in blood.
  Bibliography.
  Includes index.
  1. Christianity—Southern States.   2. United States
—History—Civil War, 1861–1865—Religious aspects.
3. Southern States—Civilization.   I. Title.

BR535.W54   277.5   80-126
            ISBN 0-8203-0515-4
            ISBN 0-8203-0681-9 (pbk.)

Paperback edition, 1983

TO MY PARENTS

CONTENTS

Acknowledgments viii

Introduction: Origin and Overview 1

Chapter One
Sacred Southern Ceremonies: *Ritual of the Lost Cause* 18

Chapter Two
Crusading Christian Confederates: *Religious Myth of the Lost Cause* 37

Chapter Three
Abiding Children of Pride: *Theology of the Lost Cause* 58

Chapter Four
A Southern Jeremiad: *Lost Cause Critique of the New South* 79

Chapter Five
Morality and Mysticism: *Race and the Lost Cause* 100

Chapter Six
J. William Jones: *Evangelist of the Lost Cause* 119

Chapter Seven
Schooled in Tradition: *A Lost Cause Education* 139

Chapter Eight
A Harvest of Heroes: *Reconciliation and Vindication* 161

Notes 183

Bibliography 227

Index 251

Acknowledgments

My greatest intellectual debt is to William H. Goetzmann. His personal encouragement and the example of his historical writing have inspired my own efforts; I first wrote on the topic of this study in his seminar on American intellectual and cultural history. Robert M. Crunden offered valuable assistance, helping to exorcise grammatical demons, as well as shaping my views on interdisciplinary studies. When I toiled in what James Dickey has called the "dark, satanic mills" of graduate school, I profited from the guidance of many professors at the University of Texas, both in Austin and in El Paso, especially Norman Brown, Howard Miller, Wayne Fuller, Kenneth Shover, and Yasuhide Kawashima. Kenneth K. Bailey shared his profound knowledge of Southern religious history with me and offered frequent encouragement, as did Carl T. Jackson, who first awakened my interest in intellectual history. I am also grateful to the generous graduate students, some of whom read preliminary chapters, I knew in the departments of American studies and history at the University of Texas at Austin, especially Joseph C. Porter, Thomas W. Cutrer, Mark Smith, Georgia Xydes, William Childs, Richard Tansey, and George Ward. My brother the attorney, C. Martin Wilson III, transcended his status to provide valuable free editorial aid. The dedication of this book to my parents is in grateful acknowledgment of their moral and financial support at crucial times.

Parts of this book originally appeared in the *Journal of Southern History* and the *Tennessee Historical Quarterly*, and appreciation is due the editors of those journals for permission to use the material.

Introduction

ORIGIN AND   OVERVIEW

Thus saith the Lord . . . ask for the old paths, where is the good way, and walk therein, and ye shall find rest for your souls. —Jeremiah 6:16

Apparently they can learn nothing save through suffering, remember nothing save when underlined in blood.
                    —William Faulkner, "The Bear"

THIS IS A STUDY of the afterlife of a Redeemer Nation that died. The nation was never resurrected, but it survived as a sacred presence, a holy ghost haunting the spirits and actions of post–Civil War Southerners. Embodying the dream of Southerners for a separate political identity, the Confederacy was defeated by Father Abraham and an apparently more blessed, as well as more self-righteous, Redeemer Nation. But the dream of a separate Southern identity did not die in 1865. A Southern political nation was not to be, and the people of Dixie came to accept that; but the dream of a cohesive Southern people with a separate cultural identity replaced the original longing. The cultural dream replaced the political dream: the South's kingdom was to be of culture, not of politics. Religion was at the heart of this dream, and the history of the attitude known as the Lost Cause was the story of the use of the past as the basis for a Southern religious-moral identity, an identity as a chosen people. The Lost Cause was therefore the story of the linking of two profound human forces, religion and history. This study examines the product of this connection in the South from the end of the Civil War until the end of World War I. It was a Southern civil religion, which tied together Christian churches and Southern culture.

The religion of the Lost Cause originated in the antebellum period.

Religion's central role in the South did not emerge early in Southern history. To be sure, the first settlers at Jamestown brought their Anglicanism with them, and a strong religious-moral tone existed in Virginia's earliest years, as in the Puritan colonies of New England. Despite the best efforts of clergymen and civil authorities, religion in the South did not become as vital a force as it was in Massachusetts Bay Colony. With the American Revolution, the Church of England in the new United States became the Episcopal church, and its position as the established church of the South ended. A new voluntary system of religious affiliation began in the South, as in the rest of the country, giving rise to the distinctive American denominational configuration. In Dixie, the Baptists and Methodists, who had only moved into the region in the late colonial period, and who had effectively participated in the challenge to the idea of an established church, emerged as the dominant denominations by 1800. This was primarily due to their role in the Great Revival of 1787 to 1805. The revival, which began in Kentucky in 1800, quickly spread to other areas of the South, bringing outcroppings of millennial thought centering on the South and establishing a central evangelical belief system.[1]

After 1805 the revival ebbed but did not dissipate, as spiritual awakenings periodically occurred thereafter. Schisms grew out of this revival era, but the important point was that by 1830 an evangelical unity had settled on the South, accompanied by a conservative orthodoxy of doctrine. While the Baptists and Methodists were numerically dominating the Southern religious picture, the Presbyterians managed to hold their own in terms of influence because their ministers were well educated and their congregations tended to include prominent societal leaders. Similarly, the Episcopal church was the church of the planter class, concentrated in Virginia, coastal South Carolina, and the Mississippi delta. It adapted to the Southern scene by becoming Low Church, giving more attention to morality than to the mysteries of the ritual. In fact, in some areas the church was evangelical in orientation, like the other Southern denominations. Despite the variations between genteel Episcopalians, theologically oriented Presbyterians, and the intensely evangelistic popular denominations, all were united in opposition to rationalism, thus preventing the growth of the Unitarianism that was making inroads among Northerners. "What the Southerner desired above all else in religion," said Richard M. Weaver, "was a fine set of images to contemplate. . . . The contemplation of these images was in itself a discipline in virtue, which had the effect of building up in him an inner restraint." By 1860 a religious culture had been established, wherein a religious outlook and tone permeated society. At a time when Northern religion was becoming increasingly diverse, the Southern denominations remained orthodox in theology and evangelical in orientation.[2]

While these developments were occurring in religion, similar events were changing Southern society's contours and self-image. By 1830 the formerly liberal political South of Thomas Jefferson had become conservative. Intellectually, as William Taylor has shown, it developed a new image of itself as a chivalric society, embodying many of the agrarian and spiritual values that seemed to be disappearing in the industrializing North. The cult of chivalry developed, focusing on manners, women, military affairs, the ideal of the Greek democracy, and Romantic oratory. A plantation legend became the cultural basis for the South's collective action. Of the South's regions, Virginia first developed a distinctive cultural consciousness, deeply infused by themes from the European Romantic movement. In the 1820s the center of Southern power shifted from Virginia to South Carolina, just at the time when the South was becoming aware of its minority status. In South Carolina the dream of Southern nationalism emerged, but not until the 1850s. Although it came from indigenous sources, it closely resembled the ideas of Romantic nationalism then popular in Europe. In the 1850s Southern leaders began more consciously drawing from European ideas. Southerners came to believe in "cultural nationalism," the longing of a homogeneous people (of the same blood and lineage, and possessing common artifacts, customs, and institutions) for national political existence. The stress was on the idea of "peoples," the builders and transmitters of distinct cultures.[3]

Southern religious leaders were not among the major formulators of the dream of Southern nationalism, but they had done their part in creating the conditions for it by encouraging the growth of sectional churches. A major contribution to the preservation of sectional consciousness came in the 1840s, when the two leading denominations, the Baptists and the Methodists, split from their Northern brethren over the issue of slavery. The New School Presbyterians underwent a similar division in 1857, and in 1861, after the start of the war, the Old School Presbyterians of the South formed the Presbyterian Church in the Confederate States of America, with which the New School synod merged in 1864. The Episcopalians did not formally divide, although during the Civil War the Southern dioceses functioned under a separate organization, the Protestant Episcopal Church in the Confederate States of America.[4]

Southern religion also contributed to the defense of Southern society against the growing criticisms of it by militant abolitionists in the North. In the 1840s and 1850s Southerners advanced a pro-slavery argument that defended their society as a high achievement of civilization and attacked the Northern industrial, free society as an inhumane one. Southerners by this time were united in the defense of slavery on the grounds of protection of property and public safety, and these intellectuals who articulated the pro-slavery argument suggested the positive benefits derived from a slave civilization. South Carolina was the leader in this defense, with Southern clergymen playing a prominent role. The pro-slavery argument leaned more heavily on the sanction of the Bible than on anything else. Ministers cited biblical examples of the coexistence of Christianity and slavery, quoted Old Testament approvals of slavery, and interpreted a passage from Genesis to mean that blacks were descendants of the sinner Ham and destined to be forever bondsmen.[5]

By 1861 Southern churches, like other regional institutions, had thus laid the basis for secession. For a generation they had preached of slavery's divine nature and the need to protect it. Unionist sentiment did exist among ministers, and those in the border states urged a policy of moderation after Lincoln's election. But in the crisis of secession and the attack on Fort Sumter in the spring of 1861, Southern clergymen and their institutions made clear their commitment to what they believed was God's cause. Like their counterparts in the North, Southern clerics preached that their cause was a holy one; they interpreted battle victories as God's blessings, and defeats as God's punishments for their failings. A recurring phrase in the Confederate religious lexicon was "baptism of blood." In his sermon "Our National

Sins," preached on November 21, 1860, before Lincoln's inauguration, the distinguished Presbyterian theologian James H. Thornwell called for secession, even though "our path to victory may be through a baptism of blood." In 1862 the Episcopal Bishop Stephen Elliott observed, "All nations which come into existence at this late period of the world must be born amid the storm of revolution and must win their way to a place in history through the baptism of blood." "A grand responsibility rests upon our young republic," said the Episcopal rector B. T. Lacy in 1863, "and a mighty work lies before it. Baptized in its infancy in blood, may it receive the baptism of the Holy Ghost, and be consecrated to its high and holy mission among the nations of the earth."[6] This evocative, powerful terminology suggested the role of war in bringing a redemption from past sins, an atonement, and a sanctification for the future.

Possessing the mechanisms for molding public opinion—clerical leadership, local churches at the heart of the Southern community, higher organizations such as synods, conferences, and associations, and the denominational press—the Southern churches became the most effective morale-building agencies. One of the most ubiquitous ways of reaching the Southern masses was through the declaration of a day of fasting, in humiliation or thanksgiving. Jefferson Davis proclaimed nine of these, and so many more were declared by Congress, state legislatures, and religious bodies that strict compliance with them "might have saved enough food to feed Lee's hungry army," in the words of James W. Silver. Moreover, identifying the Confederate cause as God's cause, preachers rarely criticized it. Although harsh comments about Jefferson Davis filled the secular press, the churches did not judge the Confederate leader. In the last months of war, notes of despair and depression did appear in sermons, as one would expect; nevertheless, ministers retained much more enthusiasm and conviction of ultimate victory than they were able to instill into their congregations. Until the end, they remained an important factor in maintaining law and order and in approving unpopular war measures. While historians have shown that one reason for the Confederacy's collapse was a failure of the will to win, this could not be said of the region's religious leaders.[7]

Southern religion also contributed to the Confederacy through the chaplaincy. The Confederate government made only a half-hearted effort to encourage an effective chaplain system, but the churches took the initiative and coordinated much of the work. The chaplains extended religion's influence into the ranks of the Confederate armies by preaching, praying, counseling, baptizing, confirming, celebrating the sacraments, delivering Bibles and religious tracts, and comforting the wounded. Sometimes they took an active part in the fighting—as in the case of I. T. Tichenor, of an Alabama regiment, who killed a Union colonel, a major, and four privates. Tichenor was only slightly wounded, but many chaplains received severe injuries in battle. Most officers, even if irreligious, wanted chaplains in order to build morale.[8] For the chaplains themselves, as for the soldiers, the war was the greatest personal experience of their lives, and it understandably influenced their later activities. Civil War chaplains had the experiences and made the acquaintances that became the basis for the postwar emergence of an organized movement to remember the past. These chaplains logically became the main celebrants of the Lost Cause rituals after the war.

Christian ministers directed the revivals that occurred in army ranks, especially in Lee's Army of Northern Virginia. In the early months of the war, religion did not play a large role in the camps, but as casualties increased, the Southern soldier showed more interest in matters of the spirit. The first revival erupted in the Army of Northern Virginia in the winter of 1862–63, following the battle of Fredericksburg. After this, revivals came in cycles, decreasing during the times of active campaigning and returning with fervor when the army paused for rest and regrouping. Another awakening occurred during the winter of 1863–64, when Lee's army was camped along the Rapidan River, and the final phase of the Virginia revival came among the troops in the siege along the lines from Richmond to Petersburg in the last months before Appomattox. Meanwhile, smaller and less frequent revivals were occurring in the Army of Tennessee. No revival occurred in the winter of 1862–63, but in the fall of 1863 a memorable one did break out near Dalton, Georgia, where General Joseph Johnston's army went into winter camp. In May, 1864, the movement of Grant against Lee in Virginia ended the revival temporarily, and that of Sherman against Johnston in the West all but finished it. Numerous factors promoted spiritual awakenings: the well-organized efforts of the denominations to supply chaplains and religious materials to the soldiers; the character of the troops, who had come from a revivalistic religious tradition; the decline of confidence following the increasing losses after the second year of conflict; and the ubiquitous spectre of death. The revivals exercised a potent influence on the postwar Southern religious mind. Preachers could recall the memory of communal religious possibility, of a profound religious occurrence in the midst of a profound social event. The Lost Cause profited from these experiences.[9]

At the end of the Civil War, Southerners tried to come to terms with defeat, giving rise to the Lost Cause. "The victory over Southern arms is to be followed by a victory over Southern *opinions*," said the Macon, Georgia, *Christian Index* in March, 1866; others echoed this call for wariness. Fearing that crushing defeat might eradicate the identity forged in war, Southerners reasserted that identity with a vengeance. In *The Lost Cause* (1866), the Richmond editor Edward A. Pollard called for a "war of ideas" to retain the Southern identity. The South's religious leaders and laymen defined this identity in terms of morality and religion: in short, Southerners were a virtuous people. Clergymen preached that Southerners were the chosen people, peculiarly blessed by God. "In a word," says Samuel S. Hill, a leading historian of Southern religion, "many southern whites have regarded their society as God's most favored. To a greater degree than any other, theirs approximates the ideals the Almighty has in mind for mankind everywhere." This attitude helped wed Southern churches to Southern culture. As Hill points out, the "religion of the southern people and their culture have been linked by the tightest bonds. That culture, particularly in its moral aspects, could not have survived without the legitimating impetus provided by religion. Their co-existence helped enable southern values and institutions to survive in the face of internal spiritual contradictions and external political pressures. For the south to stand, its people had to be religious and its churches the purest anywhere."[10] Unfortunately, the self-image of a chosen people leaves little room for self-criticism. This deficiency has led to the greatest evils of the religion-culture link in the South.

Southerners interpreted the Civil War as demonstrating the height of Southern virtue, as a moral-religious crusade against the atheistic North. In light of defeat, the ministers cautioned against decline: they feared throughout the late nineteenth century that their society would not measure up to its past heroic standards of virtue. They feared that, in present and future crises, Southerners would not meet the challenges. They saw that their own age produced only men, not saints—a disturbing thought, when measured against the past. Religious leaders continued the wartime military-political battle for virtue on a new level, by the creation of a civil religion. The antebellum and wartime religious culture evolved into a Southern civil religion, based on Christianity and regional history.

All of this was intimately related to what was happening in the churches themselves. Before the war, an evangelical consensus had been achieved in the South; however, as Samuel Hill observes, "This consensus of the southern population in a single-option religious culture . . . preceded widespread institutional commitment to a religious vision of reality, which did not occur until the period between 1870 and 1930." After the war, Southerners assumed a societal obligation to join their sectional churches. By joining, they were affirming the South's distinctive religious approach. The Baptists and Methodists extended their institutional control, although by 1900 the former had surpassed the latter as the largest regional denomination. An increase in expression of religiosity, at both the personal and organizational levels, accompanied the increased enrollment in the evangelical sects. After the war Southern churches also extended a pervasive puritanical moral code throughout the region.[11] The churches' powerful role in the Civil War, and their expansion and dominance after 1865, suggest that if the Confederacy before dying was baptized in blood, Southern religion was likewise symbolically baptized, born again in a fiery sacrament that gave it new spiritual life. The Southern churches thus profited from the holocaust.

Antebellum Southern religious leaders had proclaimed the doctrine of "spirituality of the church," which meant that the church's role was in religious affairs, not in political and societal matters. As their role in the slavery and secession questions demonstrated, they never followed this idea strictly, and after the war the churches were never as otherworldly as the Bible Belt stereotype might suggest. While Southern religious leaders and their institutions had a sense of social responsibility, they believed in the preservation of the status quo. Social concern, in short, meant a conservative interest in the preservation of religious, political, societal, and economic orthodoxy. Thus the churches organized and agitated for moral reforms enforced by the power of the state, and they avoided any involvement in such social issues as the rights of labor, the poor, and blacks. Ironically, the two dominant Southern denominations, which had begun as dissenting, non-established sects, emerged as virtually the recognized religion of the South. They learned to use the state to gain their goals.[12]

As a result of the evangelical consensus, a lack of pluralism and diversity came to characterize the Southern religious scene. While early nineteenth century American churches had, in general, known this same evangelical unity, new religious forces had entered the picture even before the Civil War, and this trend accelerated in the late nineteenth century. Heterogeneity characterized the Northern religious scene, but the South remained as it had been for decades. To be sure, intense denominational debates and squabbles occurred among the various Protestant sects in the South, but this should not be allowed to obscure the fundamental agreements of the churches. "On such concepts as heaven and hell, God and Satan, depravity and redemption, there was little dispute," writes Kenneth K. Bailey. "Few Southerners doubted the literal authenticity of the Scriptures or the ever-presence of God in man's affairs."[13] This environment fostered the growth of the interdenominational Lost Cause movement; it, in turn, contributed to furthering the atmosphere. The ministers active in the Lost Cause brought with them their own denominational attitudes and ideas, contributing them to the Lost Cause civil religion. At the same time, the experience broadened their own sectarian attitudes.

One should note that, despite their homogeneity, shared values, and moral role in society, the Southern churches were insecure amidst this seeming invincibility. Just as the clergymen worried that Southern society in general would fall into decline, so they dreaded the same development in their own ranks. As John L. Eighmy has pointed out, the Southern Baptists, fearing their own loss of separate status, struggled throughout the late nineteenth century for a distinctive identity

apart from the dead slavery issue, which had been the crystallizing factor in their emergence.[14] This fear in fact existed in the other Southern churches, and it focused especially on the North—its churches, its
religious movements, its immigrants, its power in the American nation—as the underminer of Southern religious hegemony. Southerners brooded that the Civil War had unleashed powerful forces that
would descend from the North, or perhaps even emerge indigenously,
and destroy the Southern Zion they were building. As Eighmy suggests, the Southern Baptists were culturally captive, because they
needed a consensus of separate values from the North in order to
maintain a separate identity. This fear, then, helped mobilize the
churches and enabled them to extend extraordinary influence in preserving the South's status quo.

Judged by historical and anthropological criteria, the civil religion
that emerged in the postbellum South was an authentic religious expression. As Clifford Geertz has said, the anthropological study of religion (in this case, the Lost Cause religion) is a twofold undertaking:
first, one must analyze the symbols and the myth of the Southern faith
for the meanings they embody; second, one must explore the relationship of these meanings to "social-structural and psychological
processes." The South faced problems after the Civil War which were
cultural but also religious—the problems of providing meaning to life
and society amid the baffling failure of fundamental beliefs, of extending comfort to those suffering poverty and disillusionment, and of encouraging a sense of belonging in the shattered Southern community.
The anthropologist Anthony F. C. Wallace argues that religion origi-
nates "in situations of social and cultural stress," and for postbellum
Southerners such traditional religious issues as the nature of suffering,
evil, and the seeming irrationality of life had a disturbing relevancy.
Scholars stress that religion is defined by the existence of a sacred symbol system and its embodiment in ritual. As Geertz has said, the religious response to the threat of disorder in existence is the creation of
symbols "of such a genuine order of the world which will account for,
and even celebrate, the perceived ambiguities, puzzles, and paradoxes
in human experience." These symbols create "long-lasting moods and
motivations" which lead men to act on their religious feelings.[15] At
the heart of the religion of the Lost Cause were the Confederate he-

roes, who came to embody transcendent truths about the redemptive power of Southern society. In fact, the Lost Cause had symbols, myth, ritual, theology, and organization, all directed toward meeting the profound concerns of postwar Southerners.

In addition to fulfilling the role of religion as, in Geertz's words, interpreter of "social and psychological processes in cosmic terms," the Lost Cause religion also fulfilled another function of religion by shaping these processes. Southerners used the Confederate past for their own purposes in the late nineteenth century. Businessmen and politicians employed the glorious legacy for their own needs; Southern ministers did the same. As the guardians of the region's spiritual and moral heritage, they used the Lost Cause to buttress this heritage. This study stresses that Christian clergymen were the prime celebrants of the religion of the Lost Cause. They were honored figures at the center of the Southern community, and most of them had in some way been touched by the Confederate experience. Not all Southern preachers were celebrants of the religion of the Lost Cause, but those who were true believers were frequently prominent church leaders; the phrase "minister of the Lost Cause" identifies those who were most clearly committed to it. These ministers saw little difference between their religious and cultural values, and they promoted the link by constructing Lost Cause ritualistic forms that celebrated their regional mythological and theological beliefs. They used the Lost Cause to warn Southerners of their decline from past virtue, to promote moral reform, to encourage conversion to Christianity, and to educate the young in Southern traditions; in the fullness of time, they related it to American values. Anthony F. C. Wallace has speculated that all religions originate as cultural revitalization movements, and it is clear that Southern ministers and their churches achieved this revitalization by shaping their culture. While some revitalization movements have been utopian, looking to the future, the Lost Cause religion was a revivalistic movement, aiming, as Wallace has said, "to restore a golden age believed to have existed in the society's past."[16]

Race, of course, was of fundamental importance to Southern culture. Indeed, Samuel Hill argues that Southern "racial traditions and practices have served as the cement for the South's cultural cohesion," and that white supremacy was the "primary component" of Southern culture.[17] This study explores another component providing cultural cohesion: the link between Southern history and religion. Race was intimately related to the story of the Lost Cause but was not the basis of it, was not at the center of it. In recent years the needed concentration on the racial dimensions of religion's relationship to culture in the South has left the impression that the secular culture entirely modified and distorted religion. It should now be (and is) historical orthodoxy to assert that the Southern churches were culturally captive. By focusing on this related but still separate issue of the role of religion and history in Southern culture, one can see that the churches exploited the secular culture, as well as vice versa. The culture was a captive of the churches.

The Southern civil religion assumes added meaning when compared to the American civil religion. Sociologist Robert N. Bellah's 1967 article on that topic and his subsequent work have focused scholarly discussion on the common religion of the American people. Bellah has argued that "an elaborate and well-institutionalized civil religion" existed, which was "clearly differentiated" from the Christian denominations. He has defined "civil religion" as the religious dimension of a people "through which it interprets its historical experience in the light of transcendent reality." Like Sidney E. Mead, Bellah saw civil religion as essentially prophetic, judging the behavior of the nation against transcendent values. Will Herberg has proposed that the civil religion has been a folk religion, a common religion emerging out of the life of the folk. He has argued that it grew out of a long social and historical experience that established a heterogeneous society. The civil religion came to be the American Way of Life, a set of beliefs that were accepted and revered by Protestants, Catholics, and Jews. "Democracy" has been the fundamental concept of this civil religion. Scholars have identified the sources of the American public faith in the Enlightenment tradition and in the secularized Puritan and Revivalist traditions. Clearly born during the American Revolution, it was reborn, with the new theme of sacrifice and renewal, in the Civil War.[18]

In the post–Civil War and twentieth-century South, a set of values existed which could be designated a Southern Way of Life. Those values constituted the basis for a Southern civil religion which differed from the American civil religion. Dixie's value system varied from the one Herberg discussed—Southerners undoubtedly were less optimistic, less liberal, less democratic, less tolerant, and more homogeneously Protestant. In their religion Southerners stressed "democracy" less than the conservative concept of "virtue." The Enlightenment tradition played no role in shaping the religion of the Lost Cause, while the emotionally intense, dynamic Revivalist tradition was at its center. The secularized legacy of idealistic, moralistic Puritanism also helped form its character. While the whole course of Southern history provided the background, the Southern civil religion actually emerged from Dixie's Civil War experience. Just as the Revolution of 1776 caused Americans to see their history in transcendent terms, so the Confederate experience led Southerners to a profound self-examination. They understood that the results of the Civil War had clearly given them a history distinct from that of the North. The story of the civil religion included the founding of Virginia in the colonial period, the Southern role in the American Revolution and World War I, and the myths of the Old South and Reconstruction. These aspects were adjuncts to the religion of the Lost Cause, which contained ritualistic, mythological, theological, institutional, educational, and intellectual elements that were simply not present in the other aspects of the civil religion. Without the Lost Cause, no civil religion would have existed. The two were virtually the same.

A civil religion, by definition, centers on the religious implications of a nation. The Southern public faith involved a nation—a dead one, which was perhaps the unique quality of this phenomenon. One of the central issues of the American faith has been the relationship between church and state, but since the Confederate quest for political nationhood failed, the Southern faith has been less concerned with such political issues than with the cultural question of identity. Because it emerged from a heterogeneous immigrant society, the American civil religion was especially significant in providing uprooted immigrants with a sense of belonging. Because of its origins in Confederate defeat, the Southern civil religion offered confused and suffering Southerners a sense of meaning, an identity in a precarious but distinct culture.

The institutional aspect is perhaps the most controversial part of the civil religion debate. The civil religion possesses a basic conceptual ambiguity: Has it been a separate religious tradition? Or simply an aspect of other societal institutions? Recent historical studies have cast doubt on Bellah's assumption of the continuing existence of the American public faith in permanent organizations. Scholars increasingly believe the term "civil religion" should be used to denote episodes of religious nationalism, heavily influenced in the nineteenth century by evangelical Protestantism. This study of the religion of the Lost Cause extends the conceptual debate on this controversial issue of the civil religion. Bellah's original insight seems to have qualified validity for the South; the Southern public religion was not a formal religion, but it was a functioning one. It possessed well-defined elements—mythology, symbolism, theology, values, and institutions— which combined to make a religion. Its elements were not unrelated parts, but interactive aspects of a well-organized, multidimensional spiritual movement. Even more than in the North, a strong connection existed between the Southern civil religion and the Protestant churches. Although support of the Lost Cause was indeed a prominent theme of Southern Protestantism, certainly not all religious leaders supported it. This volume is a study of the Southern civil religion and should not be seen as a study of Southern Protestantism. Its conclusions do not apply to all Southern clergymen; in addition, many important concerns of Southern Protestantism did not touch on the Lost Cause.

The religion of the Lost Cause, moreover, had its own distinctive structure of institutions. John Wilson has shown that voluntary associations have been perhaps the key organizational embodiment of the American public faith, and similar groups (the Confederate veterans' groups and the Ku Klux Klan, as well as the churches and denominational schools) expressed the religion of the Lost Cause. Because of this complex structure of well-defined, interactive institutions, the Southern civil religion, again, should not be seen simply as the equivalent of Southern Protestantism. Southern ministers who believed in the Lost Cause were the indispensable individuals who mediated between their own denominations and the other institutions of the Lost Cause. They were frequently members of these voluntary associations and directed their organizational and ritualistic activities.

While they shaped the religion of the Lost Cause in the image of Southern Protestantism, organizationally the two were not precisely the same.[19]

The persistent Bible Belt image suggests that the South has been long regarded as a sacred society. To be sure, secular values have been potent, especially in the twentieth century; nevertheless, the South's historical development resulted in longer dominance of an "old-time religion." The pioneering sociologist Emile Durkheim argued that all societies have a sacred quality, a spiritual dimension, and that members may even regard their society itself as holy. But postbellum Southerners saw their culture, rather than their society, as enduring. The reality of Southern culture's alleged sacredness was less important than the Southerner's conviction that his regional values and cultural symbols were holy. Another of Durkheim's insights helps to clarify further the question of the South's sacred or secular quality. He pointed out that religion divides existence into two realms, the sacred and the profane, based upon the perception of holiness, rather than upon the inherent qualities of the sacred items. Sacredness depends not on the item itself, but on the perception of its holiness by a religious person or group. The South was sacred to its citizens because they saw a sacred quality in it. The religious culture in Dixie, including the Confederate memory, promoted the self-image of virtue and holiness and thus helped maintain the cohesiveness of Southern society in a critical postwar period.[20]

As historians and novelists have shown, the Southern historical experience that was the basis of the civil religion has been an existential one. Defeat, poverty, guilt, disillusionment, isolation, dread of the future—all have characterized the Southern past. Samuel Hill has recently urged Southerners to look to this past for an authentic religious revelation to set beside their literalistic reading of the biblical revelation. "Surely living this way," he says of the Southern experience, "provokes acknowledgement of the transparency of earthy events to the depths, to ultimate meaning."[21] In fact, Southerners have tapped this existential religious resource in their Lost Cause religion. Taking a profound historical experience based in suffering and linking it with the deeply felt Christian forms resulted in institutionalizing a distinctly existential outlook among Lost Cause devotees.

However, the mythmaking or religious frame of mind represents an effort to overcome existential chaos, substituting a simplified, more comprehensible view of life for the ambiguities and contradictions that give rise to existentialism. Existentialism is a philosophy, attempting to interpret human activities in cosmic terms—but most people are not philosophers. Human beings seem to need some way to control events, if only symbolically; this is what religion does, which distinguishes it from philosophy. Southerners have indeed been existentialists, but (like other human beings) they could not bear their experience without the support of religion—the Lost Cause religion. They have remembered their suffering and have cultivated the memory, in order to affirm that it was not meaningless.

Samuel Hill compassionately hopes that the recovery of the existential dimension of the Southern experience by today's Christian churches in the South will make them somehow wiser and more humane in race relations. One might hope that would be true; however, in the Lost Cause religion the perception of transcendence in the Southern experience did not make the participants in the spiritual mysteries ethically wiser, mainly because Southern ministers tied the Lost Cause religion to the religion of the Southern churches—evangelical Christianity. On the racial question, indeed, the Southern historical experience as embodied in the Lost Cause provided the model for segregation that the Southern churches accepted. In short, the Lost Cause religion did not have the prophetic, ethical dimension that Hill calls for. Its prophetic aspects were not focused on racial issues. As the Southern churches did not judge regional racial ethics from the standpoint of the Christian love ethic, so the Lost Cause religion failed to judge the society's racial patterns. The Southern civil religion also failed after 1900 to perform a prophetic function in regard to the American civil religion. Rather than questioning the nation's purposes in terms of transcendent values, Southerners showed an eagerness to identify with the sometimes self-righteous dreams of glory and virtue of the American nation. Robert Penn Warren has observed that the Confederates offer the lesson that human dignity and grandeur are possible, even amid human weakness and vice. The lesson of the ministers who constructed a religion of the Confederate past is perhaps that they should have paid more attention to human weakness and vice, to the moral ambiguities and uncertainties of life, to the possibility that their society, indeed, any society, might not be virtue incarnate.[22] Southerners, then, made one attempt to utilize the spiritual resources of their historical experience, but, as in all things human, they fell short of perfection.

Chapter One

SACRED SOUTHERN CEREMONIES  RITUAL OF THE LOST CAUSE

RICHMOND REMEMBERED. It had been the capital of the Southern Confederacy, and when the drive for independence failed, Richmond became the eternal city of Southern dreams. It, in turn, preserved the memory of its past and catered to the activities of the Lost Cause. Appropriately, therefore, one of the first large postwar gatherings of defeated Confederate veterans occurred in the city in October, 1875, a decade after the war's end and one year before the nation's centennial celebration. The Confederates met for a celebration, but not of the American nation: they celebrated ritualistically the Confederate nation that still lived in their minds. "Memory-fraught Richmond, the soldier's Mecca," as one Southerner later described it, was the site on October 26, 1875, of the dedication of the first statue in the South to Stonewall Jackson.[1]

As the South's monument-making obsession gathered momentum, days like this one became ever more frequent, reaching a peak between 1890 and 1910. Richmond augmented its position as the capital of the Lost Cause. By 1920 the city boasted a sixteen-acre Hollywood Cemetery, holding the graves of 16,000 Confederate soldiers, including 3,000 from the Gettysburg battlefield; the Hollywood Cemetery Monument, a massive, ninety-foot-high Egyptian-like pyramid of James River granite; the Soldiers' and Sailors' Monument in Libby Hill Park, a seventy-two-foot-high shaft, topped by an eighteen-foot-high bronze Confederate; the Confederate Memorial Institute, known as the South's Battle Abbey; the White House of the Confederacy, which had been made into the United Daughters of the Confederacy Museum; and a carefully maintained Monument Boulevard, with statues of J. E. B. Stuart, Stonewall Jackson, Robert E. Lee, and an elaborate Jefferson Davis monument, dedicated in 1907 before 200,000 people, the largest crowd ever to assemble to honor the Confederates.[2] The 1875 gathering thus represented a beginning of the movement that lasted for generations. Its events and tone were representative of the hundreds of future dedications. It was a truly region-wide meeting to celebrate and to mourn the Confederacy. The Lost Cause was an intellectual attitude, with a marble embodiment in the monuments that proliferated throughout the South after 1875.

Ironically, the first Southern statue dedicated to Stonewall Jackson was the result more of English than of Southern effort. After Jackson died on the battlefield of Chancellorsville in 1863, Virginians immediately began plans to honor him. A group of English gentlemen had the same thought—plus the money to finance it. They subscribed the money for a statue and persuaded the sculptor T. H. Foley to undertake the work.[3] Other projects prevented Foley from completing the statue until the mid-1870s, but, as it turned out, that may have been the most propitious time for it. When they elected Brigadier General James L. Kemper, who had been wounded in Pickett's famous charge at Gettysburg, as governor in 1874, Virginians ended the era of Republican Reconstruction in their state. Earlier, in 1872, members of the Association of the Army of Northern Virginia had expressed concern that the Reconstruction government would be unfriendly to the idea of a statue to a Confederate hero. After Kemper became governor, the Virginia legislature appropriated $10,000 to defray the cost of transporting and setting up the monument. Although Lexington and Winchester competed against Richmond for the honor of being the statue's home, the capital city was the destined choice.[4]

The day of the dedication displayed a curious mixture of joy and sadness, perfectly capturing the essence of the Lost Cause itself. Balmy Indian summer weather contributed to a festive summer atmosphere among the people; but one could not escape noticing that the year was dying, and that the Indian summer was only postponing death. General Daniel Harvey Hill wrote that the autumn winds sang "a requiem to the 'Lost Cause,' and the dead leaves falling on the base of the pedestal seemed to be Nature's tribute to the lost hero." Richmond spared no expense in decorating for the occasion, but the decorations also contributed to the mixed mood. The American flags on the streets were all new, with deep, rich colors, while the Confederate flags, torn and faded, were authentic ones used in the Civil War. One observer noted, "The flag that floats over the Capitol-grounds is the flag of the conqueror. The conquered banner is wrapped around the dead hero's body in the dead hero's grave." The Confederate veterans dressed in their gray uniforms. Many of the city's decorations blended religious and military motifs; one of the most striking was the Grand Arch at a downtown corner. A Richmond reporter described it:

It was thirty-two feet high and sixteen wide. It was constructed with two tur-reted towers covered with evergreen, with an arch connecting them. On the west side of the arch was inscribed in large letters 'Warrior, Christian, Pa-triot.' Just above this was a painting representing a stone-wall, upon which was resting a bare sabre, a Bible, and a Confederate cap, with the angel of peace ascending, pointing heavenward; and on the pinnacle of the arch, just above this, was a pennant bearing the cross, as the emblem of Christianity. This picture, with the emblem above, was a beautiful design figurative of the blissful rest which our departed hero has long since enjoyed.[5]

The setting might have been that of a popular outdoor religious drama.

The activities began early, with the city's natives and numerous visitors scurrying to obtain the best places from which to view the events of the day. At eleven o'clock the procession (the largest Richmond had ever seen) started moving through the streets, arriving at the capitol grounds an hour and a half later. Almost 50,000 people had gathered for the occasion. Stonewall Jackson was the quintessential Confederate martyr-hero to Southern ministers, so when the first statue to him was dedicated they helped make the occasion a religious one. The procession had included representatives from the Baptists' Richmond College and from denominational societies. Seated on the platform were several clergymen: Robert Lewis Dabney, the unreconstructed Presbyterian theologian who had served on Jackson's staff; the Reverend J. D. Smith, also of the General's staff; Methodist Bishop D. S. Doggett, who gave the invocation; and the day's orator, the Reverend Moses Drury Hoge.[6]

The ceremonies began with Doggett's prayer, which was significant in affirming God's benevolence and omnipotence despite the Confederate defeat. Doggett acknowledged that God always acted in the best interests of His subjects and to the glory of His name, and he thanked Providence for gifted men who fulfilled the "benevolent purposes" of the Creator. Jackson, said Doggett, was such a man. At the heart of Doggett's prayer was a passage relating the day's events directly to religious concerns:

Grant that the monument erected on this spot, to the honor of thy servant, may ever stand as a permanent memorial to thy praise, and a perpetual incentive to a high and holy consecration to thy service, in all the avocations of life. May it silently and effectually inculcate noble ideas and inspire lofty sentiments in all spectators for all time to come. Above all, may it teach the youth of the land the solemn lesson of thy word, that the foundation of true greatness is fidelity to thee.

Governor James L. Kemper then delivered a short address, in which he referred to Jackson as a "Christian warrior," and noted that for all mankind Jackson's career would be an "inspiration, teaching the power of courage and conscience and faith directed to the glory of God." The day's religious rhetoric was obviously not limited to the clergy.[7]

To give the featured oration, the Virginia legislature had unanimously chosen Moses Drury Hoge, pastor of Richmond's Second Presbyterian Church. Tall, lean, and muscular, Hoge stood erect, with the bearing of a military man. Although he sported a stylish mustache as he stood before the crowd, his thinning hair betrayed his advancing age. The son and grandson of eminent Presbyterian clergymen, Hoge was educated at a leading Southern Presbyterian school, Hampden Sydney College of Virginia. He played an important role in the Confederacy, which he believed was waging a war for "civil and religious freedom." While continuing to preach to his Richmond congregation, Hoge at the same time served as a spiritual adviser to many Confederate leaders; he led the daily opening prayer at the Confederate Congress, and served as a volunteer chaplain at the training camp outside Richmond. In that latter position he preached at least three times a week, and sometimes daily, to a total of 100,000 soldiers just before they embarked on their first combat experiences. In 1862 his service to the Confederacy took him abroad. Hoge ran the Northern blockade of the South at Charleston, South Carolina, and sailed to England to obtain Bibles and religious pamphlets for the Southern armies. He superintended the transport of over 300,000 items, which arrived in the Confederacy after again running the blockade. The Southern defeat crushed Hoge. In May, 1865, one month after Appomattox, he wrote to his sister that "God's dark providence enwraps me like a pall." Shattered were his dreams of "a gospel guarded against the contamination of New England infidelity"; as a result, he felt "like a shipwrecked mariner thrown up like a seaweed on a desert shore." His depression and accompanying physical illness continued for a year or so, but eventually he reassured himself that, despite defeat, the South had not been wrong in the war.[8]

On this October day in 1875, then, his own history had prepared Hoge to address the issue of the abiding meaning of the Confederacy. As he faced the gray-clad Confederate veterans, he may have sensed that he was in a time warp—back in the glory days when all things seemed possible for those who loved the Lord and trusted Jefferson Davis. Hoge could not deny defeat, but, as on all such communal Southern occasions, the participants seemed to believe that a holy Confederate spirit descended and touched those present.

Hoge began by comparing the day's activities to the ceremonies of the ancient Greeks. Although peace was the theme of Hellenic festivals, and of this Southern event, Hoge saw a crucial difference between the two in their motivations. The Greek festivals were deficient in morality. Hoge made certain the same could not be said of the monument dedication. In his speech he frequently referred to the day as the inauguration of a new era: a new age of hero-making, of mythmaking. He praised Virginia's heroes of the American Revolution, and he predicted that the Confederate heroes would join them in immortality. "We lay the corner-stone," he said, "of a new Pantheon in commemoration of our country's fame." Southern mythmaking was not always a subtle process.[9]

Hoge then proceeded to the central figure of the day, Stonewall Jackson. Each Confederate hero had a somewhat different image, but in Hoge's speech Jackson functioned as the symbol of the Confederate crusade. Admitting that this general was the "most unromantic of all great men," the preacher said that he still became the "hero of a living romance." Hoge's explanation for this came from an examination of the qualities of Jackson's character. First, he had the traits of a born leader: "strong, adventurous, and indomitable." At the same time, he was as tender as a child. "The eye," he said, "that so often sent its lightning through the smoke of battle, grew soft in contemplating the beauty of a flower." The key to Hoge's oration lay in his discussion of another element of Jackson's character, his piety. Admitting that Jackson would have been great without religion, the preacher insisted that the General's faith made him "purer, stronger, more courageous, more efficient." Hoge cautioned against confusing Jackson's belief in Providence with fatalism, and he denied that any denominational bigotry affected his religion. He also noted that Jackson was a believer in the supernatural, despite his training in physical science. Hoge illustrated the desire of Southerners to purify their heroes of any stain, especially in the crucial area of religion.[10]

After considering the hero himself, Hoge grappled with the central, precipitating factor of the Lost Cause—the meaning of Southern defeat in the Civil War. Success was always pleasant, conceded Hoge, but pleasure was not everything. In a sentence that summed up the Southern religious interpretation of the Confederacy's defeat, Hoge said, "Defeat is the discipline which trains the truly heroic soul to further and better endeavors." Hoge saw hope for the future, and he praised the Southern people, especially the Confederate veterans, for their postwar behavior. Hoge ended his oration with an obligatory statement of the South's willingness to accept defeat, and of its desire for a fair reconciliation with the North; he noted, however, that the federal union was no longer the same as it had been in 1787. He then verbalized the fear of a catastrophe that haunted many Southerners, especially Southern preachers accustomed to thinking in apocalyptic terms:

And if history teaches any lesson, it is this, that a nation cannot long survive when the fundamental principles which gave it life, originally, are subverted. It is true republics have often degenerated into despotisms. It is also true that after such transformation they have for a time been characterized by a force, a prosperity, and a glory, never known in their earlier annals, but it has always been a force which absorbed and obliterated the rights of the citizen, a prosperity which was gained by the sacrifice of individual independence, a glory which was ever the precursor of inevitable anarchy, disintegration, and ultimate extinction.[11]

When Hoge finished, to the applause of the audience, soldiers hauled in the halyards attached to the canvas covering the statue, unveiling the monument to the accompanying sounds of musket and artillery blasts. After a brief pause the members of the Richmond Philharmonic Association performed a hymn of Luther's, "A Castle of Strength Is Our Lord." By three o'clock the official ceremonies were completed, but this was not the real conclusion of the day's events. At the end of the ceremonies Governor Kemper introduced Stonewall Jackson's daughter, Julia, described by a reporter as "a sweet-looking girl of thirteen," to the survivors of the Stonewall Brigade. They removed their hats, stood quietly, and then loudly cheered the hero's child. After she walked to the statue and placed a bouquet of flowers on the pedestal, she returned to her carriage and spoke individually to the men who had fought under her father's command. Some of them cried softly when they met her.[12]

The sacred ceremony of October 26, 1875, was the ritualistic expression of the religion of the Lost Cause. Ritual is crucial to the emergence of a religion, because, as Clifford Geertz has argued, it is "out of the context of concrete acts of religious observance that religious conviction emerges on the human plane." "The primary phenomenon of religion is ritual," says Anthony F. C. Wallace. In a chaotic world, ritual embodies a symbol system that is "simple and orderly." The Lost Cause ritual celebrated a mythology which focused on the Confederacy. It was a creation myth, the story of the attempt to create a Southern nation. According to the mythmakers, a pantheon of Southern heroes, portrayed as the highest products of the Old South civilization, had emerged during the Civil War to battle the forces of evil, as symbolized by the Yankee. The myth enacted the Christian story of Christ's suffering and death, with the Confederacy at the sacred center. In the Southern myth the Christian drama of suffering and salvation was incomplete: the Confederacy lost a holy war, and there was no resurrection. But the clergy still insisted, even after defeat, that the Confederacy had been on a righteous crusade.[13]

As Mircea Eliade has said, "It is not enough to *know* the origin myth, one must *recite* it." While other Southern myths could be seen in literature, politics, or economics, the Confederate myth reached its true fulfillment after the Civil War in a ritualistic structure of activities that represented a religious commemoration and celebration of the Confederacy. One part of the ritualistic liturgy focused on the religious figures of the Lost Cause. Southern Protestant churches have been sparse in iconography, but the Southern civil religion was rich in images. Southern ministers and other rhetoricians portrayed Robert E. Lee, Stonewall Jackson, Jefferson Davis, and many other wartime heroes as religious saints and martyrs. They were said to epitomize the best of Christian and Southern values. Their images pervaded the South and were especially aimed at children. In the first two decades of the twentieth century, local chapters of the United Daughters of the Confederacy undertook successfully to blanket Southern schools with portraits of Lee and Davis. Lee's birthday, January 19, became a holiday throughout the South, and ceremonies honoring his birth frequently occurred in the schools. Lee's picture on the wall was the center, the altar, for the event. The effect of these images could be seen in an anecdote concerning Father Abram Ryan, the poet-priest who wrote elegies about the Confederacy. He saw his young niece standing before a painting of the death of Christ, and he asked her if she knew who the evil men were who had crucified her Lord. "Instantly she replied, 'O yes I know,' she said, 'the Yankees.'"[14]

An explicit linkage between Confederate images and religious values was made in the stained glass windows placed in churches to commemorate Confederate sacrifices. One of the earliest of these was a window placed in Trinity Church, Portsmouth, Virginia, in April, 1868, while federal troops still occupied the city. The window portrayed a biblical Rachel weeping at a tomb, on which appeared the names of congregation members who had died during the war. One church, Biloxi, Mississippi's Church of the Redeemer, "the Westminster of the South," was particularly prominent in this activity at the turn of the century. St. Paul's Episcopal Church in Richmond, which had been the wartime church of many Confederate leaders, established a Lee Memorial Window, which used an Egyptian scene to connect the Confederacy with the stories of the Old Testament. Even a Negro Presbyterian congregation in Roanoke, Virginia, dedicated a Stonewall Jackson memorial window in its church. The pastor had been a pupil in Jackson's Sunday school in prewar Lexington, Virginia.[15]

Wartime artifacts also had a sacred aura about them, with Bibles that had been touched by the Cause being especially holy. The United Daughters of the Confederacy kept under lock and key the Bible used when Jefferson Davis was sworn in as president of the Confederacy. More poignantly, a faded, torn overcoat belonging to a Confederate martyr named Sam Davis was discovered in 1897; when it was shown to a United Daughters of the Confederacy meeting, the response was, said an observer, first "sacred silence" and then weeping. One Presbyterian preacher, James I. Vance, noted that, "like Elijah's mantle of old, the spirit of the mighty dwells within it." Museums were sanctuaries containing such sacred relics. The Confederate Museum in Richmond, formerly the White House of the Confederacy, contained a room for each seceding state. These rooms housed medals, flags, uniforms, and weapons from the Confederacy, while the Solid South Room contained the Great Seal of the Confederate States.[16]

If the Southern civil religion had its reverent images and its sacred artifacts, it also had its hymns. One group of hymns sung at postwar Confederate gatherings was made up of Christian songs straight from the hymnal. "Nearer My God to Thee," "Abide with Me," and "Praise God from Whom All Blessings Flow" were popular, but the favorite of this category was "How Firm a Foundation," which was sung at Stonewall Jackson's funeral and at the funeral of every member of Jefferson Davis's family after the Civil War. It was the official hymn in the United Daughters of the Confederacy's "Ritual."[17]

Another group of Confederate sacred songs was created by putting new words to old melodies. The spirit of "That Old-Time Religion" was preserved when someone retitled it "We Are Old-Time Confederates." Several Southerners, including one minister, wrote new versions of the classic "Dixie," but conservative veterans' organizations rejected this tampering with tradition. J. B. Stinson composed new verses for the melody of "When the Roll Is Called Up Yonder I'll Be There":

When this time with us shall be no more and final taps shall sound,
And the Death's last cruel battle shall be fought;
When the good of all the armies shall tent on yonder camping ground,
When the roll is called up yonder, let's be there.

A change from the original lyric was the phrase "let's be there," rather than "I'll be there," indicating a more communal "redemption" in the Confederate version. The next verse used Confederates as evangelical models of behavior:

On that mistless, lonely morning when the saved of Christ shall rise,
In the Father's many-mansioned home to share;
Where our Lee and Jackson call us to their homes beyond the skies,
When the roll is called up yonder, let's be there.

The last verse gave the invitation to obey the call of righteousness:

If all's not well with thee, my comrades, for thy entrance at the gate,
Haste thy calling and election to prepare;
You will find that precious peace, sweet peace,
When the roll is called up yonder, let's be there.[18]

Of special significance was the hymn "Let Us Pass Over the River, and Rest Under the Shade of the Trees," which was officially adopted by the Southern Methodist church. The words in the title were the last words spoken by the dying Stonewall Jackson. Two other hymns, "Stonewall Jackson's Requiem" and "Stonewall Jackson's Way," made similar appeals. At some ceremonial occasions choirs from local churches, or a joint choir representing all the town's denominations, sang hymns. In 1907 Southerners organized the United Confederate Choirs of America, and soon young belles from Dixie, clad in Confederate gray uniforms, were a popular presence at ritual events.[19]

These liturgical ingredients appeared in the ritualistic expressions of the Lost Cause. In the years immediately after the war, Southern anguish at Confederate defeat was most apparent during the special days appointed by the denominations or the states for humiliation, fasting, prayer, or thanksgiving. These special days could be occasions for jeremiads calling prodigals back to the church, prophesying future battles, or stressing submission to God's mysterious providence in the face of seemingly unwarranted suffering.[20] Although Southerners usually ignored the national Thanksgiving Day, complaining that Northerners used that day to exploit the war issue and to wave the bloody shirt, they did celebrate thanksgiving days designated by their own denominations. In general, however, the days of humiliation, fasting, and prayer were more appropriate to the immediate postwar Southern mood.[21]

Southern reverence for dead heroes could be seen in the activities of another ritual event, Confederate Memorial Day. Southern legend has it that the custom of decorating the graves of soldiers arose in Georgia in 1866, when Mrs. Charles William, a Confederate widow, published an appeal to Southerners to set apart a day "to be handed down through time as a religious custom of the South to wreathe the graves of our martyred dead with flowers." Like true Confederates, Southern states could not at first agree among themselves on which day to honor, but by 1916 ten states had designated June 3, Jefferson Davis's birthdate, as Memorial Day. Women played a key role in this ritual, as they were in charge of decorating the graves with flowers and of organizing the day's other activities. It was a holy day, "The Sabbath of the South." One Southern woman compared her sisters to the biblical Mary and Martha, who "last at the cross and first at the grave brought their offerings of love." Another noted that the aroma of flowers on Memorial Day was "like incense burning in golden censers to the memory of the saints."[22]

A third ritual was the funeral of a wartime hero. The veterans attending the funerals dressed in their gray uniforms and acted as pallbearers, or honorary ones, and provided a military ceremony. Everything was done according to the "Confederate Veteran's Burial Ritual," which emphasized that the soldier was going to "an honorable grave." "He fought a good fight," said the ritual, "and has left a record of which we, his surviving comrades, are proud, and which is a heritage of glory to his family and their descendants, for all time to come." These ceremonies reiterated what Southerners heard elsewhere—that, despite defeat, the Confederate experience proved them a noble, virtuous people. Moreover, the Confederate funeral included the display of the Confederate flag, the central symbol of the Southern identity. Sometimes dramatically placed over the hero's casket just before it was lowered into the ground, at other times the folded battleflag took the floral form of "a pillow of immortelles" under the hero's head. Even when Southerners again honored the American flag, they continued cherishing the Stars and Bars as well.[23]

The dedication of monuments to the Confederate heroes was a fourth ritualistic expression of the Lost Cause. In 1914 the *Confederate Veteran* magazine revealed that over a thousand monuments existed in the South; by that time many battlefields had been set aside as pilgrimage sites containing holy shrines. Preachers converted the innumerable statues dotting the Southern countryside into religious objects, almost idols, that quite blatantly taught Christian religious and moral lessons. "Our cause is with God" and "In hope of a joyful resurrection," among the most directly religious inscriptions on monuments, were not atypical. El Dorado, Arkansas, erected a marble drinking fountain to the Confederacy; its publicity statement said—in a phrase culled from countless hymns and sermons on the sacrificial Jesus—that the water in it symbolized "the loving stream of blood" shed by the Southern soldiers. Drinkers from the fount were thus symbolically baptized in Confederate blood. The dedication of monuments became more elaborate as the years went on. Perhaps the greatest occurred in 1907, when an estimated 200,000 people gathered in Richmond for the dedication of a statue to Jefferson Davis. Governor Claude A. Swanson made a featured address as 12,000 members of Confederate veterans' groups marched in the parade to the site on Monument Boulevard. Richmond was the Mecca of the Lost Cause, and Monument Boulevard was the sacred road to it.[24]

Rituals similar to these existed as part of the American civil religion. In both instances, to use Claude Lévi-Strauss's categories, they were partly commemorative rites which re-created the mythical past, and partly mourning rites which converted dead heroes into revered ancestors. Both common religions confronted the precariousness and instability of collective life; they provided a way for the community to help its citizens meet their individual fears of death. As the sociologist W. Lloyd Warner has said, "Whenever the living think about the deaths of others they necessarily express some of their own concern about their own extinction." By the continuance of the community, the citizens in it achieve a kind of immortality. For Southerners, the need for such a symbolic life was even greater than for Northerners. Union soldiers, too, had sacrificed, but at least the success of their cause seemed to validate their deaths. Postwar Southerners feared that the defeat of the Confederacy had jeopardized their continued existence as a distinctively Southern people. By participating in postwar Lost Cause rituals, Southerners tried to show that the Confederate sacrifices had not been in vain. While similar rituals existed to honor the Grand Army of the Republic, the key point was that Southern rituals began from a very different starting point and had a different symbolic content than Northern ones.[25] Within the bounds of the United States, there was a functioning civil religion not dedicated to honoring the American nation.

Anthony F. C. Wallace suggests that, just as liturgies form ritual, so rituals themselves make up "cult institutions." The permanence of the Lost Cause religion could be seen in its structural-functional aspect, in the institutions which directed its operations, providing ongoing leadership and institutional encouragement.[26] One organizational focus was on Confederate veterans' groups. Local associations of veterans existed in the 1870s and 1880s, but Southerners took a step forward in this activity with the establishment of the United Confederate Veterans in New Orleans in 1889. In 1896 the heirs of the Lost Cause formed another group, the United Sons of Confederate Veterans, which provided more energy for the movement. The frequent meetings held by local chapters of these organizations were an important social activity for Southerners, especially those in rural areas. They also had their holy elements, mostly in the rhetoric used in orations. The highlight of the year for the veterans was the annual regionwide reunion, held in a major Southern city. It was one of the most highly publicized events in the South. Railroads ran special trains, and the cities lavishly welcomed the grizzled old men and their entourage of splendidly dressed young women sponsored by the local chapters. Tens of thousands of people invaded the chosen city each year to partake in a few days of the past. The earliest reunions were boisterous gatherings, but that spirit did not prevent an equally religious tone from existing, especially as the veterans aged. In 1899 the reunion was held in Charleston; a city reporter noted that while the veterans were lighthearted at times, they also were as devout as any pilgrim going "to the tomb of a prophet, or a Christian knight to the walls of Jerusalem."[27]

Each day of the reunion began with a prayer, which usually reminded the aging Confederates that religion was at the heart of the Confederate heritage. The Presbyterian clergyman Peyton Hoge, in a prayer at the tenth reunion in 1900, was not subtle in suggesting his view of the typical Confederate's afterlife. He prayed that those present "may meet in that Heavenly Home where Lee, Jackson and all the Heroes who have gone before are waiting to welcome us there."[28] After the invocation, a hymn was usually sung; one favorite was the "Doxology," which ended with the explicitly Christian reference, "Praise Father, Son and Holy Ghost." A memorial service was held each year at a local church as part of the official reunion program that directly linked Christianity and the Confederacy. At the 1920 reunion, for example, the Baptist cleric B. A. Owen compared the memorial service to a Christian sacrament, Holy Communion. In the Communion service, he said, "our hearts are focused upon Calvary's cross and the dying Lamb of God"; in the Confederate sacrament, "we hold sweet converse with the spirits of departed comrades." The dead heroes were "the aristocrats of suffering and sorrow," he said, in a curious phrase that seemed to blend the image of Jesus with that of an Old South planter. In any event, in order to coordinate their work at memorial services and elsewhere, the ministers of the Lost Cause organized a Chaplains' Association before the Atlanta reunion in 1898.[29]

The Nashville reunion of 1897 was probably the single most religiously oriented Confederate meeting. The veterans met at the downtown Union Gospel Tabernacle, which later would be known as Ryman Auditorium, the home of Southern music's Grand Ole Opry. A new balcony was added to the Tabernacle for the 1897 convention, and it was dedicated as a Confederate memorial. Sitting on hard church pews, facing the altar and the permanent baptismal font, the veterans had a rollicking yet sacred time in the sweltering summer heat of the poorly ventilated Tabernacle. Each reunion ended with a long parade, and the 1897 procession was one of the most memorable. The reviewing stand was set up on the campus of the Methodists' Vanderbilt University, where the old veterans paused before continuing their march. The reunion coincided with Tennessee's centennial celebration, which saw the unveiling in Nashville's new Centennial Park of the Parthenon, the replica of the ancient Greek temple, and a mammoth statue of the Greek goddess Athena. The Confederate parade ended in Centennial Park; as the old soldiers entered the grounds, the bells from a nearby tower chimed the hymn "Shall We Gather at the River?" Apparently unintentionally, the ceremony evoked comparisons with the annual Panathenaic Procession in ancient Athens, which went from the lower agora to the Acropolis (the citadel of the city) and then to the Parthenon (the temple of Athena). A difference, however, was that while the ancient rite initiated young Athenian men into the armed forces and thereby into adult status in society, the Nashville procession consisted of old soldiers renewing their status as society's heroes.[30]

If religion pervaded the United Confederate Veterans, it saturated the United Daughters of the Confederacy. The importance of Christianity to the Daughters could be seen in the approved ritual for their meetings. It began with an invocation by the president:

Daughters of the Confederacy, this day we are gathered together, in the sight of God, to strengthen the bonds that unite us in a common cause; to renew the vows of loyalty to our sacred principles; to do homage unto the memory of our gallant Confederate soldiers, and to perpetuate the fame of their noble deeds into the third and fourth generations. To this end we invoke the aid of our Lord.

The members responded, "From the end of the earth will I cry unto Thee, when my heart is overwhelmed; lead me to the rock that is higher than I." After similar chanted exchanges, the hymn "How Firm a Foundation" was sung, followed by the reading of a prayer composed by Episcopal Bishop Ellison Capers of South Carolina, himself a Confederate general before entering the ministry. After the prayer, the president then read the Lord's Prayer, and the meeting or convention began its official business.[31]

The Daughters provided an unmatched crusading zeal to the Lost Cause religion. A typical local chapter motto was that of the Galveston, Texas, group: "With God Everything, Without God Nothing." The members rarely seemed to doubt that God was on their side. Cornelia Branch Stone entitled her 1912 pamphlet on Confederate history a "U.D.C. Catechism for Children," a title which suggested the assumed sacred quality of its contents. The Daughters took an especially aggressive role in preserving the records of the Southern past. These were sacred documents, viewed by the women in a fundamentalist perspective. Mrs. M. D. Farris of Texas urged the organization in 1912 to cooperate in guarding its archives, "even as the children of Israel did the Ark of the Covenant."[32]

The second organizational focus for the Southern civil religion was the Christian churches. The religion of the Lost Cause and the Christian denominations taught similar religious-moral values, and the Southern heroes had been directly touched by Christianity. The God invoked in the Lost Cause was distinctly biblical and transcendent. Prayers at veterans' gatherings appealed for the blessings of, in J. William Jones's words, the "God of Israel, God of the centuries, God of our forefathers, God of Jefferson Davis and Sidney Johnston and Robert E. Lee, and Stonewall Jackson, God of the Southern Confederacy." Prayers invariably ended in some variation of "We ask it all in the name and for the sake of Christ our dear Redeemer." At the 1907 veterans' reunion, the Reverend Randolph McKim, like other preachers before and after him, invoked the third person of the Christian godhead, praying for "the blessing of the Holy Ghost in our hearts." The references to Christ and the Holy Ghost clearly differentiated the Southern civil religion from the more deistic American civil religion. The latter's ceremonies rarely included such references because of the desire to avoid potential alienation of Jews, who were a small percentage of the Southern population. In Dixie, the civil religion and Christianity openly supported each other. To Southern preachers, the Lost Cause was useful in keeping Southerners a Christian people; in turn, Christianity would support the values of society.[33]

Certainly, the most blatant connections between religion and the Confederacy were made during Confederate rituals. The evidence is that, in their normal Christian services, Southerners did not worship the Confederacy. Nevertheless, Southern religious journals, books, and indeed pulpits were the sources of Lost Cause sentiments. Church buildings were the most frequently used temples for Memorial Day activities, funerals of veterans, and memorial meetings held when prominent Confederates died. Such gatherings were interdenominational, with pastors from different religious bodies participating. A spirit of interdenominationalism had existed in the wartime Confederate armies, and it survived in the postbellum South in the attitudes of the Lost Cause. The overwhelmingly Protestant character of Southern religion facilitated the growth of the ecumenical Lost Cause religion, which, in turn, furthered Protestant ecumenicism. Although predominantly Protestant, Southern religion was not manifested in one church, but was ecclesiastically fragmented. The Lost Cause provided a forum for ministers and laymen from these differing churches to meet as participants in a common spiritual activity. Preachers occasionally made reference to particular denominational beliefs, but since Southerners shared so many of the same doctrines a basis for cooperation existed. Moreover, despite the Protestant orientation of the Lost Cause, Catholics and Jews were not excluded from it. Members of these faiths joined the Confederate groups, and priests and rabbis occasionally appeared at Lost Cause events. Catholics and Jews accepted the Protestant tinge of the religion of the Lost Cause and made their own contributions to it.[34]

The Southern churches proved to be important institutions for the dissemination of the Lost Cause. Despite the opposition of some clerics, on Sunday morning, November 27, 1884, congregations across the South contributed to a well-promoted special collection to finance a Robert E. Lee monument in Richmond. The denominational papers approvingly published such appeals from Confederate organizations for support, editorially endorsed Lost Cause fund raising, recommended Confederate writings, and of course praised the Lost Cause itself. The Confederate periodicals, in turn, printed stories about Christianity which seemed unrelated to the usual focus on the Civil War. Richmond, the center of Lost Cause activity, was also a religious publishing center. The Episcopalians, Baptists, Methodists, and Presbyterians all published periodicals there, and the Southern Presbyterian Publishing House was located in the city. Nashville was a religious publishing center as well, with the same Confederate-Christian mixture. *Confederate Veteran* magazine, the most important organ of the Lost Cause after 1890, had its offices in, and was published by, the Publishing House of the Southern Methodist church in the city.[35]

The close connection between the churches and the Confederate organizations could be seen in terms of the central experience of Southern Protestantism—evangelism. Confederate heroes were popular choices to appear at Southern revivals. The most influential Southern evangelist, the iconoclastic Georgia Methodist Sam Jones, was a master at having Confederates testify to the power of Christianity in their lives, preferably its inspirational effect on the battlefield. At the same time, a significant feature of the religious rhetoric of the reunions was the insistence on a response from the veterans. The invitation to follow Christ, which was made during the memorial services, was also an invitation to follow once again Robert E. Lee, Stonewall Jackson, and Jefferson Davis. Some of these reunions thus resembled vast revivals, with tens of thousands of listeners hearing ministers reminding them of the imminence of death for the aged veterans, and of the need to insure everlasting life.[36]

One of the most important conclusions about the Christian-Confederate connection was that, despite their suspicion of popery, Southern Christians in the Lost Cause religion invested profound meaning into their Confederate artifacts and symbols. This was an indication that the most ascetic and fundamentalist Southern Christians were not in control of many activities of the Lost Cause. While Methodists and Baptists openly endorsed and participated in the religious atmosphere of the Lost Cause rituals, the Episcopalians played an especially prominent role in the Southern civil religion, particularly in its rituals. This stemmed partly from their position in Southern society: the Episcopal church was the church of the antebellum planter class, and after the war the Episcopalians helped make the Lost Cause a defense of aristocratic values. The role played by the Episcopalians in the Lost Cause also came from their leadership role in the Confederate cause. Jefferson Davis, for example, was a Baptist in Mississippi, but when he moved to Richmond during the Civil War his Episcopal wife persuaded him to change denominations, as much for social as for religious reasons. Bishop John Johns baptized him in the Confederacy's Executive Mansion and later confirmed him at St. Paul's Episcopal Church. St. Paul's was almost the official church of the Confederacy, because of the number of influential men who worshipped there. The army's leadership was laced with Episcopalians, including Lee, Leonidas Polk, and Ellison Capers. During the war Polk baptized or confirmed Generals William J. Hardee, John B. Hood, and Joseph E. Johnston. The denomination also claimed a disproportionate number of chaplains. While the Methodists led all groups, with 200 chaplains, the Episcopalians had at least 65, only 35 fewer than the Baptists. Four Episcopal chaplains later became bishops, and others had done voluntary war work in the army ranks. Again, this wartime participation laid the basis for postwar involvement in the religion of the Lost Cause. Additionally, as the most ritualistic of Southern Protestants, Episcopal churchmen may have been a logical choice for prominence in the highly ritualized religion of the Lost Cause.[37]

In any event, all of the rituals and institutions dealt with a profound problem. The Southern civil religion emerged because the experience of defeat in the Civil War had created a spiritual and psychological need for Southerners to reaffirm their identity, an identity which came to have outright religious dimensions. Each Lost Cause ritual and organization was tangible evidence that Southerners had made a religion out of their history. As with all ritualistic repetition of archetypal actions, Southerners in their institutionalized Lost Cause religion were trying symbolically to overcome history. By repeating ritual, they recreated the mythical time of their noble ancestors and paid tribute to them.[38] Despite the bafflement and frustration of defeat, Southerners showed that the time of "creation" still had meaning for them. The Confederate veteran was a living incarnation of an idea that Southerners tried to defend at the cultural level, even after Confederate defeat had made political success impossible. Every time a Confederate veteran died, every time flowers were placed on graves on Southern Memorial Day, Southerners relived and confronted the death of the Confederacy. The religion of the Lost Cause was a cult of the dead, which dealt with essential religious concerns. Having lost what they considered to be a holy war, Southerners had to face suffering, doubt, guilt, a recognition of what seemed to be evil, and above all death. Through the ritualistic and organizational activities of their civil religion, Southerners tried to overcome their existential worries and to live with their tragic sense of life.

Chapter Two

CRUSADING CHRISTIAN CONFEDERATES  RELIGIOUS MYTH OF THE LOST CAUSE

LIKE ALL RELIGIOUS RITUALS, that of the Lost Cause had its mythology. While related to the myths of the Old South and Reconstruction, the myth of the Lost Cause was a distinct one, having to do primarily with the Civil War itself. While most Southerners paid homage to the Lost Cause, they saw different meanings in it. Politicians and political philosophers, for example, interpreted the Lost Cause as a defense of states' rights, and they waved the gray shirt to enable former Confederates to win election. The most profound and lasting interpretation of the myth of the Lost Cause was the religious one. To distinguish it from other meanings, one can label the religious interpretation of the Lost Cause as the myth of the Crusading Christian Confederates. Myths represent one formulation of a religion's belief system, and at the center of this myth was the idea of virtue. Realizing that Confederate defeat jeopardized what they believed to be essentially religious and moral values, Southern preachers developed a set of symbols of virtue and an overarching myth which embodied the threatened values.

Although time did not radically alter the contours of the myth, changes in Southern intellectual history from 1865 to 1920 did influence the myth's development. The years from 1865 to 1880 were ones of poverty, confusion, and disorganization in Southern life, including its cultural activity; however, during this period the Lost Cause myth emerged. In these years many Southerners, especially military leaders, bickered over defeat and lambasted allegedly disloyal Southerners. Southern ministers, who had been perhaps the most unswervingly loyal of all Confederates, did not generally participate in this bickering, instead maintaining that the Confederacy was a glorious fight for virtue and liberty. Eventually their view triumphed throughout the South. Southern romanticism had never vanished, and the 1880s saw a resurgence, a reintensification, of romanticism with particular importance in sentimentalizing the Confederacy. The 1880s also witnessed the development of the New South creed, which paradoxically both supported and contradicted the myth of the Lost Cause. A third trend in Southern intellectual life was the steady growth of sentiment toward reconciliation with the North. The withdrawal of federal troops in 1877, the Spanish-American War, and World War I were the most important landmarks in this coming together of North and South, and the ministers of the Lost Cause gradually came to share this spirit.[1]

The existence of several Southern myths in the post–Civil War years pointed to the region's special need for mythology in that period. Anthropologists, psychoanalysts, literary critics, and folklorists agree that a myth is an attempt to unify the contradictory, ambiguous experience of a people. In this view, myth is not irrational but is an attempt to impose one's will on a world that is not always logical. In Mark Schorer's words, "It is the chaos of experience that creates [myths], and they are intended to rectify it." Psychoanalysts especially stress the function of myth as a form of "ego defense" against threatening conditions. The defeat of the Confederacy created such chaos, especially in values, and for the ministers it activated the fear of even greater moral anarchy if traditional Southern values died. The myth of the Crusading Christian Confederates enabled the clergy to assert that the Confederacy's values survived the war and would be a stable basis for Southern society.[2]

The psychoanalytic conception of myth as, in Henry A. Murray's words, "a collective dream or fantasy" is also relevant in this context. In a study of frontier mythology, Richard Slotkin has suggested that myth evokes a "sense of total identification and collective participation." Students of culture emphasize that a myth is a cultural artifact, the common possession of a people; it binds a civilization together, just as material artifacts do. Identifying their civilization as distinct from the rest of the United States, and believing that status threatened, Southerners were particularly susceptible to the communal appeal of myth. As Ruth Benedict has said, "Mythology has notoriously represented its makers as chosen people or as the first and uniquely created human beings." Her statement takes added significance in light of the tendency of Southern Protestants to identify themselves with the biblical chosen people, the Israelites.[3]

A myth and its accompanying symbols also provide models of behavior. Mircea Eliade goes so far as to state that "the foremost function of myth is to reveal the exemplary models for all human rites and all significant human activities," which thereby "gives meaning and value to Life." For him, mythology represents "a genuinely 'religious' experience," since it transcends "the ordinary experience of daily life."[4] Southern ministers employed their myth in precisely this way, pointing in their sermons and moral lessons to the behavior of the Confederates as parables of Christian conduct.

One should note that a myth is not a symbol or an image. The phrasing of the myth of the Crusading Christian Confederates conveys the essential fact that a myth is a story, "a novelistic tale," in Ruth Benedict's classic definition, that embodies and orders a people's history. "Myth narrates a sacred history," concluded Eliade. The Confederate myth included symbols and images such as Robert E. Lee, Stonewall Jackson, Jefferson Davis, and Confederate army camp meetings, but it was more all-encompassing than these. It expressed in story form the Southern view of its past.[5]

An important aspect of Southern mythmaking was the tendency of ministers to place their myth in the context of other legends and past history, suggesting that they were aware of their function as mythmakers. Clergymen alluded to the Arthurian tales, visualizing the Confederates "on a field of chivalry more glorious than any since the Round Table." Southerners identified with another lost cause, the failed Scottish rebellion immortalized in the novels of Sir Walter Scott. Another popular comparison was with the ancient Greek heroes. In a 1905 oration the Episcopal minister and Confederate veteran Randolph McKim claimed that the Southern heroes were not matched by Agamemnon, Achilles, Ulysses, Ajax, Militiades, "nor by Leonidas himself at Thermopylae." After considering the ancients, the Baptist preacher S. A. Goodwin, at the time of Jefferson Davis's funeral in 1889, insisted that "In all the galaxy of fame there is no brighter constellation than that of the 'Heroes of the Lost Cause.'"[6]

Ministers of the Lost Cause identified the Confederate crusade with the virtuous American Revolution, especially by linking the names of George Washington and Robert E. Lee as the highest products of Southern civilization. The two were said to share deep religious faith, moral character, and superiority to adversity. Ministers stressed blood ties, real or fantasized, between Confederate and Revolutionary heroes, and they noted that in both wars the virtuous had been invaded and had fought defensively. Clergymen believed that the Confederates had struggled for the same principles as the Americans of 1776. "Putnam and Greene and Washington in 1776 made it absolutely certain that Gordon and Jackson and Lee would come in 1861," said Methodist Bishop Warren A. Candler of Georgia. "The issues involved and the men engaged were wonderfully alike." Another Methodist bishop, Oscar P. Fitzgerald, even blamed the nation's founders for establishing principles that led to war in 1861. Tongue in cheek, he noted that it was "too late to hang any of them on a sour apple tree." Moses Drury Hoge said that those who praised the Revolutionary generation did "homage to virtue," and that the same virtue pervaded the Confederacy.[7]

Southerners took inspiration from identification with the noble ancestors, but they portrayed their wartime adversary in harsh terms. The Yankee represented the monster against which heroes must always contend. In the minds of the ministers of the Lost Cause, the Yankee monster symbolized a chaotic, unrestrained Northern society that had threatened the pristine, orderly, godly Southern civilization. The marauding Yankee, sweeping through and devastating the South, was seen as a typical figure from Northern society. General William Sherman's march to the sea and his devastation of civilian life was the image that Southerners remembered. Just after the war, ministers dwelled on "the deeds of dark and damning atrocity," as Methodist Bishop James O. Andrews phrased it. Going to the marrow of the Southern clergy's attitude, the *Christian Advocate* wrote that the behavior of the Union soldier was a "gross violation of the moral law." The Yankee monster had challenged the moral basis of society. The ministers of the Lost Cause did not soften their views, despite the passage of a half-century or more. In 1913 the Presbyterian pastor James H. McNeilly, noting the growing spirit of North-South reconciliation, remarked that a spirit of good will by the South should not be "interpreted as condoning the barbarities of burning and butchery with which the war was conducted against our people."[8]

Southern clerics charged that the abolitionist Yankee suffered from the same moral failure as the marauding Yankee—an undisciplined, unrestrained liberty. To be sure, Northern abolitionists believed in the sacredness of conscience, as did their Southern brethren; but Dixie's clerics characterized abolitionism as a distortion of conscience, an excuse for license. James H. McNeilly, for instance, in 1901 admitted that the conflict was "a war of conscience against conscience—a conflict of moral ideals"; he added, however, that the Northerners had "a perverted conscience," which resulted in injustice toward the South. An 1871 poem in the Methodist-supported *Southern Review* portrayed early America as an Eden which by 1860 had been spoiled by the appearance of the serpent in the guise of unlimited liberty. The poet lamented the abandonment of biblical revelation as a guide to conduct, and its replacement by "the higher law" of the abolitionist as "the rule of right." A Methodist minister raged that the abolitionist was "a wild fanatic, an insane anarchist, a law-breaker, a wicked intermeddler in other men's matters, who was disloyal to the laws of God and of man." Writing in 1866, the Presbyterian preacher Donald Frazer advised that the abolitionist pretended to be "more humane than God," and he feared that abolitionism had survived the war. As Northern reformers abandoned the South at the end of Reconstruction, the Southern clergy's fear became less acute, but the wartime Yankee remained a symbol for the shattered bonds of divine authority.[9]

Against this enemy, the Southern heroes quested for the holy grail of virtue. "Sublime" was the reverential word Southern religious leaders used most frequently to describe these heroes and their inspirational Confederate crusade.[10] The Confederates were sublime because they fought a war of principle, a war whose lesson was that one should follow conscience despite the risks of defeat. One aspect of this lesson was the traditional American admiration for heroes who follow the call of duty.[11] The inscription on the Confederate Monument in Arlington National Cemetery, written by the Episcopalian Randolph McKim, taught that the Southerners fought not "for fame or for reward," nor "for place or for rank"; instead, they campaigned "in simple obedience to duty." Moses Drury Hoge stressed the religious nature of duty when he insisted that Confederate soldiers "at the sacred call of duty" had "for principle sacrificed all, committing their souls to God and their memories to us who might survive them." The Reverend Carter Helm Jones of Louisville phrased the idea in a revealing way, stating that the Southerners had obeyed a "small voice in their bosoms, the voice of God, which was the voice of duty." Pegram Dargan, a Baptist minister from Darlington, South Carolina, captured the sentiment in a poem:

> There's but one *cause, and they who fight*
> To *set their* conscience *in the right,*
> Tho' Hell *sent forth her friends to aid*
> The *foe, unconquerable is made*
> The *dying patriot's might!*

Dargan suggested that those who fought in response "to *that* battle call," of conscience, could never die in vain. [12]

No Southern minister expressed this idea better than Richard Wilmer, the Episcopal bishop of Alabama but a Virginian by birth and training. Consecrated as bishop by the Confederate Episcopal church and later confirmed by the reunited Episcopal church, Wilmer earned notoriety during the early years of Reconstruction by refusing to lead the Episcopal prayerbook's prayer for the President of the United States. In his autobiography, Wilmer expounded the ministerial belief in the Confederacy's moral and religious significance. He wrote that there were "not only questions of constitutional principle, but deep questions of morals" involved in the war. Wilmer believed that North-ern radicalism was "a pestilent heresy" which had threatened the sanctity of Christianity. "It was this moral and religious feature of the movement in question which called into active opposition the clergy of the South, and forced them to become prominent in the conflict which soon ensued." He frankly argued that Southern ministers sup-ported the Confederacy "to maintain the supremacy of the Word of God, and the teachings of universal tradition." To him, the Con-federates were "a noble army of martyrs"; even more revealing, they were "a small remnant," the saving remnant of the nation, who had fought for righteousness. [13]

The Confederate army itself had a significant role in the story of the Confederacy as a religious-moral crusade. Southern ministers portrayed the army as a carrier of the contagion of morality and of evangelical Christianity. The clergy insisted that the typical Southern soldier came from a religious family and was therefore receptive to spiritual influences. The pervasive image of the mother with her Bible, as well as that of the stern but loving clergyman teaching righteousness to Southern youth, explained this religiosity. Religious leaders agreed that the Confederate soldier emerged from the war even more religious. Despite the demoralizing influences, the Reverend P. D. Stephenson still concluded in 1909 that "the moral tone of our army was exceptionally high." "Thousands," he said, "came out of Christian homes and retained their integrity; thousands became Christians in the army."[14]

The comparison with the Israelites again came to mind. One minister claimed that the army had been protecting a Southern Ark of the Covenant, just as the biblical chosen people did in their wanderings. Writing at the turn of the twentieth century, G. W. Anderson of Nashville also linked the nomadic Confederate army with the Israelites: "As the Israelites at every stop were wont to set up the tabernacle and offer sacrifices to the God of battles, so at every stop (especially with the infantry) Confederates would arrange at once for religious worship—their sacrifies [sic] the souls of brave men, who might fall in battle the next day, offering themselves to God by faith. Doubtless thousands were born of God." Since the Southern people were like one family during the war, the Reverend Randolph H. McKim said that the best analogy was with "the communal life in the early [Christian] Church."[15]

Two books were especially influential in promoting the image of the army as a religious force. William W. Bennett in 1877 published *A Narrative of the Great Revival Which Prevailed in the Southern Armies*, and in 1887 John William Jones, "the Fighting Parson" of the Confederacy, published his *Christ in the Camp; or, Religion in Lee's Army*. Bennett's book was the better written and covered a wider geographical area, but Jones's volume exhausted its subject and proved more influential, touching off a series of reminiscences by others. Both men used the same cliché in describing religion in the army as the "silver

lining of the dark and heavy cloud of war." Both also claimed that religion's greatest role was in raising the morale of the soldiers, preparing
them for holy combat. Both men selected Oliver Cromwell's followers
as the closest to the Confederates in religious motivation, thereby re-
versing the usual Puritan-Cavalier stereotype in regard to the North
and South. In fact, the use of the analogy aptly indicated the adaptation of the Southern self-image to the increasingly moralistic-ascetic
nature of late nineteenth century Southern middle-class religion.
Bennett and Jones agreed on the authenticity of the army's religious
revivals, asserting that Christian laymen and ministers throughout the
South had "entered the battle against the powers of darkness" because
of the revival's influence. They conceived of the Confederate army as
carrying morality and religion into the postwar world, as well as maintaining those elements during the war itself. Such a belief reassured
the clergy that the old-time Confederate virtue continued to influence
Southern souls.[16]

Joseph Campbell, in *The Hero with a Thousand Faces*, notes that one
stage of the hero's journey involves an inner odyssey toward self-un-
derstanding. In the myth of the Crusading Christian Confederates,
the soldier's confrontation with Christianity in the army represented
such an inner journey. The Southern soldier as hero had to renew or
to tap for the first time the religious source of his identity—the Southern identity—by retreating into his soul, in preparation for combat
with evil. The religious revival in the army's ranks was one way of doing this. But the hero traditionally also receives a call to adventure
which takes him to a new spiritual center, such as a forest or the
underworld. Another way for Confederate heroes to achieve deliverance for themselves and their society was in combat itself, with the
battlefield serving as a spiritual center. Combat, in short, had spiritual
significance. The Mississippi minister George C. Harris admitted in a
sermon that while the Confederates, like all men, had been sinners,
those sins were "washed away under the baptism of blood." "Greater
love hath no man than this," he added, "that a man lay down his life
for his friends." The communal aspect was again crucial: the shedding
of blood cleansed all of Southern society, as well as its individual
soldiers.[17]

Clergymen compared the sacrificial, redemptive deaths of the Confederates to the passion of Christ. Carter Helm Jones of Louisville reminded his audience of war veterans of "the memories of your Gethsemane" and "the agonies of your Golgotha." The Reverend H. M. Wharton, through the voice of a fictional clergyman in his novel *White Blood*, made the same point, likening the fate of the South near the war's end to "the blessed Saviour who passed from gloomy Gethsemane to the judgment hall, through the fearful ordeal of being forsaken by His friends, and then on to the bloody Cross." Such Christian references and terminology were more direct in relation to some of the major heroes, such as Lee and the young martyred spy Sam Davis, than to others; still, the basic framework was put forward by ministers to explain the role of the heroes in the myth of the Crusading Christian Confederates.[18]

The Southern clergy could make such a Confederate-Christ connection because of the similarity in their minds between military and religious virtues. The Reverend T. B. Latimore touched on this theme in a 1901 sermon at the Tennessee Confederate Soldiers Home, during which he told the old men that the Bible taught that "God's Church is an army, and that every member of it is a soldier." He pointed out that the rules of enlistment and obedience were the same in the Christian army as in the Confederate one. The Presbyterian Walter B. Capers, in his 1912 biography of his father, Episcopal Bishop and Confederate General Ellison Capers, listed the virtues that he considered both Christian and soldierly: "obedience, endurance, fortitude, bravery, religious belief, kindness and self-sacrifice." Capers and other Southern clergymen stressed that "the militant Christian" was the epitome of righteousness, and that the Confederate army offered many examples of his existence. T. V. Moore, a Methodist pastor, in an 1870 Nashville sermon observed that religion always has inspired military prowess in battle, because a man who thinks his cause is that of God "will feel girded by a more than human power, and shielded by a more than human protection, so that there shall descend npon [*sic*] him in the terrible shock of contending squadrons a baptism of fire that will nerve him to dare in the hour of peril what seems to mere human resources, impossibilities." Moore's phrase "baptism of fire," like "baptism of blood," suggested that combat could be a sanctifying experience.[19]

In the myth of the Crusading Christian Confederates, Southern

preachers suggested that the people of Dixie were particularly virtuous. Fearing a decline in the moral and spiritual quality of Southern
civilization, they urged their contemporaries to maintain the old-time
virtue. The highest symbol of Southern virtue was the Confederate
woman. (Woman is central in mythology because she represents the
totality of attainable knowledge and wisdom.) For Dixie's mythmakers, woman was a threefold image of virtue. In the first place, like
Southern soldiers and leaders, her wartime behavior had been heroic.
Examples of this heroism cited by the clergymen included nursing
wounded soldiers, supervising agricultural work, and making clothing
for fighting men. Episcopal rector DeB. Waddell of Meridian, Mississippi, argued that the courage of Southern women in the Civil War
showed a "moral heroism" that was even greater than that of the Confederate soldier. In a 1901 address, George C. Harris of Mississippi
pointed to the communal aspect when he lauded the "abnegation of
self" shown by Southern women. Such qualities as they had exhibited
differentiated the hero and the heroine from other people, and "this is
what makes a saint."[20]

Southern ministers also viewed woman as virtuous because she was
the symbol of home and family. One can gauge the importance of the
family from the words of the Methodist pastor Albert T. Goodloe, who
called the family "the first and most important divine institution
among men. The family first; the church next." In his 1912 book, *The
Women of the Confederacy*, the Presbyterian minister J. L. Underwood
concluded that "the inspiration of the knightly hearts of the Confederacy was home and the inspiration of a pious home was godly
woman." "The arm of the hero," he said, in a biblical cadence, was
"nerved by his heart, and the heart of John was Mary, and Mary was
the soul of the South." Equally revealing was the 1898 tribute of James
H. McNeilly to Winnie Davis, "the Daughter of the Confederacy." He
wrote that she represented the "old order of things" and embodied
"the sacred memories and the high aspirations for which we fought."
McNeilly warned of the "many forces of this commercial and material
age" that "would degrade our idea and contemn it as mere sentiment."
He especially feared those women who desired to be "a competitor of
man in the struggle of life, in the affairs of business." "God keep the
South true to this mighty sentiment of the past," said the Reverend

James I. Vance, in another tribute to the symbol of Confederate virtue, Winnie Davis, "and may the shaft which rises above the grave of
the Daughter of the Confederacy be another sentinel pointing the
faith of the people upward to that which may be intangible, but is
eternal!" The *Confederate Veteran* magazine printed these tributes, il-
lustrating them with a religious picture captioned "Madonna and
Child."[21]

In mythology, noble knights often fight for the sexual purity of fair
damsels; the same was true in the Southern myth. Ministers identified, in J. L. M. Curry's words, "the purity of our women" with the
purity and the virtue of Southern civilization, and by standing between the Yankee invader and their women Southerners could symbolically preserve their civilization's virtue. Southern ministers and
their women spoke in revealing terms of protecting "the virgin white-
ness of our South," and of preventing assault on the "snow-white citadel of one Southern woman's virtue." John L. Underwood concluded
that the most important effect of the Confederate loss was to un-
shackle black men to lust after "the Paradise tree of the forbidden
fruit—the white women beyond their reach." William Felton, a
Georgia Methodist minister and postwar politician, in a "Sermon on
Lee" praised the General because he had stood between Southern
women "and ruined innocence." His wife, Rebecca, a prominent
churchwoman and later the first woman United States senator, praised
the Confederates for shielding "innocence and virtue from rape and
ruin." Throughout her life she nurtured hate for Yankee "soldiers that
outraged Southern women."[22]

Sexual purity was thus a socially moral virtue, as well as an individually moral one. The point was especially important because of the
Southern clergy's insistence on the need for a manly Christianity. The
Confederates may have been Christian heroes and saints; nonetheless,
they failed to protect their women—and, symbolically, their civilization—from rape by the Yankees. Did the fault lie in an unmanly
religion? The Episcopal divine I. W. Grimes denied the accusation,
saying that "Christianity emasculates no man, makes no man effemi-
ate [sic], depreciates no manly virtue." In contemplating the Confederacy, Underwood summed up the Southern clergy's belief that "a
people's manhood" was its most valuable possession. The Methodist

Christian Advocate agreed, stating that one Stonewall Jackson displayed "manhood enough to outweigh a legion of conceited little fellows" who looked on Christianity as unmanly. To be sure, the ministers consciously conceived of manhood primarily in terms of character, rather than sexuality. But the clergy's preoccupation with the problem of manliness, the symbolism of virtuous woman, and the undeniable loss of self-esteem from defeat suggested that the sexual virtue of their women was a holy idea to Southern religious mythmakers.[23]

While Southern woman symbolized virtue, the Lost Cause myth focused on the crusading Confederate soldier who quested to attain virtue against the wicked Yankee. In mythologies, a hierarchical pantheon of heroes usually exists, and at the apex of the Lost Cause pantheon was Robert E. Lee. To Southern ministers, Lee was the Christian knight representing a romantic Christianity. Father E. C. De La Moriniere, of Mobile's Spring Hill College, in a 1910 address described Lee as the incarnation of his cause, "the Christian Chevalier whose white plume waves before us wherever we cast our eyes." Even "the fatherlands of Sidney and Bayard never produced a nobler soldier, gentleman, and Christian than Robert Edward Lee." Preachers cited anecdotes about Lee's religious life, apocryphal stories about his behavior, and biblical quotations to honor him and to compare him with Christian saints. A revealing allusion was the analogy with Moses, who led his people as Lee led his. Neither man reached the promised land. Christianity was the basis of Lee's "sublime integrity of character," which to the ministers constituted his greatness. They considered him "a model of manhood," and his story became a moral tale. Christian imagery was especially strong in relation to him. Laymen and preachers alike compared Lee's 1861 decision at Arlington to reject the offered command of federal forces with the temptations of Christ. Lee's temptations were money, power, and fame, which he abandoned for principle and honor. One minister described the time before Appomattox as "the anguish-fraught hour of [Lee's] Gethsemane." Lee's postwar image as the sad but proud man seemed to epitomize the Man of Sorrows.[24]

By virtue of his being the supreme Southern cavalier, Lee possessed the chivalric knight's usual duality of masculine-feminine traits. While Southern Christianity posited a close tie between military and religious values, and while it pictured Lee as a bold military man, it paradoxically saw its central hero as supremely gentle. The Lee of the preachers reminds one of the pale, gentle Jesus described in Southern Sunday schools for generations. The Presbyterian cleric Henry A. White characterized General Lee as a "perfect man"; as proof of that perfection he cited Lee's tenderness with children and his patient nursing of his mother before her death. R. Lin Cave, a chaplain in the Army of Northern Virginia, sketched a typical portrait of Lee that lacked only a halo. He praised "his uprightness as a boy, his purity at West Point, his large-heartedness under all conditions, his sympathy and tenderness for the weak and the oppressed—even dumb animals—his great feats of physical and moral courage . . . his ability to resist temptation, his calmness and self-possession, and his reverence for all holy things—a symbol of the highest type of manhood and womanhood to which the world has ever attained." In an understatement, one minister commented that Lee was pure enough to have founded a religion.[25]

Randolph McKim was Lee's most important ministerial interpreter after 1900. Whereas Lee became a national hero between 1900 and 1920, with writers focusing on his character rather than on his military achievements, the clergymen had concentrated on this theme all along. McKim, a soldier on Lee's staff and later rector of the Church of the Epiphany in Washington, D.C., praised Lee as a fellow Episcopal churchman; but, more important, he portrayed Lee as one of "the Christian heroes of the ages." He made the crucial point that Lee suffered with his people, noting the familiar story of Lee's opposition to slavery but love of Virginia. Even more revealing was McKim's belief that the sufferings of the Southern people had "pressed sorely upon him, a true crown of thorns, borne silently and uncomplainingly." "My brethren, in all this we see the embodiment of the deepest principle of the religion of Jesus Christ. Christ, says the apostle, died for all, that they which live should not henceforth live unto themselves." To his soldiers, Lee was "not only their commander, but their Father," he said, capitalizing a significant word. McKim's sketch stands as the finished expression of a half-century of teaching on the religious nature of Lee, the Christian knight who led his people in "a sacred cause, dearer than life."[26]

If Lee was the Christian knight, Jefferson Davis was the Christian martyr. In terms of his image, however, he had the unfortunate luck to die peacefully twenty-five years after the war, rather than sacrificing his life in battle. Davis was a controversial wartime leader, and many Southerners blamed their loss on his leadership and administration. Some people, like General P. G. T. Beauregard, who clashed frequently with the wartime President, never forgave or forgot their grievances, although most Southerners did. Davis was redeemed in their eyes because at the war's end Northern troops arrested him and placed him in irons at Fortress Monroe, Virginia. As the national government contemplated a treason trial against him, Davis symbolically assumed the South's burdens. Southern ministers repeatedly singled out this immediate postwar incident for mention, and it was the key to Davis's later impact. At his death in 1889, it was as if he had not lived past 1866; reading the eulogies to him one almost concludes that he must have been tried for treason, convicted, and probably crucified.[27]

Ministers saw Davis's imprisonment as a parable of Christian behavior. Davis sat in the silence of his prison cell "at midnight alone with his open Bible before him." The fetters he wore were "anklets of gold," and the sound of his chains had "the martyr ring." When "the overbrimming chalice was pressed" to his lips and he heard "the cries of a misguided rabble thirsting for his death," Davis could still ask forgiveness for his foes. Southerners cherished all the relics of his suffering as "Christians hold the wood of the Cross." In short, as John William Jones said, Davis suffered, went to prison, "had indignity put upon him, and was hated, slandered, maltreated and ostracized in the land he had served so faithfully—all *for them.*" Methodist circuit rider and Confederate General Clement Evans concluded that "the Southern people became more distinctively his people" when this persecution occurred, enabling Davis to outlive "obloquy." In a 1910 United Confederate Veterans reunion address, Father E. C. De La Moriniere admitted that Davis "was a thousand times greater in the fetters and confinement of Fortress Monroe than in the Capitol at Richmond." Davis's example of "Christian fortitude" was the outstanding lesson of his life. His suffering had a redemptive quality for the Southern people. The ministers were suggesting that, just as the Christians are a chosen people because of Jesus' suffering, Southerners likewise were holy because martyrs like Davis had redeemed them.[28]

In the 1890–1920 period Davis rivaled Lee as a Southern Christian saint. Davis's death and funeral in New Orleans in 1889 reawakened Southern sectionalism, as did his reinterment in Richmond's Hollywood Cemetery in 1893. Raised a Baptist, he had become an Episcopalian during the Civil War, as mentioned earlier. Both denominations claimed him, and other ministers as well praised his life for being "modeled after the Man of Galilee." The United Daughters of the Confederacy aggressively assumed Davis's cause in the 1890s. His daughter Winnie seemed to epitomize the Daughters' self-image, a fact which undoubtedly increased her father's appeal to the ladies. After 1900 the women of the South placed more stained glass windows commemorating Davis than in honor of Lee. In 1908, the centennial year of Davis's birth, the organization suggested that all Southern schools should offer courses on Davis's "public and religious life." The parable of Jefferson Davis, in other words, was not just for the churches. The national Daughters of the Confederacy convention that same year adopted a resolution urging all clergymen to "study the religious life of Mr. Davis that his pious example may appear for the edification of those under their charge and influence." While Lee was becoming a national hero between 1900 and 1920, Davis was advancing in reputation as a symbol of the South's holiness.[29]

To Southern ministers, Stonewall Jackson was like a stern Old Testament prophet-warrior. In the sentimental, romantic post-1880 period preachers did mention his gentleness, his love for little children, and his tenderness with his daughter; still, their underlying admiration for him was due to his unbending righteousness, the holy wrath he could unleash. In a poem at the 1911 United Confederate Veterans meeting, a Catholic prelate praised General Jackson because "he flung the lightning in his path." He compared this son of Mars "to a whirlwind in its wrath." John William Jones insisted that "stonewall" was a misnomer, and that "thunderbolt," "tornado," or "cyclone" more accurately conveyed his character. These images of bold action contrasted with the gentler, more feminine traits of Lee the cavalier. In fact, Southern clergymen honored Jackson as much as Lee. Curiously,

Jackson was rarely portrayed as a Christ figure, although other Confederates frequently were so pictured. His values, at least as interpreted by Southern preachers, were those of the Old Testament, and in the increasingly moralistic tone of Southern churches and Southern society the general's intense, fanatical faith had special appeal. Jackson was a puritan at heart, and while the romantic South loved the cavalier, the moralistic South could identify with the puritan.[30]

Although baptized by an Episcopal priest when he was a young officer, Jackson later became a Presbyterian with a vengeance. As the *Confederate Veteran* noted in 1917, every day from his conversion to his death "he lived with a constant sense of the presence and providence of God and a living faith in the Lord Jesus Christ." To Southern churchmen he was always "a Stonewall before evil as before the enemy." Henry A. White included Jackson as an exemplar of his denomination's faith in his 1911 *Southern Presbyterian Leaders*. White almost made him an evangelist, saying that Jackson's chief desire was to lead a "converted army."[31]

One of the greatest religious lessons of Jackson's life was the example of his death. Wounded accidentally at the battle of Chancellorsville by one of his own soldiers, Jackson survived long enough to exhibit faith in the face of death. Robert Lewis Dabney sketched the death scene in his 1866 biography of Jackson, writing that the General possessed "perfect peace" as he approached death. He had spent many of his last hours with the chaplain, discussing efforts to achieve greater army observance of the Sabbath. When his pain increased, Jackson asked his wife to sing hymns. His last words were "Let us pass over the river, and rest under the shade of the trees." He died on May 10, 1863, a Sabbath; he had always wanted to die on a Sabbath. Dabney remarked that the lessons of his death were "plain and solemn." John Esten Cooke asserted that the death showed "how a Christian soldier can die," while John William Jones characterized Jackson's demise as a "glorious death."[32]

Lee, Davis, and Jackson were heroes in the Confederacy and afterward. Although their images were not unchanging, the basic outline of each man's role in the myth of the Crusading Christian Confederates was clear by the 1880s. The most important addition to the myth was another hero, Sam Davis of Tennessee. Unlike Lee, Davis, and Jackson, Sam Davis was an obscure private soldier whom the Union army hanged as a spy. In the mid-1890s the editor of the *Confederate Veteran*, Sumner Cunningham, discovered Davis while reading a schoolboy's essay on him, and he launched a campaign to honor this non-Virginia hero. From 1895 to 1905 almost every issue of the magazine contained articles, pictures, poems, or addresses about the "Boy Hero of the Confederacy." The story of Davis's martyrdom was a popular one for Southern sermons, and the *Confederate Veteran* repeatedly urged ministers to preach more frequently about him. Cunningham requested that preachers commemorate November 27, the day of Davis's death. Southern theaters staged the "Sam Davis Drama," a story with so many religious overtones that the Southern Methodist Publishing House in Nashville published it. In 1950 Davis's story became the basis for a radio drama, "Honor Bound," which was broadcast to American servicemen overseas.[33]

Sam Davis was a Christ figure to Southerners. The focus of his story was on his execution, which was filled with analogies to Christ's crucifixion. For example, Davis's scaffold was "the Calvary whereon were exhibited the highest characteristics which belong to the Southern character." After noting that, in his last letter, Sam Davis had written his family to "tell the children all to be good," Sumner Cunningham remarked that he knew of "no greater test of character since the crucifixion of Him who counseled that all children be good." Similarly, Governor Malcolm Patterson, at the unveiling of the Davis Monument in Pulaski, Tennessee, said:

On Calvary the Son of God died with cruel nails driven through his quivering flesh, the crown of thorns pressing down upon his agonized brow, and since then the cross has been the Christian's sign in every land; and which of us has the right to say that He who created the earth and the sky and every living thing on sea and land, whose mysteries baffle, but whose providence is over all, could give the Son of Mary to teach men how to live could not also give this son of Tennessee to teach men how to die?

While many of these Christ references were made by laymen, clerics freely granted Sam Davis status as a religious hero. The Reverend J. D. Barbee saw Davis's life as a lesson in integrity, while Episcopal rector James R. Winchester said the story of "God's martyr" Sam

Davis was one of enduring suffering and remaining "faithful unto death." "He met suffering like his Lord," Winchester added, "and entered into the rewards of the just."[34]

Sam Davis shared in the praise that the clergy lavished on the common foot soldier. While their real heroes were the generals, the ministers portrayed the average Confederate soldier in the same moral and religious terms. According to the Reverend Robert C. Cave, himself a former Confederate private, the ordinary soldier was "thoroughly imbued with moral principle." Unlike his Yankee counterpart, he "left no fields wantonly laid waste, no families cruelly robbed of subsistence, no homes ruthlessly violated." The Southern soldier's behavior resulted from his native intelligence, superior education, and, above all, from his being a gentleman. "Gentleman" was a concept with moral, as well as class, dimensions. Moreover, while Jackson, Lee, and the other leaders achieved individual greatness as they fought to preserve the religious-moral identity of the South, the common soldiers did their duty collectively, symbolizing the communal aspect of the myth. Their lack of fame and reward was taken as a sign that they had fought selflessly, with no thought of mundane, materialistic matters. Writers poignantly pictured these highly moral soldiers as mere youths who had to fight when "no mother's hand was near." As if that deprivation were not enough, they achieved their spiritual triumphs despite being ill fed, ill clad, and poorly armed.[35]

The Southern clergy had a special interest in another Confederate hero, the Episcopal Bishop of Louisiana and Confederate General Leonidas Polk, who was killed in 1864 at the battle of Pine Mountain in Georgia. To describe him the ministers used such familiar terms as "a knightly soul," "the Chevalier Bayard of our history," "a man of noble presence," and a "perfectly magnificent and glorious man." His special image was that of "the Fighting Bishop." Many clergymen became soldiers in the ranks, but Polk, as an Episcopal bishop and then a Confederate general, was the most prominent of them; his decision to join the Confederacy was discussed by North and South alike. Clergymen during and after the war were sensitive to the criticisms of religious men who killed for Christ in a worthy cause. In an 1879 address, the Episcopal Bishop William Green of Mississippi suggested that while Polk obeyed his conscience in accepting a military commission, "An All-wise Providence saw fit that he should atone for the error—if error it was—with his own noble blood." Although Green sharply qualified his criticism of Polk, it remained criticism. In a private letter, Polk's daughter indignantly wrote that Green was the first Southerner "to question the purity of his motives and his conscientious sense of what was right."[36]

Most ministers, however, stressed that Polk's decision had been a righteous one. Polk's prime mythmaker was his son, William Mecklenburg Polk, who in 1893 published a biography of his father. He argued that Polk, believing the Southern cause "a righteous one," never doubted that wielding "the sword in its defense would be consistent with his vows to the Church." He cited his father's statement that he would not remove the holy robes and replace them with the sword, but would instead "buckle the sword over the gown." His conduct as a military man could only be termed holy. Preachers pointed out that he always supported missionary work among the troops, preached sermons, and longed "to return to that chosen field as the shepherd of a Christian flock." The ministers tarried over Polk's death scene, as they did with the other Confederate heroes. As J. P. B. Wilmer of Louisiana wrote, Polk "witnessed in his death to the power of the Christian faith." The hero's son noted the fact that "when the fatal shot cut him down, a blood-stained prayer-book was found next [to] his heart." Perhaps Episcopal Bishop Charles T. Quintard best epitomized the clergy's portrait of Polk when he wrote in a children's book that the general had died "in defense of the Church and the Altars to which he had been bound as a sacrifice."[37]

One Confederate military hero with ministerial connections survived to participate in his own sanctification. Ellison Capers, a Confederate general and a postwar Episcopal clergyman, was an expression of the Confederate myth and at the same time a mythmaker himself. Capers participated in the Lost Cause by serving as chaplain of his local veterans' association; his numerous orations at monument unveilings won him the title "Orator Laureate of the Lost Cause." Speaking in 1901 at the unveiling of the Confederate Monument on the Chickamauga battlefield, he said that the monuments had an "ethical value," being "the symbols of an honest and earnest people in an honest struggle." Revealing his high opinion of his own contemporaries, he insisted that if the monuments did not commemorate virtue, "the virtuous could not participate in these ceremonies." He admitted that the "odor of sanctity" about the Lost Cause spiritually renewed him. In sketching his version of the noble Confederate, Capers drew on his powerful remembrances of the war, on stories of friends killed and of soldiers questioning and then, always, reaffirming their faith in God. His recollections gave an emotional edge to his use of Confederates as moral and religious exemplars.[38]

While Capers did his part to make a myth, he also was the subject of mythmaking. Every hero needs an advocate and Capers's (like Polk's) was his son, the Reverend Walter B. Capers, who in 1912 published a biography of his father. On the cover of the volume was the imprint of a miter sitting atop a Bible, with both balancing on a sword and a scepter. The illustration accurately conveyed both the crucial combination of Capers's traits, and the precariousness of that combination. Ministers used his example to support the validity of the Lost Cause. According to the Episcopal *Southern Churchman*, Capers proved "that Lee and Jackson did not stand alone as Christian characters, but that such were the rule and not the exception in the armies of the Confederacy." A poem pictured Capers as the ultimate romantic knight, as "the Bayard of the tented field," the performer of "knightly deeds," a man with a "princely heart." The poet described him as "the Sydney of the Stainless shield," "the good Sir Galahad," and "a paladin." He was great because "his heart was pure." Capers combined the military man's virtues with those of the religious man. As one newspaper said when he died, "A dual warfare o'er, the warrior is at rest." The Reverend C. K. Nelson of Atlanta wrote that the source of Capers's influence was his manliness "preserved in studious imitation of his Divine Lord and Master." The Christianity admired here was not that of a gentle Christ, but that of a Jesus vigorously driving the unrighteous from the temple.[39]

Capers is not a major Southern hero today, but he was popular in the 1900-1920 period, particularly in the home of secession, South Carolina. Southerners did not complete their religious myth with Lee or Jackson or even Sam Davis. To an almost exaggerated degree the ministers claimed the lesser-known military figures as righteous crusaders. Even the seemingly impious, such as Nathan Bedford Forrest and Jubal Early, emerged as holy in the preachers' writings.[40]

Judging from the myth of the Crusading Christian Confederates, the religious version of the Lost Cause taught Southerners to crusade against evil, to bear the suffering which accompanied that struggle, and to die in Christian faith. If they did so, virtue would then be theirs. Lee at Appomattox, Jefferson Davis in his cell awaiting possible execution, Stonewall Jackson on his deathbed, and Sam Davis on the scaffold—all were moral lessons for Southerners on the acceptance of death and defeat. The synthesis of religious and military virtues intimated an important point about Southern religion in the post–Civil War period. Marshall Fishwick, in a study of heroes, has concluded that the world's admiration has alternately focused on the military hero and the religious saint.[41] The Confederate "Angel-Saxon" heroes combined both roles. On the one hand, the ministers used the Confederate Man of Sorrows as a moral lesson on suffering, humiliation, defeat, and death. For the beaten, impoverished Southerners, this lesson would have continuing relevance. On the other hand, the preachers reassured their brethren that the Confederate Holy Warrior-Prophet did not crusade in vain for morality and religion. Because Southerners continued throughout the postbellum years to fear the materialistic, heterogeneous Northern civilization, for many people the Yankee continued to be a monster symbolizing evil. But the clergy used the Confederate myth as the rationale for opposing any evil, and to righteous Southerners the late nineteenth century, like each age of history, seemed to be a dark age, filled with demons.

Chapter Three

ABIDING  THEOLOGY
CHILDREN OF THE
OF PRIDE LOST CAUSE

DURING THE CIVIL WAR, Southerners believed that God approved their cause, and they did not abandon that belief in the face of Confederate defeat. Defeat raised a traditional religious problem: How could the righteous man or cause be defeated when a just, omnipotent God ruled the universe? Southern ministers pondered the essential theological question of the Southern relationship to God as the war neared an end, but during the war most clergymen maintained hope of ultimate victory. To the end, they remained the Confederacy's most important morale-builders. With defeat, Southern clergymen assumed the responsibility for explaining the South's defeat in what they claimed had been a holy war. As with mythology, a theology represents a formulation of a belief system, and the theology of the Lost Cause again showed the close tie between the civil religion and the Christian denominations. The ministers of the Lost Cause elaborated on a traditional Christian interpretation of history in explaining the Confederate failure. The myth of the Crusading Christian Confederates had enacted the Christian drama, but without a resurrection and redemption to complete the myth. In the theology of the Lost Cause, one can see that Southerners still hoped the spirit of the suffering and dead Confederacy would one day have, in the words from a Confederate monument, "a joyful resurrection."

Southern ministers addressed themselves to the theological question most thoroughly in the years immediately after the war, before Lost Cause organizations emerged. The individual who best captured the mood of the South in this period was Father Abram Ryan, known as the "Poet Priest of the Lost Cause." Born in 1838 in Norfolk, Virginia, of Irish immigrant parents, raised in Virginia and Missouri,

Ryan was educated for the priesthood in St. Louis and in Buffalo, New York. He was a parish priest before serving the Confederacy as an un-official but fulltime chaplain to infantry units. After the war he founded and edited a rabidly pro-Southern newspaper, *Banner of the South*, in addition to fulfilling his ministry at St. Paul's Church in Au-gusta, Georgia. He edited briefly another newspaper, the New Orleans *Morning Star*, before moving to Mobile, Alabama, in 1870. In 1881 he left Mobile for a semi-retirement that included almost continuous travel and lecture-circuit appearances. His Confederate sympathies became even more intense with the South's defeat, and his sectional belligerence did not abate until 1878, when the generosity of North-erners during a Southern yellow fever epidemic converted him. (He published a poem, "Reunited," to reflect his change in perspective.) When he died in Louisville in 1886, he was only forty-eight years old.[1]

Ryan was a melancholy, morose figure. A sad-eyed man with stooped shoulders and curly, unruly hair that hung down his back, he was given to legend-making, and he fostered the legend of himself as a man of mystery. He cultivated his unusual appearance by wearing a faded black coat that reached to his feet. He remained a romantic, even in the harsh Southern world of Reconstruction. He praised the South as a land of ruins, a land "that is blest by the dust, / And bright with the deeds / Of the down trodden just." He loved the land "that has legends and lays / That tell of the memories / Of long-vanished days." In an 1878 lecture in Nashville, Ryan spoke on this favorite theme:

A land without ruins is a land without memories; a land without memories is a land without liberty. A land that wears a laurel crown may be fair to see; but twine a few sad cypress leaves around the brow of any land, and, be that land barren, beautiless, and bleak, it becomes lovely in its consecrated cornet of sorrow, and it wins the sympathy of the heart and of history. Crowns of roses fade; crowns of thorns endure. Calvaries and crucifixions take deepest hold of humanity; the triumphs of might are transient, they pass and are forgotten; the sufferings of the right are graven deepest on the chronicle of nations.

He was a poet of the dead, the Confederate dead. "There's grandeur in graves— / There's glory in gloom," he wrote.[2] If the plantation nur-tured prewar romanticism, the graveyard nourished that of the post-war generation.

Ryan struggled with the meaning of Southern defeat. While acknowledging that God reigned, Ryan asserted that the South had been right in its struggle. In "Prayer of the South" Ryan alternated a recitation of the South's woes with an affirmation: "O Father, may thy will be done." Observing the South, he saw "so much lost, alas, and nothing won"; he wept, and prayed not to question God's will. Admitting that his heart was "filled with anguish, deep and vast" and that his hopes were buried in the dust, Ryan asked for "peace in all my doubts and fears." He did believe that instead of being a meaningless defeat the Confederate loss would lead Southerners to stronger religious faith:

> Ah! I forgot Thee, Father, long and oft,
> When I was happy, rich, and proud, and free;
> But conquered now, and crushed, I look aloft,
> And sorrow leads me, Father, back to Thee.

In another poem, "The Land We Love" (1868), Ryan portrayed the South as a land "where only the dead are the free." However, he again asserted that adversity experienced as a result of Confederate defeat would lead Southerners to God: "Each link of the chain that enslaves, / Shall bind us the closer to thee."[3]

Ryan's most famous poem of the Lost Cause was "The Conquered Banner," which conveyed his reverence for the Confederacy:

> Furl that Banner, softly, slowly.
> Treat it gently—it is holy—
> For it droops above the dead.
> Touch it not—unfold it never,
> Let it droop, there furled forever,
> For its people's hopes are dead!

At other times he would write more belligerently about the righteousness of the Southern cause, but here the mood was simply one of quiet, proud despondency. At a parish in Knoxville when he received word of Appomattox in April, 1865, Ryan composed the dirge while the parish choir rehearsed the sacred music for Holy Week in an adjoining room. Writing of "The Conquered Banner," Hannis Taylor, a lawyer who collected many of Ryan's poems for publication, said,

"Only those who lived in the South in that day, and passed under the spell of that mighty song, can properly estimate its power as it fell upon the victims of a fallen cause." The poem was perhaps even more popular during the 1890–1920 period. Frequently reprinted in periodicals, this most famous of Ryan's poems had appeared in forty editions by 1929.[4]

Ryan and other Southerners particularly expressed their public anguish and concern on the special days appointed for humiliation, fasting, prayer, or thanksgiving. In a November 1866 sermon on the Georgia fast day, the Episcopal Bishop Stephen Elliott admitted that the South's efforts had been in vain, and that it must now turn to God in humble submission. He chastened his people for their pride. "I am afraid," he said, "that many of us have said: 'Men may despoil us of our property, of our homes, of our rights, of our privileges; but they shall not deprive us of our pride, or our associations, or our memories. We will make these our idols, and will cherish and worship these in our inmost hearts!" God had dealt harshly with this attitude, and would continue to do so. Elliott repeated the conventional Southern wisdom that adversity was a sign of God's concern: "It is better to be chastened, than to be let alone."[5]

Southerners also celebrated denominationally or state-appointed thanksgiving days, but, as has been mentioned, they were less than enthusiastic over the national Thanksgiving Day. They believed Northerners used it to exploit the war issue and to wave the bloody shirt. In 1869 D. Shaver, the editor of the *Christian Index*, a Baptist newspaper in Atlanta, noted that such days too often evoked in the Yankee "the smell (if they do not wake the thirst) of blood." He characterized the Northern Christian's behavior on Thanksgiving Day as like that of a Pharisee of old, who stood "pilloried through the ages as venting a self-complacent but empty piety." The editor of Charleston's *Southern Presbyterian* agreed, observing in 1872 that Southerners generally ignored Thanksgiving Day when it was appointed by the federal civil authorities. The editor added, though, that the Southern Presbyterian General Assembly in that year had appointed a day for thanksgiving and humiliation, and that Southerners had reasons to be both thankful and humble. Southern Christians were certainly to give thanks—only not at the decree of Yankees.[6]

Southerners could not limit their anguish or their gratitude to such ritualistic occasions. As Confederate defeat became apparent, Southerners came to have a sense of foreboding. The image most often evoked by religious people was that of entering into the darkness. In January, 1865, the editor of *Christian Index* spoke of the "darkness which hovers over our prospects." In the same month, Mrs. Mary Jones, the wife of a Presbyterian minister in Georgia, wrote in her private journal, "Clouds and darkness are round about us; the hand of the Almighty is laid in sore judgement upon us; we are a deserted and smitten people." When Lee surrendered, said Episcopal minister Randolph McKim, "the world grew dark to us. We felt as if the sun had set in blood to rise no more." Episcopal Bishop Stephen Elliott surmised that many Southerners believed that "a dark cloud seems to be gathering over us in the future." Elliott professed that Christians should not fear the darkness; rather, they should enter into it, "knowing that God often dwelleth in the thick darkness." In an 1868 letter the Presbyterian theologian Robert Lewis Dabney wrote that the situation looked "as gloomy as if it were clothed in the pall of death." The aging Methodist Bishop James Andrew reiterated this view, characterizing the postwar era as one "of peril, and of dark and threatening prospects for our country." He prayed for deliverance.[7]

Episcopal Bishop Richard Wilmer of Alabama captured the essence of the Southern sentiment when he said in May, 1865, that the present was "something like the hour of judgment." To be more precise, "it gives premonition of that dreadful day, when the secrets of all hearts shall be disclosed, and terror shall seize upon all whose treasures are not laid up beyond the reach of moth, and rust, and thieves." He might have added Yankees to his list of the enemies of temporal treasures. The Baptist preacher J. L. Burrows, who was a Richmond resident during the war, said that the end of the Confederacy was like the day of judgment, "or a day about as near like it as imagination can compass."[8]

During Reconstruction, some Southern ministers had a sense of restriction and even imprisonment. For example, Brigadier General William Nelson Pendleton, who had been Lee's chief of artillery and after the war was rector of Grace Memorial Episcopal Church in Lexington, Virginia, immediately faced conflict with the Union troops occupying Lexington. During the war Southern Episcopalians had replaced the prayer for the President of the United States with a prayer for the President of the Confederate States, and Pendleton refused to reinstate the former prayer. He was arrested on Sunday, July 16, 1865, and his church remained closed until January 1, 1866. As happened with other Southerners, such experiences during the immediate postwar years powerfully cemented Pendleton's Lost Cause sentiments. He revealingly maintained that Southerners were "related towards the government and Northern people somewhat as were our Blessed Lord and the Apostles towards the Roman authorities and population; submission but without other ties than general good inte[rest] and the common brotherhood of humanity." Given the bleak landscape of Reconstruction Virginia, Pendleton gave himself up to prewar nostalgia. In 1865 a daughter wrote that "papa is much grieved and his mind and heart seem carried out of the sad present to the careless, bright days of their happy childhood." "I am not much given to romancing in this day of trial," he admitted in an 1870 letter. "But sometimes it is very pleasant to indulge feelings in that way." With sentiments such as these, more than 10,000 Southerners went into exile after 1865. Expatriates established Confederate colonies in Mexico, Brazil, and Venezuela, wandered in Canada and from one European nation to another, and even assisted Egyptian leaders in training their army. These exiles made a major religious contribution by permanently establishing the missionary work of the Southern denominations in South America.[9]

Faced with discouraging conditions, some Southern ministers succumbed to apocalyptic visions when they attempted to explain defeat. These visions began, of course, before the war ended. In February, 1865, a writer in Richmond's *Religious Herald* told of seeing an opened book of the future that told "that heaven and earth might pass away, amid earthquakes and tempests, and thunderings and lightnings, and consuming fires," yet the Scriptures would never fail. The writer admitted that "with eager, anxious gaze" he had inquired as to the fate of Virginia and the South. He warned Southerners that "if you will not turn from your evil ways," God might place them in a captivity to the Yankees, which would resemble the Babylonian captivity of the Israelites. The clergy saw especially relevant meaning in the biblical Revelation of Saint John. One writer insisted that the Harlot of Babylon mentioned in the book of Revelation referred not to the papacy, as Southern Protestants usually said, but to the Northern churches, which seemed to "regard the scarlet woman as an example, rather than as one of the most terrible warnings of history." The clergymen complained that these Northern churches were working toward "the secularization of the Redeemer's Kingdom."[10]

Other ministers found solace in the appeals of pre-millennialism, the idea that Christ's second coming would precede a thousand-year earthly reign. Even the staid, distinguished Presbyterian cleric Moses Drury Hoge admitted in 1866 that he wanted to believe in the millennial ideas of John Cumming, a British prophet who predicted that 1867 would be the day of fulfillment. "Though I do not believe with the personal advent people," Hoge wrote, "I constantly find myself wishing their doctrine might be true; as the quickest and most certain way of putting an end to the misrule and unrest with which the world is filled."[11]

The ministers of the Lost Cause were not members of millenarian sects, and, as with Hoge, their apocalyptic thoughts were generally temporary and not the basis of their theology. The most wide-ranging prophetic vision related to Confederate defeat did not appear, however, until 1907, when the Mississippi cleric J. W. Sandell published *The United States in Scripture*. Sandell had been an officer in a Mississippi infantry regiment during the Civil War, and during the last days of the conflict he came to see the resemblances between it and the prophecies recorded in the biblical books of Daniel and Revelation. He continued pondering the similarities for forty years, publishing his conclusions after the turn of the century.[12]

Sandell saw a parallel between the Civil War and the war between Northern and Southern kings recorded in the book of Daniel. The Northern kings' abiding flaws were vanity and lack of submission to God, traits which seemed to describe the Yankee perfectly. Referring to the Revelation of Saint John, he proposed also that the American government was like the "beast having seven heads and ten horns, and upon his heads the name of blasphemy." Sandell insisted that the federal government represented "the best illustration of the symbols that has ever been impressed on my mind." He claimed that, although the beast emerged triumphant during the administration of Andrew Jackson, the Confederacy was an obstacle to its permanent ascendancy. The beast was the federal government's power, and the woman in Revelation who fled from that cruel beast symbolized the South. Sandell related his reading of biblical prophecies to the political issue of states' rights. During the Civil War itself, the principle of "the separate existence of states" emerged by God's decree. Since "God's method" was not to attain goals through "carnal warfare," the South lost the war. God, "in His unsearchable wisdom," had permitted the Devil to use the beast (the federal government) to destroy "the principles that should characterize the government of the states forming the Union." However, it was not a lost cause, since the South, "in the providence of God" and "by steadfastness to principle," could still attain an even greater influence among the nations than would have come with Confederate independence. Sandell did not elaborate on the nature of that influence, preferring merely to reiterate that the states' rights principle would "be maintained over the nations by the authority of Him who is to rule the nations 'with a rod of iron' whose power is according to the perfect law of liberty." In his view, God would authorize yet another war, and in it His enemies would be destroyed. Sandell suggested that the states' rights principle was not dead in 1907, and that to abandon it would be to betray America's founding fathers as well as the Confederate ones. In constructing a prophecy of future Southern triumph, he borrowed the images and terminology of the prophetic books of the Bible.[13]

If Confederate defeat caused some Southerners to see the South as part of a prophecy, it resulted in others experiencing a loss of faith. "'Things are pretty bad, boys. But never mind, God is on His throne,'" said a character in the novel *White Blood*, by the Presbyterian minister Henry Wharton. "'Don't know, Cap,' said a poor fellow with a wounded arm, 'looks mightily like the Devil had the upper hand about this time.'" As a result of their fundamentalist outlook, most Southern Christians believed in the literal reality of Satan, and he seemed like a powerful figure in the postwar era. A letter to the *Religious Herald* argued that God's plan could not have been to "overthrow an institution which he himself ordained, established and sanctioned." The writer continued: "Would he cause wicked men to desecrate, blaspheme and burn houses dedicated to his own worship? And not only so, but let loose fire and sword, and the wrath of an unbridled soldiery upon the innocent and the helpless, until the very earth was drunk with the blood of the victims?" His conclusion was that "it was Satan that ruled the hour." Confederate Colonel William Preston Johnston agreed, saying, "I shall never believe that it was Providence but the devil's work that defeated us." Robert Lewis Dabney concluded that "the devil is apparently triumphant." Similarly, South Carolina's John L. Girardeau blamed "Satanic influence" for his congregation's noticeable loss of confidence in prayer after the war. He preached a series of five sermons reasserting that the Devil could not stand against a holy man's prayers.[14]

Few Southern ministers succumbed to complete loss of faith, but the experience of defeat in a holy war was agonizing. Randolph McKim told his theology professor, "I feel as if I had nothing left to live for!" The famed Presbyterian cleric Benjamin Morgan Palmer of New Orleans admitted simply that he was "very sad." "Just now the earth is very dark," he said, "and I thank God that I have faith, when I cannot have knowledge." Many clergymen experienced the same emotions as Presbyterian minister John Jones of Georgia, who admitted in an 1866 letter that he was "brokenhearted, and tempted sometimes to rebel and then to give up in hopeless despair." Either extreme, he added, was wicked; "the antidote for each is a refuge in the sovereignty and righteousness of God."[15]

Southern clergymen testified to the postwar skepticism among laymen, which they attributed to Confederate defeat. Richard McIlwaine, a Presbyterian, confessed that, when defeat came, he himself "did not for one moment doubt the Divine goodness but bowed reverently in recognition of his wisdom and righteousness." His parishioners were not so tranquil. Women of "culture, intelligence and piety" were especially "wretched and had drifted far from their religious moorings"; much of his time after Appomattox "was consumed in ministering to these lovely, lonely and disconsolate creatures." In 1874 the General Assembly of the Southern Presbyterian church officially noted the loss of faith evidenced "in the oft-repeated inquiry, 'Where is thy God?'" In assessing the state of religion in the South, Episcopal Bishop Charles T. Quintard of Tennessee blamed the loss of faith on the results of the Civil War. "The license which followed our late civil war," he observed, "aggravated a recklessness in spiritual matters which began in the bitter disappointment experienced at the result of that war in the Southern mind." He believed, inaccurately, that no Southern denomination had kept pace with the overall growth of the South. At the end of the war, he said, Southerners with energy rebuilt their material fortunes, to the neglect of spiritual values, while those without pluck sank into a lethargy destructive of physical and spiritual improvement. He urged his people "to arrest the tide of unbelief and irreligion that rests upon us like a black pall."[16]

Southern clergymen warned that the loss of faith resulting from Confederate defeat could jeopardize the future of Southern religion. A writer in the *Christian Index*, for example, remarked that the war's results were a mystery and that "the faith of some good men, in the justice of God, has been shaken." The evil effect of skepticism was not just placing the individual's soul in jeopardy, but also threatening the Church itself because "it deadens zeal and excuses inertness." The Southern churches desired members who were actively crusading against evil; skepticism, since it represented a threat to this morality in action, was more than an intellectual problem. Preaching in March, 1866, at the reopening of St. Philip's Episcopal Church in Charleston, Rector W. B. W. Howe suggested a related point. Granting that the victory of evil "*tries faith*," he reminded his congregation that righteousness would not finally triumph until "our Lord's second coming." The thrust of his message was the warning that to doubt the triumph of righteousness was to surrender to atheism and to "deny the radical distinction between good and evil." Loss of faith would then lead to moral and ethical degeneration—a fact of importance in an individual's life, but of crucial significance in preserving a Southern saving remnant. His use of the Israelite comparison was revealing: "Individuals, nay, the mass, might prove untrue to the ancient covenant, but a remnant always survived, through whom, as from holy seed, the nation renewed its youth." In the immediate postwar years, Southern clergymen feared the war-engendered skepticism but hoped to preserve at least pockets of spiritual purity, with the aim of redeeming Southern society in the future.[17]

In trying to deal with postwar skepticism, Southerners brooded over

God's reasons for apparently passing a negative judgment on their region. Most church councils and assemblies did not identify specific reasons for the calamity, except to admit in general terms that Southern sins such as covetousness, worldliness, and greed, had displeased God during the war. Individual ministers bore the brunt of explaining God's displeasure. Stephen Elliott addressed himself to the problem in a fast-day sermon in 1866. A white-haired, square-jawed man, he had been a lawyer, a wealthy Georgia planter, and presiding bishop of the Protestant Episcopal Church in the Confederate States of America. His son, Brigadier General Stephen Elliott, was seriously wounded near the end of the war, dying in March, 1866. In his fast-day sermon Bishop Elliott told his congregation that, while Southerners had obviously displeased God, each person seemed confused as to what offense beset Southerners as a people. "Have we submitted to God's decision of the conflict in which we were, for so many years, engaged?" he asked. The war's results were so decisive, he added, that God's will could not be doubted. Although Elliott did not ask Southerners to change their views on the justice of the Confederate cause and the righteousness of slavery, he did implore each Southerner to consider "whether you have submitted to God's will about the termination of the conflict. I know that, in many places and in many hearts, there has been an open quarrel with God upon this point;—that He has been charged with injustice, with a false view of right and wrong, with cruelty to the innocent and the godly." This attitude, he said, only reinforced God's already apparent anger. Elliott asked his listeners to understand that "God's people must be always tried" or they would not be worthy of their status as God's special favorites. The test always seemed to be the same—"perfect trust and faith in His proceedings."[18]

Elliott ignored specific reasons why God might have tested His people between 1861 and 1865, but one reason which could not be totally overlooked by Southern ministers was slavery. Southerners refused to admit that God's displeasure with the peculiar institution was the cause of Confederate defeat. They never abandoned the belief that slavery was a divinely ordained institution, or the idea that Southerners had helped Christianize the Negroes, which seemed to them God's plan in bringing Africans to America. In an important concession, however, some Southerners did admit that perhaps they had not adequately cared for the spiritual and physical welfare of the slaves, so that God was chastising them for the failure to live up to their duty. In January, 1865, the *Christian Index* editor admitted grudgingly that Southern battle reverses might be connected to the issue of slavery. In relation to slaves, Southerners were as fathers to children—and they had neglected their "parental obligations." The failure to recognize slave marriages, obviously a sin, was only part of a larger problem. If, instead of "hoarding up wealth from the labor of our slaves," Southerners had shown themselves willing to aid the "degraded" race, then God would not have provided Northerners with the "hardihood" they had shown in "this unjust and cruel war." He recognized that many people believed the Bible sanctioned slavery, and that therefore the Confederacy could not fail; but he warned that disaster was imminent. "Let God's chastizement have its proper effect on our hearts, and we may then hope that the rod will be removed."[19]

Antebellum Southerners were certainly expedient in making the pro-slavery argument; however, many of them had a heartfelt sense of responsibility for the spiritual condition of their slaves, believing themselves God's agents in Christianization. The sense of responsibility sometimes shaded into guilt, as with the Presbyterian minister John B. Adger, who admitted that he had not fully performed "my religious duties to my slaves." He added that he had tried to do so, and in fact had spent much of his time preaching before black audiences. When it became apparent that the slaves would be freed, many Southerners assumed that God was displeased not with the institution itself, but with the Southern agents of divinity. As Robert L. Dabney said immediately after defeat, God had taken from Southerners, and given to Northerners, the responsibility for civilizing and Christianizing the heathen Negro.[20]

Southern ministers insisted that the immediate reason for their defeat was not slavery but the superior material resources of the North. The Reverend J. William Jones argued that while the South possessed spiritual strength, the Yankees' superior physical resources enabled them to triumph. While the Southern soldier suffered physically, Northern supplies "of every kind were abundant and even luxurious." Despite being undersupplied and underpaid, however, the Confederate soldier freely contributed his money to humanitarian and religious causes. Writing in 1909, R. A. Goodwin agreed with Jones, referring to the "ragged, starving heroes" of the Confederacy. "We would not have it believed that we fought on equal terms, and in the same way they fought," he said. The Confederate legacy was "that we could not be conquered, even by vastly superior numbers and inexhaustible resources, till the women and children of the South as well as the armies in the field were brought to the verge of starvation by the systematic destruction of the necessities of life." Jones and Goodwin portrayed the Northern triumph as a materialistic one, and the Southern victory as a spiritual one.[21]

Attributing the Northern victory to material might, Southerners made the corollary argument that might does not make right. John Adger wrote that during the war the Southern clergy had made the error of thinking "that God must surely bless the right." Frequently, Adger said, "in God's infinite wisdom and sovereign pleasure" he had allowed that "righteousness be overthrown." Adger cautioned against doubting Divine Providence, and at the same time he predicted Northern doom if the region learned only pride from the war. Another minister denied "the old superstition" that right must always be on the side of might. He would not "speak of Appomattox as a judgment of God." Instead, he regarded the Southern loss as another instance of "truth on the scaffold, and wrong on the throne." A woman writing in the Baptist *Religious Herald* echoed this sentiment: "History and observation have taught us the fallacy of the notion that where there is *right* there must be success." An 1866 article in the *Christian Index*, a Georgia Baptist periodical, suggested that one should not assume "that the providences of God were intended to decide, or that they *do* decide questions of rivalry among men." It was a "fatal and paralyzing error" to infer "divine displeasure" from "divine chastizement." The Episcopal Bishop J. P. B. Wilmer categorized the "might makes right" argument as an "absurd doctrine." The Southern view rested on the assumption that Southerners were people of principle and integrity, qualities whose values were untouched by temporal success or failure. As Moses Drury Hoge said, the failures of honorable men were "nobler than the successes of the unprincipled intriguer. Reproach, persecution, misrepresentation and poverty, have often been the fate of those who have suffered the loss of all for the right and true."[22]

Time did not change the argument. In several articles written after 1890, the Presbyterian cleric James H. McNeilly recalled the ubiquitous Old Testament analogy. He noted that the Bible contained accounts of God's chosen people led into captivity by heathen conquerors, "but that fact did not prove the heathen to be right in the cause nor that the Israelites were upholding a bad cause." Nor was Pilate just and Christ a failure. McNeilly, who was a chaplain during the war and pastor of a Presbyterian church in Nashville afterward, insisted that the Confederates "who poured their blood like festal wine, a libation to liberty," were not necessarily wrong in fighting the war, since "questions of right and wrong before God are not settled by success or defeat of arms." After Southerners had committed themselves and given their last drop of blood, they confidently left "the issues with God." God created such crises to test peoples: "Will they measure duty by success? Will they sacrifice principles for expediency?" Perhaps the most important question for the postwar generation, and one that showed McNeilly looking to the future as well as to the past, was, "Will they forsake truth because of defeat?" The South, he hoped, could answer "no" to all these questions. For McNeilly, integrity was the essential achievement which showed God's grace. Integrity, then, not prosperity, was God's blessing—and the Confederates possessed it.[23]

In times of adversity Christians frequently stress that suffering is a means to greater faith, and the postbellum era was no exception. Some preachers called for Southerners to draw closer together in adversity. In a typical sermon near the war's end, H. C. Hornady, a Baptist pastor, exhorted that the common suffering of Southerners should bind them together in "that best solace of the afflicted—true and steady friendship." Southern clerics told their congregations that they had experienced the great problems of existence, not in philosophy, poetry, or history, but in life itself, and that their common experiences should unite them. Stephen Elliott noted in the 1866 survey of his Georgia diocese that his people were "suffering and depressed, but united in spirit." He claimed that most Georgians believed their suffering to be "unnecessary and cruel," but in his opinion it was a condition "very favorable for religious impression of a deep nature." Suffering could lead to "unbelief and indifference"; in contrast, the clergy should use the situation to lead their followers "to the foot of the Cross, that emblem of humiliation and suffering." Elliott's eventual successor as bishop of Georgia, John Beckwith, preached a series of sermons in the immediate postwar years which attempted to explore the role of suffering as a catalyst for faith. In his view, one virtue of suffering was that it led to patience: "Without suffering there would be no room for patience, and without patience man would lose possession of his soul." Moreover, periods of prosperity and happiness were historically times of "spiritual lukewarmness and indifference," while eras of "affliction, suffering, trial and humiliation have always exhibited the church in her greatest purity, and earnestness and activity." Making yet another Southern analogy to Christ, he remarked that before Jesus "wore His crown of glory, He was pierced with one of thorns." If God wanted to ensure "our eternal ruin," Beckwith said, He would crown man's efforts "with perpetual prosperity, giving us unmarred health and insuring us against suffering: Nothing more effectively causes us to forget God than prosperity." He concluded that "it is part of our destiny to suffer," but that from suffering would emerge a stronger Christian.[24]

The war's results prompted sermons and periodical articles on the book of Job, urging Southerners to accept their burdens without murmurings. While the Baptist minister Henry C. Renfro of Texas allowed that Southerners had endured "havoc and desolation," he castigated them for their failure "to meet their calamities in the spirit and language of Job." The most popular quote from Job was "Though He slay me, yet will I trust him." Baptist minister S. G. Hillyer of Georgia decided that, in addition to Job, other biblical stories provided models for the development of Southern piety in the face of adversity. "It was," he stated, "when Isaac lay upon the altar of sacrifice that Abraham's faith was made perfect by works; it was when the Hebrew children walked in the midst of the fiery furnace that the glory of the Lord was revealed before the eyes of His enemies." Hillyer concluded that under similar circumstances "our Southern churches may make all men know that our religion is to us a sublime reality." Adversity, then, should provide an opportunity for Southern Christians to testify to their religion's truth.[25]

These reactions to defeat rested ultimately on the belief in God's

omnipotence and control of history. In this Southern context the clergymen elaborated on the traditional Christian interpretation of history—that God was working from a plan, a design, which man was
unable to understand. "God is working out larger ends than those
which concern us as a people," said Stephen Elliott. "His ends em-
brace the universe: His purposes are co-extensive with Time." Elliott
advised his parishioners that the foundation of the Christian faith was
"a scheme, which, beginning in the cradle of the world, is to go
on, until the kingdoms of this world shall become the kingdoms of
Christ." Each event in the history of a nation was a link in the chain
of events that would eventually bring the Christian's hopes to fulfillment. Given this scheme of things, the duty of the Southern Christian was to be patient and submissive in the postwar world and to take
care, in Elliott's words, "that we do not perish in the wilderness." In
an 1866 sermon Elliott's successor, John Beckwith, agreed, stating that
"the evidence of a *plan* is stamped upon the history of the world: a
plan of mercy in wh.[ich] God works for our good and turns even the
wrath of man to His own glory and the salvation of souls." The meaning of God's plan was beyond human comprehension; furthermore, it
was not important that man know that meaning. This, of course, was
a traditional Calvinist explanation, a call for faith in the benevolence
of Providence. To expect God to be accountable to man would be to
deny His omnipotence. "As the ruler of the universe, and the supreme
arbiter of events, He disposes of all things in accordance with His own
secret purposes," said John L. Girardeau. "For wise purposes," He
sometimes allowed his saints, including His Southern ones, to under-
go "apparent defeat" and to experience "a tempest of opprobrium, oppression and scorn."[26]

Girardeau's use of the phrase "apparent defeat" suggested that
Southerners clung to the hope of future vindication. Though they accepted the Confederacy's defeat as final, they repeatedly speculated
that God might allow Confederate principles to succeed in another
guise, in another time. In June, 1865, William Nelson Pendleton surmised that God had sent defeat because Southerners had become
idolatrous of their region; now they had to be a people without a country for a while. Yet he anticipated that God's order in the future would
"enable us to achieve the independence which is our birthrite and of

which we have now been despoiled by a mighty combination. . . ."
Girardeau predicted the same future in 1866, that Confederate ideals
would "in another day, in some golden age, sung by poets, sages and
prophets, come forth in the resurrection of buried principles and live
to bless mankind, when the bones of its confessors and martyrs shall
have mouldered into dust." In short, as good Christians, they left their
case with God. As a poet put it in 1871:

> From each lost cause of earth
> Something precious springs to birth,
> Tho' lost it be to men,
> It lives with God again. [27]

The Methodist minister J. L. Gilbert, writing in 1869, believed that
he knew the specific form this future success would take. He concluded that Confederate defeat was not an "unmitigated calamity," but
"a necessary disciplinary ordeal, chosen by God, in his wisdom, by
which he designed to prepare the Christian Churches of these States
for their high and holy mission, as the custodians of an unadulterated
evangelism, and as his honored instruments for the development of a
pure Christian civilization throughout this continent and throughout
Christendom." He confidently assumed that the evangelism of the
Southern churches would eventually vanquish the menace of the po-
litically oriented religion in the Northern churches. Soon all Americans would seek "a pure and unadulterated gospel from the lips of the
ministry of the Churches of our Southern States." [28]

However specifically envisioned, the general idea of future vindication became even more ingrained as time passed, so that Southerners
remained unwilling to call it a lost cause. "Can a cause be lost which
has passed through such a baptism as ours?" asked Benjamin Morgan
Palmer. "Principles never die, and if they seem to perish it is only to
experience a resurrection in the future." In 1889 Moses Drury Hoge
told Southerners not to worry about the Confederate cause, because
other Southerners would eventually put on the knightly armor "and in
God's good time vindicate the principles which must ultimately triumph." In a 1901 oration Methodist Bishop Warren A. Candler even
suggested that the goals of the Confederates had been achieved, although he (like others who made this argument) saw the achievement

as one of political goals, making the tenuous claim that local self-government was more respected in 1901 than before the Civil War.[29]

Speaking in 1897 before a church service preceding the yearly Confederate Veterans' reunion, James I. Vance, the pastor of Nashville's First Presbyterian Church, told the audience that ideals can survive defeat in war. A democratic majority could alter the externals of life, but "truth is truth, whether it have a conquering army at its back or wear the chains of imprisonment, like Paul in his cell at Rome." Vance explicitly made the connection between the Southern Lost Cause and Christianity: "His enemies could nail Christ to the cross, but they could not quench the ideals he embodied. His seemed to be a lost cause as the darkness fell on the great tragedy at Calvary, but out of what seemed Golgotha's irretrievable defeat has come the cause whose mission it is to save that which is lost." The implication was that Confederate principles might yet be the basis for a similar magnificent destiny. Vance stated that life itself is a lost cause, in a sense, because it is only preparation for certain death. As a result, human affairs had to be placed in a long perspective. "The incidents of life have more about them than the present," he said. "All the ages gather around them. Destiny is to speak a word over the lost causes of earth. Then it will appear that what we retain is not what we have acquired, but what we have become." The Confederate devotion to principle was a legacy that could inspire generations of Southerners to nobility. His analysis of how Confederate values could be vindicated in the character of Southerners was more subtle than Candler's political view. Vance's philosophical treatment of the Lost Cause was based on a more perceptive understanding of the nature of its impact.[30]

The idea that Confederate defeat was a form of discipline from God, preparing Southerners for the future, was fundamental to the belief in ultimate vindication. The report of an 1865 Southern Presbyterian church committee said as much, proposing that God had sent disasters to the South in order to develop "that spirit of liberality which distinguished the primitive churches, in like poverty, and which may be the means of uniting us as one common brotherhood for any trials or triumphs He may have in reserve for us." The same committee a year later went so far as to conclude that God's chastisement, if it yielded the desired "fruits of humility, submission, love, and forbearance," would do more than any amount of money "to promote the interests of his kingdom among men." Similarly, John Girardeau denied that all afflictions were penal, since some "constitute a salutary discipline which is intended to benefit and not to destroy." They were not so much harsh retributions from a judge as loving corrections from a father. Suffering was a crucial element of "the moral economy of the world," said William Nelson Pendleton, because without it "virtue could not be what it is." He was sure that "virtue the most approved" might be sorely tried, but that ultimately it would triumph.[31]

The metaphor used most frequently in this connection was that of the purification of metals. In March, 1866, W. B. W. Howe told his church members that their postwar sorrows should "purge us as gold and silver, that we may offer unto the Lord an offering in righteousness." James I. Vance predicted that "the period of struggle was the period of discipline. It was providence placing the idle ore in flame and forge." As a result, the South in his generation was "awakening to an inheritance that eclipses all her past." Southerners were now of great worth, as precious metals are when purified.[32]

After the turn of the twentieth century, the writings of Southern clergymen expressed faith that God's plan included an important role for the South. Randolph McKim, for example, while granting that "It was not the will of God that we should succeed," nevertheless insisted that "the Southern people were necessary then, they are necessary now, for the accomplishment of the designs of Providence." McKim guessed that "the Lord could not trust the North to fulfill His great purposes on this continent without the aid of the Southern people." According to the pastor, the common sense, conservatism, and Anglo-Saxon tradition of the South were the traits that God wanted the South to preserve in the American nation. R. A. Goodwin, in a 1909 memorial sermon, outlined an almost identical manifest destiny for the South. "God is in our history as truly as He was in the history of Israel," he commented, later adding that the defeat of the Confederacy "was a part of the wilderness through which we were led" by God. Refusing to admit that Confederate defeat was anything but evil, he reminded his audience of biblical examples of God bringing good out of evil. The good was apparent to Goodwin in 1909: the Southern destiny was to be a necessary part of the American nation. He continued:

Without the welding together of our people by the fiery trials of war, of re-construction, of threatened servile domination, we could not have been the conserving power we have been. If this government is still to stand for liberty and freedom, it will be the South which will preserve it, and in the good providence of our God, bringing good out of evil, our sufferings will help to bring a blessing to all people.

The South's real cause was not lost, since a fight for "right and truth and honor" is never lost. "The spirit of the men of '61 goes marching on!" he said.[33] And His truth goes marching on.

Confederate defeat ultimately brought a renewal of faith for South-ern Christians. The harsh lesson of evil triumphing—by God's command—strengthened an already present strain of fatalism. But Southerners learned a more important religious lesson from their de-feat in a holy war: God's chosen people did not give up that chosen status when defeated. Like the Reverend George B. Eager, they even-tually decided that "behind a frowning providence Thou did'st hide a smiling face." Southerners thus retained their pride. They believed that God would bring good out of triumphant evil: the new good would be a purer, more holy chosen people prepared to face a special destiny. The stress was on the future, the need for communal soli-darity, and the conviction that God would demand great achieve-ments from Southerners, especially Southern Christians. The relation between Southern defeat and the development of a Southern religious mind prepared to combat evil could be seen in the words of Bishop Stephen Elliott in 1866: "Arouse yourselves, children of God; and while you humble yourselves under the mighty hand of God, forget not that you are Christ's servants, bound to do His work in the church militant upon earth, and to advance His kingdom wherever He may spread the banner of the Cross. Instead of permitting suffering to over-come your faith, let it rather lead you on to perfection."[34] In the postbellum years Southern religious leaders believed that the South was almost Zion; nevertheless, they also understood that if they risked being "at ease in Zion," the punishment would be another divine chastisement, such as had occurred when their Confederate crusade against evil failed. They would have to demand even higher standards of themselves and their society. As a result of facing defeat in a holy war, therefore, Southerners emerged with a paradoxical blend of fatalism and a heightened sensitivity to the need to combat evil.

Chapter Four

A SOUTHERN JEREMIAD ✝ LOST CAUSE CRITIQUE OF THE NEW SOUTH

IN ADDITION to the ritualistic, mythological, and theological aspects of the Lost Cause, a prophetic dimension also existed. Certain ministers, the prophets of the Lost Cause, warned their brethren of the dangers in abandoning traditional Southern values and failing to meet the high standards of the Confederate past. The greatest danger to traditional values was seen as coming from the increase in commercial and industrial economic activity in the South. The New South movement urging industrialism and laissez-faire capitalism as the solutions to Southern problems became prominent in the 1880s, and that movement became the focus for the preachers' criticisms. They contrasted the materialism of the New South with the spirituality of the Confederacy and concluded that the South had declined since the Civil War. Their critique of the New South was based partly in the antebellum pro-slavery arguments of George Fitzhugh and others; while Fitzhugh had analyzed the shortcomings of the emerging Northern industrial society, the postbellum clerics fearfully warned that these shortcomings were emerging in the South. In addition, the Lost Cause critique was based on the Old Testament prophetic writings, and it drew upon the secularized legacy of idealistic and moralistic Puritanism.

The attitudes of the clerical Cassandras can be better understood by placing them within the context of a concept from American Puritan history. Perry Miller has suggested that, in the late 1600s, the second and third generations of Puritan ministers warned their brethren of decline from the virtues of New England's founding fathers. Economic developments had by that time created conflicts with Puritan ideology. The clergymen developed a special sermon form, the jeremiad, which dwelled upon the sins and afflictions of New Englanders and the need for repentance in order to prevent future punishment. Having succeeded in building their city on a hill, the Puritans had to face the question of their identity, to redefine their "errand into the wilderness." The jeremiad was a ritualized public confessional, psychologically representing "purgation by incantation." In explaining this "stylized self-denunciation," Miller argued that the ministers were the voice of a community expressing its fears about itself in a transitional period. He believed that, by confessing the society's moral and religious failures in a ritualized way, the jeremiad actually encouraged New Englanders to persist in the very economic and social activities that were being condemned. In this way the Puritans "launched themselves on the process of Americanization." Sacvan Bercovitch has pointed out that the Puritans had changed the traditional meaning of the jeremiad, which had existed as far back as the Middle Ages. Whereas traditionally it had been "a dirge over the irrepressible agencies of common providences," in New England it was "a celebration of God's promises" for a saintly people. The Puritans' sense of their mission as a chosen people, in other words, modified the jeremiad's pessimism and bitterness.[1]

Just as the Puritans had altered the jeremiad, so postbellum Southern clergymen adapted it to their situation. Basically the two jeremiads were similar in their concern for the question of identity, although the source of this common concern was different. Both groups were descendants of noble ancestors; however, for the New Englanders success had engendered the issue of identity, while for Southerners the problem of Confederate defeat had raised the issue. Like the Puritans, Southern Christians after the Civil War thought of themselves as a chosen people. The Confederate experience established a covenanted identity among Southerners, and it became the basis for the sense of Southern mission. Southerners believed they had fought a holy war in the Confederacy, but how does a self-defined chosen people lose a holy war? Ministers explained that this affliction was a trial from God. After the war, defeat had brought another trial: the introduction of Northern economic and social forms into the weakened, vulnerable South. Southern ministers associated with the Lost Cause warned of the dangers to traditional Confederate-Christian values from an industrial, commercial society. Like the Puritans, the Lost

Cause prophets listed the evidence of decline from past "virtue," which was the central value of the Lost Cause religion. Because defeat of the Confederacy had challenged the very notion of a separate Southern identity, the Lost Cause jeremiad asserted the importance of this identity and the need for constant vigilance to preserve it. The North played an important role in this process. By the time of the Puritan jeremiad in the late 1600s, New Englanders were defining themselves less and less in terms of Europe; in contrast, Southerners continued after the war to define themselves in relation to the North. They nurtured the self-perception of regional difference. A major theme of the Lost Cause jeremiad was the wickedness of the Yankees. In addition to warning Southerners of their own decline, the jeremiad cautioned Southerners to learn from the evil North. The danger of the South's future degradation was readily embodied in the North's image, with some ministers even teaching that the South must serve as a model to the corrupt North. By maintaining Confederate virtue in the postbellum world, the South would be an example to the North in future days of reform. This was a Southern mission worth achieving.

Historians have suggested that the critique of the New South was half-hearted, ineffective, and short-lived, but they have failed to grasp its religious dimensions. Paul Gaston, in his study of *The New South Creed*, wrote that the preservation of old values and the criticism of the New South was conducted "by a small band" of Lost Cause champions. C. Vann Woodward has pointed out that by the late 1800s the churches were so dependent on money from the wealthy that they did not criticize the new order. Robert Little, in a study of "The Ideology of the New South," similarly argued that after 1900 Southerners expressed little "disapproval of the evils of the New Southern materialism," adding that the Southern churches "became more and more non-social" and otherworldly.[2] These are at best partial truths, but historians of the Lost Cause have not corrected them. It is not enough simply to dismiss the religious critique because some ministers and churches accepted the benefits of material improvements. The jeremiad reflected the deepest fears of Southern preachers, who continued to warn against the dangers of New South materialism and worldliness at least through World War I. The Lost Cause was the foundation for this critique. The ministerial critics were not a "small band." True, they were church leaders, not newspapermen or businessmen; but churchmen had extraordinary influence in the post–Civil War South. Although the two groups of leaders had different constituencies and used different forums for expressing their views, the critics of the New South remained vigilant into the twentieth century.

A key to the effectiveness of the New England jeremiad was its ritualized setting. Among the Puritans, the jeremiad was delivered on specially appointed fast days, militia days, election or execution days. The Lost Cause jeremiad had just as ritualized a setting, namely, an occasion when the Confederacy was mourned or celebrated. The dedications of monuments, the burials of veterans, Confederate Memorial Day, fast and thanksgiving days, meetings of the local and regional Confederate veterans' groups—all brought forth the Lost Cause sermon, prophesying Southern doom if virtue was not preserved. Tens of thousands of people gathered for the most noteworthy of these events; their pervasiveness in the small towns and rural areas also testified to their importance. Evangelical churches and denominational colleges were at times forums for Lost Cause sermons, and the themes of the jeremiad were written into media articles and editorials, as well as in published histories and biographies. Miller showed that the New England jeremiad was not limited to public preaching, and the Southern jeremiad similarly transcended the sermon form. It could be found throughout the religious literature of the age.

The Puritan ministers looked back to the virtue of the founding New England fathers, while the Confederates stood at the center of the Lost Cause jeremiad. They were moral and spiritual models, used by the preachers like biblical figures. Clergymen argued that they represented the true moral standard by which Southerners should be judged, insisting that it was sacrilege for sin to be tolerated in a society that had produced a Robert E. Lee. Lee's postwar decision to become an educator rather than to seek financial gain was a popular parable. Southern clerics even opposed pensions for veterans because the money might be a corrupting force. As the editor of Nashville's *Christian Advocate* remarked in 1889, accepting proposed pensions from the federal government "would be bartering much manhood for a little money." His underlying assumptions were that the Confederate heroes had been ennobled by poverty, and that Northerners were trying to buy off the veterans with corrupting gold. Similar was a letter from a "Limping Confederate," which appeared in 1887 in the Richmond *Religious Herald*. The author observed that, while his Northern friends were receiving large pensions, "how much larger I am receiving, if I did belong to the losing side." His deliverance had come when he found a virtuous woman who would accept "a penniless soldier and sinner and lead him along gently to Christ. Is this not greater than all the pensions Congress can appropriate?" Of special concern was the maintenance of Confederate veterans' groups as moral leaders. "If any body of men on the earth should be heroic and steadfast, it is the remnant of the Confederate army," said Sumner Cunningham, founder of *Confederate Veteran*. As a result, Southerners were sensitive to any hint of impropriety by the saving remnant.[3]

Throughout the postwar world, Southern preachers perceived the danger of decline. Even during the poverty-stricken Reconstruction years, the prophets of the Lost Cause anticipated the dangers of materialism and worldliness. Episcopal Bishop J. P. B. Wilmer of Louisiana noted disapprovingly, in an 1875 address to his diocese, that "in no age have men been so eager to combine for purposes of worldly gain." The Presbyterian cleric Joseph B. Stratton conveyed the same message in an 1875 college address, telling the young people that "The question 'what will it pay' has come to be so currently asked in this mercenary age, that the use of it has bred a disposition to make literal 'pay' the motive to every exertion, and to swell the appetite for 'pay' to such inordinate bounds that contentment has become an impossible or, an obsolete virtue." In an 1872 address, "The Present Crisis and Its Issues," delivered at Washington and Lee University in Virginia, the Presbyterian minister Benjamin Morgan Palmer foretold "the impending crisis" of the social effects of industrialization in the South, and he predicted that the traditional Southern sense of honor would be destroyed, "to be followed by the swift decay of virtue." "The spirit of materialism," he continued, with classic prophetic imagery, "infused into all the transactions of business and common life, is the Angel of Pestilence dropping the seeds of death from its black wing wherever it sweeps. It is this subtle and dangerous spirit which is at the bottom of that fearful demoralization that has spread like a leprosy over the land."[4]

The most influential critic of materialism in the 1870s was Albert Taylor Bledsoe, one of the most anguished and embittered Lost Cause ministers. Author of prewar pro-slavery documents and Confederate propagandist in Britain, Bledsoe in 1866 published *Is Davis a Traitor?*, a legal defense of Jefferson Davis's role in secession. Possessing few of the orator's talents, he made his contribution to the Lost Cause in his writing. In 1867 he founded the *Southern Review*, a belligerently pro-Southern journal, in Baltimore; in 1871 it became officially aligned with the Southern Methodist church. In the decade after the war this was the most important forum for diehard defenders of the Confederacy. In Bledsoe's opinion, the postwar moral threat facing the South came directly from the defeat of a moral-spiritual force, the Confederacy. The South was now vulnerable to the invasion of Northern ideas. "The great defect of Northern civilisation is its materiality," he wrote. "It is of the earth, earthy; and ignores the spirituality of our nature. Its grand motive and object is the accumulation of money; and its prime boast is of the things money can buy—'the lust of the eye, the lust of the flesh, and the pride of life.' Mammon is its god; and nowhere has he more devout and abject worshippers, or has set up a more polluted civilisation than in the North." While admitting that Southern civilization had its defects, he insisted that it was "a civilisation seeking a spiritual elevation over matter and money, which is in the right road of Christianity." Although defeated, the South should appreciate its poverty "as far less corrupting than wealth in its influence on public liberty, or national character." He predicted Northern attempts to corrupt Southern principles by bringing material prosperity to the South, and he warned Southerners to beware Yankees bearing gifts.[5]

The sharpest criticism of materialism and accompanying worldly values began in the 1880s. Earlier warnings of the Southern preachers against mammonism were general and unfocused, but after 1880 they gained a specific Southern target, the New South movement. Ironically, the plans for a New South were popularized in the same period that saw the triumph of the myths of the Old South and the Lost Cause. By the second decade after Appomattox, the New South advocates had a well-developed program for rebuilding the South; they proposed increased industrialization, urbanization, improved education, harmonious race relations, and a more nationalistic orientation. Leaders of the movement were primarily businessmen and newspapermen, but some ministers, like Methodist Bishop Atticus Haygood, were also important boosters. Despite their rhetoric and undeniable changes, the vision of a New South was only partially realized. Until World War I the South remained agricultural, rural, illiterate, racially divided, and sectionally oriented.[6]

The New South movement did, however, evoke concerned reaction from those who viewed it as a threat to traditional values. Drawing upon accumulated sermons, the Congregational Synod of 1679 had compiled a list of sins and afflictions besetting the Puritans. Although no Lost Cause Synod catalogued such a list for the South, it was inherent in the Lost Cause sermons. To be sure, the list would not be a literal replica of the Puritan list; the latter detailed departures of individuals from Christian morality, while the Lost Cause sermons were concerned with departures from what the ministers identified as Confederate virtue. At the head of the list was the general sin of mammonism, the spread of materialistic values. As the Reverend A. W. Magnum said in 1887, "the lauded change in the South consists mainly in the *money-mania*." The standard for evaluating human worth by the "blatant portion of the New South" was "the *brazen* standard of money making."[7] This perception confirmed the fears of clerics who increasingly viewed the New South as an intrusion of Yankee ideals and programs.

In 1882 one of the most bitter advocates of the old ways, the Presbyterian theologian Robert Lewis Dabney, addressed himself to the issue of a New South in a commencement speech at Hampden Sydney College in Virginia. Touching on several themes which later critics of the New South would reiterate, Dabney grudgingly admitted that the defeat of the Old South had been inevitable, a sacrifice to progress; he saw the coming of a New South as equally unavoidable. He hoped to use the benefits of industrialism to increase Southern cultural independence, for without wealth the South would be "dependent and subordinate," despite its "martial virtues." Wealth, then, could be the means to a greater end, the preservation of a distinct Southern civilization. But Dabney warned against the accompanying byproduct, materialism. The North stood as a fearful warning to Southerners on the precipice of change. Dabney cautioned Southerners against think-ing that "the surest way to retrieve your prosperity will be to BECOME LIKE THE CONQUERORS." He predicted that the North faced an "ap-proaching retribution," and he admonished Southerners not to "share, for a few deceitful days, the victors' gains of oppression." Dabney urged caution because he doubted the ability of Southerners to man-age their wealth without being corrupted. Wealth always sought "il-legitimate forms," he claimed, and in "obeying the inevitable impulse" it corrupted the land. "Mammon wills it so, and Mammon rules."[8]

Dabney saw Lost Cause values as the only hope for preserving Southern virtue. Wealth usually weakened "manhood with costly pomps and luxuries," but the Confederate heroes were forever a warn-ing against this spirit. "The problem you have to learn," he told his young Southern audience, was "how to combine the possession of great wealth with the personal practice of simplicity, hardihood and self-sacrifice. That people which makes selfish, material good its God, is doomed. In this world of sin the spirit of heroic self-sacrifice is the essential condition of national greatness and happiness." In a stark conclusion, he prophesied, "If the generation that is to come ever learns to be ashamed of these men because they were overpowered by fate, that will be the moral death of Virginia, a death in which there will wait no resurrection." Dabney later recalled that, when he had finished his sermon, "the whole audience was in tears."[9]

Dabney was not alone in warning against the dangers of New South materialism. "Alas! the trouble is that the love of gain, the root of all evil, absorbs the hearts and minds of our men," proclaimed Episcopal Bishop Richard Wilmer of Alabama. He insisted that the church's main threat was "*Mammonism!* Mammonism, which blinds the minds of them that believe not, and dazzles the minds of them that believe, and thus the light of the glorious Gospel, and the glory of heralding its tidings, is hidden from the souls of our people." He complained that Southerners were "in a craze," and that the spirit of speculation had made "wise men mad." The Methodist preacher John C. Calhoun Newton, in *The New South and the Methodist Episcopal Church, South* (1887), recognized the inevitability of a New South. He defined the South's problem as one of assimilating the sudden wealth that would soon be produced, money which would not be coming "*slowly and nor-*

mally from within," but which would result from the "sudden and immense influx of capital from abroad." He contrasted the threat of the New South with the noble Southern past. Whereas the Old South had been a variant of feudalism, "and therefore chivalric, and intensely unmercenary," the New South threatened to be "a low mammon worship." Another Methodist critic of the New South materialism in the 1880s was Oscar P. Fitzgerald, a popular figure at Confederate veterans' gatherings. His influence stemmed from editing the *Christian Advocate* from 1878 until 1890, and thereafter he became a Methodist bishop. Fitzgerald believed that "the profane babblings of materialism" were the most important threat to traditional Southern values. He pointed out that the business-industrial aspect of the New South was predominating over other goals. "When Mammonism thus possesses the people they soon become prepared to make almost any concession of moral principle to the demands of commercial expediency," he said. "Cursed be the wealth which comes to us at such a price!"[10]

Prophets of the Lost Cause warned of mammonism and worldliness in the 1880s, but they went beyond this general criticism in later years, to engage in a wide-ranging discussion of the cancer spreading through the South. Perhaps the chief devil of Southern Protestants was Demon Rum, and the Lost Cause prophets warned against the worldly sin of drunkenness. Drinking had increased during the Civil War, and after 1865 it was a frequently noted problem among the demoralized Southerners. The preachers pointed to the Confederate as the model of right behavior. H. A. Scomp, in *King Alcohol in the Realm of King Cotton* (1889), claimed that Southern soldiers drank less liquor than any "other English-speaking army of modern times." A favorite hero in this connection was Stonewall Jackson. When the clerics preached against liquor, their text was sometimes his words: "I am more afraid of King Alcohol than of all the bullets of the enemy." Although Jackson was the preachers' favorite because his ascetic, moralistic puritanism fitted their need exactly, they also cited Lee, Jefferson Davis, and other heroes as models of sobriety. After 1900 the Anti-Saloon League established a Lincoln Legion to promote total abstinence, but it soon changed the name to the Lincoln-Lee Legion, in order to please Dixie.[11]

Southerners claimed that the liquor interests were Northern based, and thus an alien, corrupting force. Scomp, of the Methodists' Emory College in Georgia, surveyed the earlier temperance efforts in the South, concluding that the postwar liquor crusade grew directly from prewar Southern antecedents. He thus countered the Northern charge that the postbellum temperance campaign had been introduced by reform-minded Yankees during Reconstruction. Scomp praised the Confederacy's attitude toward alcohol, contending that it had tried to suppress the distillation of liquor. On the other hand, blame for the power of the liquor lobby in the Gilded Age was, Scomp concluded, due directly to the taxation of alcohol by the Union government, which inadvertently created a potent liquor lobby in response to the action. One historian of prohibition has concluded that some Southern reformers believed that "in this reform lay the chance of revenge." The North had abolished chattel slavery in the South; the South would now abolish whiskey slavery in the North.[12]

Southerners also condemned a peculiarly visible regional symbol of the sins of materialism and worldliness, the Louisiana Lottery. The Lottery Company had been established in 1868 with a twenty-five-year charter. Ministers opposed it from its beginning, and throughout the 1870s and 1880s they spearheaded efforts to have it abolished. They argued that the Lottery was objectionable because it represented gambling. Even though it might seem innocuous, gambling was as sinful, said one cleric, as being in a New Orleans brothel. The fearful preachers believed that, during the poverty-ridden Reconstruction years, the temptation for Southerners to participate in the Lottery was greater than it ordinarily would have been; they urged the unwary to be on their guard. Later opponents of the Lottery, playing on the sectional theme, stressed that it had been sneaked in by Yankee carpetbaggers and Southern scalawags during Reconstruction and had since become rooted in the self-interest of Louisiana citizens, whose moral scruples had been overcome by the search for wealth.[13]

As on the liquor issue, the clerics cited the Confederate hero as the model of correct behavior. The use of Confederate heroes in this connection was complex. Southern railroads and businesses frequently hired Confederate generals to give their efforts respectability; the same was true with the Lottery Company, which announced in the 1870s that Generals P. G. T. Beauregard and Jubal Early would be its spokes-men. As symbols of integrity and honor, their demanding job was to sit on the platform during the Lottery ceremonies and to supervise the spinning of the Lottery wheel. Opponents of the Lottery Company re-alized the appeal of these men, and they believed that they were be-traying the Lost Cause, betraying the moral and spiritual values that the Confederacy had represented. The editor of the *Texas Baptist Her-ald* observed in 1879 that Beauregard and Early might be famous war heroes, but he asserted that they had failed the South in peacetime by lending their names to the Lottery evil. Concluding that "the true pa-triot" should "respect the moral sentiment of a community," he called the managers of the Lottery "wicked men," who knew the value of "a brilliant name" and obtained the best Southern names money could buy. Though some ministers granted that the heroes may have unwit-tingly allowed their names to be used to support "this form of sin," most agreed with an article in *Southern Presbyterian*, which charged that the sole object of the two generals was "to *fill their own pockets*." The author was "surprised and grieved" to see men of "such high char-acter" lending support to immorality.[14] The clerics had discovered that decline even affected some Confederate heroes.

Realizing that they could not allow the Lost Cause to be preempted by their opponents, Southern clerics asserted that the Confederate heritage was on their side. The head of the Anti-Lottery League was a Confederate colonel, and ministers related his heroic past to his noble reform efforts. Louisiana Governor Francis Nicholls, who had lost an eye, an arm, and a leg in battle, was a crusading opponent of the Lot-tery, and the ministers perceived him as a Confederate knight trying to slay the Lottery dragon. They praised people like General Edmund Kirby Smith, who had rejected the presidency of the Lottery Com-pany in favor of remaining an educator at the University of the South. Smith died, deeply in debt, eight days after refusing the company's healthy financial offer, thus giving rise to a parable of virtue. Oscar P. Fitzgerald called the Lottery "one of the most demoralizing institutions in this country," and he charged that, as a result of the participation of Beauregard and Early, "the men that followed Robert Lee and Sidney Johnston have cause to hang their heads." Fitzgerald contrasted the behavior of the Lottery generals with that of Lee. The latter's activity as a poor educator was "preferable to five times the amount received by 'a hero' for the use of his name to sell tickets in a lottery."[15]

The clergymen went beyond these specific signs of Southern decline to engage in a broader analysis. They were disturbed by the emerging shape of Southern society itself. Having a hierarchical, paternalistic, moralistic, non-materialistic conception of the good society, they were troubled by the social changes accompanying industrialization and urbanization. "A pure democracy is the dream of the idealist," said Howard M. Hamill, chaplain general of the United Confederate Veterans, "and would be unprofitable even in the millennium." He praised instead the paternalistic aristocracy of the Old South as one of "wealth, of blood, and of honor." Ministers criticized New South businessmen, the "swarm of idlers," for their lack of an ethical code and their "nauseating display" of wealth, contrasting this with "the inflexible code" and open-hearted hospitality of earlier Southerners. James McNeilly raised an explicit class issue in his critique of the New South, noting that "when greed for gain is the controlling motive, as it is in a commercial commonwealth, then there is no limit to the oppression that men will inflict for money." Writing during the depression of the 1890s, he pointed out that expanding Southern capitalism had created a class of unemployed tramps who wandered the countryside, visible symbols of declining Southern virtue. Equally disturbing were the cruelties of child labor; the white slave trade, which existed to satisfy "the lust of the idle rich"; and the growing labor movement, which held its members "to a slavery as tyrannical as that of its opponent." His image of society was that of "a growing chasm between the classes, a lack of sympathy that bodes no good." The real concern of the clergymen was the impact of these societal developments upon individual virtue. The clear result of "the congestion of wealth, the result of war," was "the debasing of character." McNeilly lamented that "the tendency of enormous wealth" was "to make virtue in woman and honor in man commodities to be bought and sold in the market." His troubled conclusion was that "the doom of the nation is sealed," because of the class division and its effect on virtue.[16]

The foreign immigrant also seemed to threaten a virtuous Southern society. Oscar P. Fitzgerald saw the foreign immigrants as "red-handed anarchists and God-defying atheists" who had corrupted the North. Most immigrants had settled in the North, making that section "rich and strong." But Fitzgerald believed that Northerners "would be willing to have grown more slowly if, having less money, they had purer morals; and having a smaller population, it were more homogeneous and peaceful." He warned the South to profit from the North's experience. Visualizing the foreign immigrant as Catholic and urban, the ministers portrayed him as a moral threat to the South's civilization. James Gambrell foresaw a mission for Southern religion, predicting that the South was "yet to play a great part in saving American institutions from the foreignizing deluge in the north." More specifically, he proposed that one day Southern Baptists would "send multitudes" of missionaries north to aid in the struggle "with a constant in-pour of immigrants." To fulfill this destiny, the South had to remain uncontaminated by foreign influences.[17]

The clerics were agrarians at heart, and they hoped to avoid materialistic dangers in a New South by advising young Southerners to stay on the land. Since the Lost Cause ministers had no specific, practical political or economic program, the agrarian argument was a limited one. On the other hand, the Lost Cause was not the only protest against business dominance in the Gilded Age South. In the 1890s Populism emerged, with its agrarian-based critique of the new order. The agrarianism of the Lost Cause was aristocratic and conservative, while the agrarianism of Populism was democratic and reformist. For the Populists, the main point of contention was economic, but to clergymen the moral-religious issue of virtue was even more important. Ultimately, neither protest would prevail against the New South.[18]

The prophets of the Lost Cause also saw decline in politics. "We have fallen on evil times," said the editor of the *Christian Advocate* in 1898 when assessing politics. After the Civil War, the plantation aristocracy lost its political ascendency to a new elite—a business elite of industrialists, large merchants, and railroad officials. The ministerial defenders of the Lost Cause identified these business-oriented politicians as one symbol of the New South. Believing in a hierarchical, paternalistic, moralistic, non-materialistic society, they were consequently hostile to the dominance of politics by the *nouveaux riches*.

The preachers insisted that this business class and its political representatives had no conception of the need for virtue and morality.
They repeatedly portrayed the New South's business-oriented politicians as crassly materialistic and corrupt, contrasting this with the allegedly higher tone of politics in the Old South and the Confederacy.
Preachers spoke of the "almighty dollar politics of the bloated bond-
holder and the trusts, the one-idea craze of the silver mine-owner,"
"the tariff greed of the manufacturer," and the "bribery and corruption" in politics. Suffrage was "degenerating into a mere commodity
having a commercial value, just as cotton or tobacco!" Robert L.
Dabney believed that, in a morally decayed environment like the
postwar South, the demagogue was inevitable; he appears just "as the
vulture comes where the carcass is." Claiming that paid political managers, bosses, ward heelers, and the partisan press had not existed in
the Southern past, Howard M. Hamill concluded that "these latter-
day importations and inventions of 'peanut' politics would have mer-
ited and received the unmeasured contempt of the politicians of the
Old South." Criticism even extended to noting the corruption within
the Democratic party. Hamill urged the region to free itself "from
thirty years of subserviency and emasculation" to the party, so that it
could once again "assert and maintain the integrity and high principles of the Democracy of the fathers." By 1893 Dabney was predicting
that "the Democratic party will be dissolved by its own putrescence."[19]

Many of the politicians aligned with business interests had been
Confederate leaders, and this complicated the views of the ministers.
As with the Lottery, some ex-Confederates seemed to have fallen prey
to the corrupt temptations of the age. Dabney condemned Con-
federate General and postwar Virginia Governor William Mahone,
asserting that the latter's only motivation in politics was personal
financial gain. The Mahone era in Virginia was a "carnival of corrup-
tion," and Dabney's only hope was the traditional one of the prophet:
"God is the judge; he will avenge." Pastors continued to honor any
Confederate saint who had maintained a purity of soul. Methodist
Bishop Warren A. Candler of Georgia, for example, in a eulogy to
Georgia Governor and United States Senator Alfred H. Colquitt in
March, 1894, said that Colquitt was "knightly and Christian in an un-
chivalrous age." Living in a time "when vast fortunes have been easily

acquired," Colquitt held political positions "where a less scrupulous man would have grasped large wealth. But he has died poor. I think he was a little proud of his poverty." Candler claimed that the key to Colquitt was his belief, fostered by the Old South and tested in the Confederacy, that the first and last duty of every human being was "morality; virtue, virtue, always virtue." Candler insisted that politicians like Colquitt vindicated the Southern past and provided a force for virtue among his corrupt New South peers. In reality, Confederate veteran politicians like Colquitt were frequently more committed to a New South than to preserving the past; Colquitt, for example, had speculated in railroads, textile mills, a fertilizer factory, and coal mining. Nevertheless, some ministers downplayed such connections, focusing instead on the past virtue shown by the politicians when they were Confederate heroes.[20]

The prophets of the Lost Cause also saw a decline in education. They attacked the idea of a utilitarian education and criticized "the cheap and tawdry 'business college.'" In contrast, students in the Old South had learned to read, think, analyze, judge, debate, "and in short to master whatever subject one might come upon." Howard Hamill admired the discipline of the past schools and the teachers who had "molded us into the image of the gentleman of the Old South." Many sermons addressed the young, urging them to reject the false values of the New South and, as the Reverend H. D. C. Maclachlin said in a 1917 sermon, to learn the "gentle art of being ladies and gentlemen, of chivalry to women and honor between men, of the old-fashioned courtesy which takes time to be polite—that spirit born in the purple which is the most precious of all the legacies which your fathers left you when they sealed their testimony with their blood." Hamill urged the Southern young to "shun as sacrilege" the ideas of the New South. In an emotional Memorial Day address in 1914 at Nashville's Mount Olivet Cemetery, he urged Southern parents to let the "old-time rule of honor and gentleness, of unfailing courtesy and high breeding, become the law of life to our boys and girls."[21]

Finally, the prophets of the Lost Cause warned that religion itself was in crisis because of the spread of materialism. The fear of religious decline had been a major theme of the New England jeremiad, and the same was true in the South. The Southern fear was not of declining numbers, as in New England, but that the churches themselves would be compromised because of their prosperity. Churches were criticized for increasingly relying on membership figures and material resources as signs of health. "When this mammonism has once invaded the Church of God," said John C. Calhoun Newton, "made the pews vain and worldly, frivolous and luxurious, and when it has once contaminated the pulpit, disarming it of honest utterance, then we shall wish that the iron furnaces, and the rolling mills, had never come." Baptist pastor James Gambrell agreed, pointing especially to the large city churches. "What are they more than Sunday Social Clubs?" he asked. They might claim "great numbers, intelligence, social influence and wealth," but they lacked the essential spirituality that evangelical churches needed. Despite the great sums of money spent on religion, the ministers were convinced that not enough went to promote evangelism, which they believed was the primary function of the church. The very size of congregations seemed to undermine the church's mission. "It is an age of organization," said the Reverend McNeilly, "and when men are incorporated in a body they are apt to lose their sense of personal responsibility, which is the foundation of real high character."[22]

The ministerial analysis of the postbellum South was thus a troubled one. Still, the attitudes seem to contradict the realities of the expansiveness of Southern religion and of the Confederate groups after the Civil War. Believers in conservative religion and regional tradition marched from victory to victory. One can perhaps again gain insight from the New England jeremiad. Perry Miller noted that the cultural anthropologist must read the jeremiads with a certain skepticism, because their total effect was "not at all depressing: you come to the paradoxical realization that they do not bespeak a despairing frame of mind." These ritualistic sermons were "purgations of the soul," which enabled the second and third generations of Puritans to accommodate themselves to the inevitable changes that had occurred in their American experience. They came to realize that their mission was no longer to represent an extension of the Protestant Reformation, but to achieve an American mission. They still retained, most importantly, their sense of mission as a chosen people.[23]

When reading the sermons of older Lost Cause ministers like Dabney, Palmer, Wilmer, and McNeilly, one does see despairing minds at work. McNeilly was a good example. Born the son of a slaveowner, he served as a chaplain to Tennessee troops in the Civil War, and was partially blinded in battle. Afterward, he served as a Presbyterian pastor in Nashville for over forty years. From the 1890s until his death at eighty-four in 1922, McNeilly, a short-haired man with bushy eyebrows and a long, wiry goatee that fell straight down to his chest, steadily recorded his Confederate memories and in the process revealed himself to be a sad, poignant figure. He was the aging Confederate who knew he was out of place in the New South. McNeilly worried that the younger generation of Southerners was rejecting the Southern heritage; he was convinced that they ignored or contemptuously dismissed the ideals of the prewar era. Insisting that these ideals could "never become outworn," McNeilly complained that "the present generation seems ready to set them aside for material ideals which are the idols of the pit." Although men of the new order ridiculed the men of the Old South, he said during a monument dedication, "the blood of one of these men of the 'Old South,' shed on yonder fateful field, was richer than the life current of the whole race of sneering, money-seeking, materialistic apostles of the 'new' South." The Confederates were the supreme products of the Old South's civilization, and they vindicated that society. They proved their nobility, even though "the fledglings of a new day decry and ridicule." Their achievement was one of principle and idealism. McNeilly argued that the Confederate heroes had "achieved a finished testimony, a consistent record against mere materialism." This was especially important in an age when everything was "measured by money values." His hope was that their example would "endure in the spiritual upbuilding of our people."[24]

To understand fully the Lost Cause jeremiad, one must distinguish between the first-generation Lost Cause ministers, like McNeilly, who had matured before the war and played a leadership role in it, and the children of the cause, the second and third generations of ministers committed to the defense of the Confederate memory. The latter group was more open to the potential for religious advancement via New South wealth. As C. Vann Woodward has pointed out, the churches increasingly relied on the wealth of the new order to finance their operations and programs. Many ministers praised industrialists and businessmen for their support of Southern religion. These younger prophets of the Lost Cause were part of dynamic, expansive denominations which were in the process of extending their dominance over Southern culture. James B. Gambrell, for example, who was president of the Southern Baptist Convention, had been a Confederate scout as a youth; he played a major role in publishing and organizational activities of his denomination. Believing in expensive missionary work and moral reform efforts, he urged larger contributions to Baptist churches. The son of one of Georgia's largest slave-owners, a brother to Coca-Cola magnate Asa Candler, and a frequent Lost Cause orator, the Methodist Bishop Warren A. Candler had a Midas touch for his denomination. As president of Emory College and later as chancellor of Emory University, Warren gained contributions of over $7 million from his brother.[25]

Nevertheless, the reliance of ministers like Gambrell and Candler upon the wealth of the New South did not preclude their criticizing the postbellum world. They struck the same themes as the older clerics, but with something more—a hopefulness and a confidence in the future. Their hope was embodied in words that revealed a questing, a crusading spirit. "A great forward movement is demanded at this time, especially in the South, to save us from a mere material civilization," Gambrell warned in an 1892 sermon before the Southern Baptist Convention. "Undoubtedly, the South is to become vastly rich, and riches have always had a materializing tendency." Recognizing the inevitability of change, he hoped to control, rather than to obstruct, the force. Candler attributed change to "that fell destroyer and arch-demon of evil," the Civil War, which had left Southerners so poor and demoralized that many of them hungered inordinately for wealth. "Our main concern should be to fix our moral convictions so deeply that our consciences will not drag anchor in the tidal wave of commerce that is impending," he wrote in 1908. "It will bring great dangers to moral life." Noting that "our human nature is no better than that of other people," he cautioned that the temptation for Southerners would be to "subordinate principle to commercial expediency." He predicted that "settled principles of morality and righteousness" would be "derided as obsolete puritanism." At this point in his argument, he summoned the inevitable Confederate example. Claiming that the virtuous Confederate experience was particularly relevant because the virtuous elements of man were imperiled in his age by the materialistic, selfish pursuit of wealth, he called for "a new crusade and a higher chivalry" that would insure the survival of traditional spiritual and moral values in the new Southern world.[26]

Beneath the surface lamentations about the dangers of Southern decline was a great hopefulness, based on the clerics' paradoxical belief that the Civil War, despite being in some ways cataclysmic for religion, had not disturbed fundamental continuity with the Old South. God's chosen people still had a mission to fulfill, and it was not contained simply in an inward, otherworldly theology. The crusading religious zeal of the Confederacy, stifled during Reconstruction, erupted thereafter. The Southern religious world, like the rest of the South, lost its battle with Northern evil in the war; however, in the 1880s the religious-political fervor that had not really been spent even in 1865 was rechanneled into opposition to internal Southern evil. Southern Christians of the 1865–1900 period expected that their day of trial would come, and they prayed that, like their forebears, they would be equal to the task. With each baptism of blood in combatting evil they renewed their faith. Perry Miller showed that the Puritans of the late 1600s were redefining their mission and identity into American terms. Similarly, the Lost Cause prophets were applying the Confederate-Christian crusading spirit into building a Southern identity with essential foundations combining religion and regional history. A frequently recurring phrase in the literature of postbellum Southern religion was "our Southern Zion."[27] The Lost Cause was to be at the heart of it. Whereas the second- and third-generation Puritans had lost control of their society, Southern ministers of the late nineteenth and early twentieth centuries were profoundly shaping theirs. They successfully led crusades using the power of the state to achieve moral reform. By 1890 every Southern state had adopted local option laws, so that prohibition of liquor existed at the local level in most places. In the 1890s the Louisiana Lottery was not rechartered and thus died. The denominations expanded their educational work and their overseas and domestic missions. Revivalism was a pervasive aspect of Southern communities, enabling the Baptists and Methodists to extend their numbers and influence.

Ultimately, then, the second- and third-generation postwar Southern ministers had good reason not to despair. Candler understood one strand of the Southern theology when he warned that Southern human nature might not be able to remain uncorrupted in the face of wealth; but the Baptist leader Victor I. Masters explained another strand—the confidence in Southern superiority. It was based in Southern history. From defeat in war and humiliation in Reconstruction, Masters said, Southerners had developed "a great gentleness of spirit which was worth more than all the billions we have now gained." The challenge from New South industrialization was whether Southerners, "chastened and refined by suffering," could control the lavish wealth that was now theirs. "If we really had all the greatness of soul we believe we had, we would be able to show it by using our wealth for service, instead of spending it for power and pleasure." He argued that the South had a better chance than other sections "to win the victory over dollar-lust and the machine." The South had "a peculiar responsibility" to demonstrate to the nation its moral and spiritual superiority. If Southerners succeeded in the quest, they would vindicate their past by drawing upon it for inspiration in the struggle against materialism.[28] By serving as an example to the rest of the nation, even Northern redemption might rest upon Southern wisdom.

The Southern sense of mission thus tempered the force of the Southern jeremiad. As in New England, the jeremiad form, the warning against decline, helped reconcile Southerners to the process of Americanization—meaning, in this case, economic and societal changes from the North. By suggesting, albeit with fear and danger, that Southerners might be able to control the impact of the New South changes, Southern ministers promoted the very process they feared. The sense of mission, of hope, of continuity with the regional past persuaded Southerners that they might manage their new American prosperity. But, paradoxically, the jeremiad also served to nurture a Southern identity. Only by drawing upon the heritage of the Southern past, on an identity forged in the Civil War and thereby separate from the American identity, could corruption be avoided. The North was a continual reminder of what Southerners must not become. The Lost Cause jeremiad thus touched deep emotions of the Southern people. The hope was that a cultural identity based on religion and regional tradition could be the answer to Southern fears of decline. The full impact of the jeremiad has not yet been assessed, though. One aspect of the fear of decline requires a more extended discussion, because it involved still deeper fears stemming from the South's greatest social problem: the question of the black's role in the Southern Zion.

Chapter Five

MORALITY AND MYSTICISM ✝ RACE AND THE LOST CAUSE

WHITE SUPREMACY was a key tenet of the Southern Way of Life, and Southern ministers used the Lost Cause religion to reinforce it. The implications of the Lost Cause for racial relations were disturbing. The Ku Klux Klan epitomized the use of the Confederate experience for destructive purposes. The Klan represented the mystical wing of the Lost Cause, as the most passionate organization associated with this highly ritualized civil religion. Its mysticism was attained not through a disciplined meditation, but through the cultivation of a mysterious ambience, which fused Confederate and Christian symbols and created unique rituals. The racial views expressed within the context of other Lost Cause institutions were more moderate than the Klan's. Race itself did not play a large role in the Confederate myth, where the central focus was on the virtue of the Confederates. Southerners insisted that they had fought for principle, not for slavery, and the Negro's wartime loyalty was a respected part of the Lost Cause myth. The special concern of Lost Cause ministers was the obstacle that postbellum blacks presented to the preservation of a virtuous Southern civilization. The ministers' views on this subject thus reflected the essential concern of the jeremiad; one could see here, as elsewhere, that the Lost Cause vision of the good society was paternalistic, moralistic, well ordered, and hierarchical.

The post–Civil War years saw segregation emerging to replace slavery as the South's solution to the "race problem." Southerners were united in believing in white supremacy, but historians have identified several different positions within the general acceptance of white dominance. After the instability of Reconstruction, the position that dominated the 1880s was the paternalist-conservative one, closely aligned with the New South business philosophy. The paternalists typically rejoiced at the demise of slavery, but they nostalgically praised the harmonious race relations of the antebellum period. They saw no black moral or cultural decline after the Civil War, and they stressed that the races had continued their harmonious relations. The second position, which came to dominate after 1890 and especially after 1900, was of negrophobia. The Southern position partly reflected the nationwide growth of Anglo-Saxon racism in this era. The extreme racists of the South believed that the Negro was a beast, and that he had sunk to a morally degenerate condition when the discipline of slavery had been removed. They advocated rigid repression and control, which meant strict public segregation at the least, and which sometimes even extended to the justification of lynching.[1]

Southern ministers were among the leading defenders of white supremacy. As H. Shelton Smith has suggested, racial heresy was more dangerous to a preacher's reputation than was theological speculation. White Southerners perceived dissension on the racial issue as a threat to the social order itself, and clergymen made clear their commitment. One could find ministers whose views fell into each of the two major racial positions, although few religious leaders succumbed to extreme racism. Most typically the clerics preached acceptance of Negro inferiority and white supremacy, while working to mitigate the harshness of the system through individual cases of charity and kindness. The attitude of ministers of the Lost Cause did not precisely fit either of the two dominant categories; they were paternalists, but their attitudes came from a different source than those of the New South paternalists. Lost Cause belief focused on the moral retrogression of blacks after emancipation, but preachers articulated this idea before the extreme racism of the end of the century made it a dominant article of faith. The belief in moral retrogression stemmed from the legacy of slavery, the blacks' behavior in the Civil War, and the Reconstruction experience.[2] The fear of Negro decline was the basis for both racial positions associated with the Lost Cause—the extreme Ku Klux Klan viewpoint, and the more moderate paternalistic-moralistic position. The Klan represented negrophobia, while the Lost Cause paternalists tried to find a substitute for slavery as a way of insuring Negro virtue and thus Southern virtue.

After the Civil War, prominent antebellum clergymen restated the argument that slavery was a God-ordained, spiritual institution. They believed that God had rescued the Negro from savagery, so that Southern whites could train him in Christian civilization. Slavery had thus opened a missionary field of four million people to Southern white evangelists. In explaining emancipation the Methodist Albert T. Bledsoe, among others, concluded that blacks had been "in the protecting matrix" long enough: God had allowed them to be freed so they could return to Africa, in order to spread Christianity and civilization. The Presbyterian cleric John B. Adger, a prewar evangelist to the slaves in South Carolina, was typical in claiming that "the South has no tears to shed" over the end of slavery, which he said represented the "deliverance from a very serious and weighty responsibility." But just as typically he added that the religious principles underlying slavery "cannot die."[3]

While the clerics thus stressed that slavery Christianized the blacks, they also admitted the closely related point that slavery provided a valuable system of moral and social discipline. The key word was "order." As the Methodist pastor Albert T. Goodloe remarked, slaves "were contented and orderly"; the Episcopal prelate William B. W. Howe added that slavery was a blessing to blacks because they led "comfortable and well-ordered lives." The preachers portrayed slavery as an expression of a profound eternal truth, the need for order in society and in individuals. William Harrison, in his novel *Sam Williams: A Tale of the Old South*, summed up the institution as one with "a firm but mild authority on the one hand, and a confiding obedience on the other." Through it, a commendable hierarchy had been achieved. Methodist minister George Smith, in his novel *Boy in Gray*, observed that slaves "were not permitted to do as they wished, and alas! I have found that when people, young or old, black or white, are permitted to do as they wish, many of them wish to go wrong. They were made to work, and alas! it is a sad fact that many people will not work unless they are made to do so." His words reflected his opinion of the contemporary world as well as the Southern past. Episcopal Bishop Richard Wilmer of Alabama praised slavery for bringing order to white Southerners and black slaves alike. At first, he said, slavery was based on the economic considerations of the white planters; but soon religious motives touched the slaveowners, and "the relation between them and their servants became less and less mercenary, and more and more patriarchal." For their part, Wilmer continued, African blacks had been "heathen savages" until Southern slavery civilized them: "Their habits of subordination to their earthly master inclined them to an easier submission to the will of God." He concluded approvingly that, in this properly ordered condition, obedience soon "went forth to every object of reverence and authority." He contrasted this antebellum society of subordination, submission, reverence, and authority with the postwar South, which experienced "conflicts of races, animosity and distrust, jealousy of capital, suffrage without sense, religion without morals, service without reverence."[4]

The frequent reassertions of the religious and moral principles of slavery suggested that the preachers were still defensive about the institution. Throughout the late nineteenth century, and especially during Reconstruction, Northern denominations irritated their Southern counterparts by uncompromisingly attacking it. Southern denominational assemblies were concerned enough with the issue to justify slavery long after its demise. As late as 1876 the Southern Presbyterian Church Assembly was reaffirming that "domestic servitude is of Divine appointment" because its essential principle was that of submission, which was "an essential element" in every society, government, and family. The Southern Baptist Convention reasserted slavery's religious dimensions in 1892. While urging reconciliation with the North, Baptist editor James B. Gambrell typically responded with anger when he heard Northern criticism of the Southern past: "If we are to be told that our fathers were barbarous in holding in servitude a people committed to them in a state of slavery, we are sufficiently human to resent it as unjust and untimely."[5]

As a result of the war and Confederate defeat, Southern ministerial defenders of the Lost Cause in effect extended the pro-slavery argument to include new elements needed to justify the prewar institution and, later, segregation. For example, they portrayed blacks' behavior in the Civil War as a vindication of slavery. "They were quite as loyal to the Confederacy as their masters, and to them we are indebted for the fact that the war lasted four years," said the Georgia *Christian Index*. Another *Christian Index* contributor, Richard Carroll, in 1917 pointed out that blacks had contributed to the Confederacy by feeding the soldiers, constructing fortifications at the battlefront, and guarding women and children on the home front. Albert T. Bledsoe in the *Southern Review* made black behavior seem even more significant when he accused the North, with its "advanced Christian civilization," of trying to provoke slaves into a bloody rebellion. "These devilish instigations failed however," he said, "and the poor semibarbarous negroes proved themselves to be more civilized than their instigators." The Episcopal Bishop Stephen Elliott evoked a concept from the myth of Confederate virtue when he said that the behavior of slaves in the war was "the sublimest vindication of the institution of slavery" that could have been given.[6]

To the defenders of the old order, the heroism of Southern white men and women had reached its peak in the Confederacy; likewise they conceded that blacks, as slaves, reached the height of their dignity as a race in the war. If the Confederate heroes were noble, heroic, and honorable, the key word to describe the black role in the Confederate myth was "loyal." Blacks had achieved dignity, said Methodist Rebecca Felton, "by reason of discipline and habit, restraints on idleness, and [the] good example" of white slaveowners. They had remained in their allotted order in society and had been exalted by their loyalty. One clergyman went further than most when he argued that blacks had developed "a genius for religion" through contact with whites in slave times, and that the slave's religious "influence was afterward felt in the religious tone of the Confederate armies." In making such comments, Southerners were careful to attribute the virtuous wartime conduct of blacks to the antebellum influence of slaveowners.[7]

Throughout the late nineteenth century Southerners praised and even romanticized "the old-time Negroes" produced by the plantation. Southern religious leaders and laymen were perhaps even more prone to this view than most people in Dixie; they sentimentally reminisced about the influence of the old uncles and beloved mammies, freely granting that the chivalrous character of Southerners owed much to the spiritual example of these old slaves. Betsy McKeethen had served the Leonidas Polk family all of her life, and when she died in 1874 they praised her as an embodiment of the principles of the

Episcopal church, as a teacher of her own upright children, and as one who had nurtured the character of the Polks themselves. A few ministers professed, in retrospect, to having had doubts in childhood about slavery because of its effects on their black nurses and friends. Sumner Cunningham, the editor of *Confederate Veteran* magazine, proposed in one of his first issues that old blacks who had been slaves for twenty years should be given homes in honor of their service.[8]

Surveying the Southern landscape, the Reverend A. H. Gilmer in 1896 went so far as to observe, "So many monuments, yet how strange no one has thought of these dear old mammys and faithful servants." In fact, at the turn of the century the Confederate groups did debate the question of building a monument to the slave's loyalty in the war. Methodist cleric Howard M. Hamill described one such proposed statue as "a trinity of figures to be carved from a single block of Southern marble, consisting of the courtly old planter, high-bred and gentle in face and manner; the plantation 'uncle,' the counterpart in ebony of the master so loyally served and imitated; and the broad-bosomed black 'mammy,' with varicolored turban, spotless apron, and beaming face, the friend and helper of every living thing in cabin or mansion." The issue was controversial. Indeed, one Daughter of the Confederacy, Mrs. W. Carleton Adams, was outraged at the suggestion. Noting that the South was "already black with their living presence," she insisted that Negroes deserved no monument. The trusted slaves were well rewarded for their wartime loyalty, she continued, and she suggested that money for a slave statue could be better spent in building a home for Confederate women. Her final argument seemed to her to be insurmountable. Writing in 1904, she noted that every Southern town was "in mourning for some beautiful woman whose life has been strangled out by some black fiend." Who, she asked, could propose in light of this situation a tribute to blacks?[9]

Nevertheless, the United Daughters of the Confederacy pledged $1,000 for a Negro monument. A spot at Harpers Ferry was chosen, where Heyward Shepherd, a former slave employed as a railroad night watchman, had refused to join John Brown's raid. A 900-pound boulder was chosen, and a contract was given to the Peter Burghard Stone Company of Louisville. Opposition to the project came from the city council and from students at a nearby Negro institution, Stoner College. Not until 1937 was the memorial boulder placed and dedicated at Harpers Ferry on land contributed for that purpose. The inscription said that the stone was a "memorial to Heyward Shepherd, exemplifying the character and faithfulness of thousands of negroes, who, under like temptation, throughout subsequent years of war, so conducted themselves that no stain was left upon a record which is the peculiar heritage of the American people and an everlasting tribute to the best in both races."[10]

The ministers of the Lost Cause believed strongly that slavery had provided essential order, discipline, and morality in Negro life, qualities which were seen in the Civil War experience. But when slavery ended, they consequently came to believe in the moral retrogression of blacks. As Rebecca Felton put it, the black race "was more honest, more upright, and more virtuous in the South, at the time of the surrender at Appomattox, than they are today." Her use of the word "virtuous" pointed to the concern among Lost Cause religious figures that the traditional virtue of the South was endangered after the war. Black immorality, it was feared, could destroy Southern virtue.[11]

The preachers themselves praised the Negroes whose character had been molded by slavery, but they feared the young blacks growing up in freedom. In an 1893 editorial on recent lynchings, the editor of the *Christian Advocate* asserted that those lynched were rapists. He warned that they were not "the old slaves who watched over their masters' families with so tireless a fidelity in the dark days of 1861–1865"; instead they were "the representatives of a new generation, intoxicated by a liberty which they have not known how to use." Instead of being hard-working, moral, and religious, they were now "indolent, sensual, devilish." Similarly, the Reverend John Paris warned that when blacks gained their freedom it soon became license. These "simple minded people," he said, believed they had been "freed from the restraints that servitude had thrown around them," so they "abandoned themselves to a cause of reckless disappation [sic]." In his words was the assumption that people, and especially blacks, could never legitimately abandon "restraints." Howard M. Hamill made the same point. While freedom was "an inestimable boon," he said, the "care-worn faces of the remnants of old-time negroes" indicated that they had discovered the limitations of freedom. "I take exception," Hamill said, "to the much-vaunted doctrine of liberty as the panacea for all human ills." [12]

Robert Lewis Dabney was surprisingly frank about the sexual dimensions of his fears. The young black woman seemed to him to symbolize Southern doom. He wrote that, without slavery, black girls in the antebellum era would have "grown up the besotted victims of brutal passions." With Southern defeat the restraints of slavery were gone, and he saw only predictable results. Black women "breed the future incubus of your descendants," he wrote a friend. His solution was to make the South's problem the North's problem, by urging young black women to go North, "out in a steady stream upon Washington City, Philadelphia, New York, Boston, etc." The relationship between his fears and the Confederate heroes was painfully clear in the speech he gave in November, 1867, at the Presbyterian Synod in Virginia:

Yes, sir, these tyrants know that if they can mix the race of Washington and Lee and Jackson with this base herd which they brought from the pens of Africa, if they can taint the blood which hallowed the plains of Manassas with this sordid stream, the adulterous current will never again swell a Virginian's heart with a throb noble enough to make a despot tremble. But they will then have, for all time, a race supple and grovelling enough for all the purposes of oppression.

In 1891, in one of his last letters, Dabney was still unrelentingly warning of the black presence as "an eating cancer" that imperiled the South. [13]

Southern clergymen especially worried over the alleged decline of black religion after emancipation. Southerners had contended in the pro-slavery argument that slavery was a Christian, missionary institution that allowed white Christians to bring the glad tidings to the heathen. Whites had, in fact, exercised great supervision of slave religion, but after the war the situation changed. While most religious leaders wanted to retain blacks within the existing denominations, they refused to give equal status to blacks in church offices and worship services. Consequently, by the end of Reconstruction, Southern Christians were segregated into black and white denominations. [14] Southern white religious leaders soon concluded, though, that freedom in religion had resulted in blacks sinking into "moral and spiritual darkness." They complained that the Negro's innate emotionalism had resulted in a false religion. "Colored people being naturally very excitable," said Richard Wilmer, "their meetings become the scene of the wildest orgies, savoring much more of heathenism than the peaceful work of the Spirit." To such observers, it seemed to be a short step from "a seeming religious exaltation to the lowest act of sensuality and vice." Another pastor, John Paris, conceded that blacks were faithful worshippers, but he added that they believed "some of the most glaring absurdities." The Reverend J. M. Rittenhouse charged that Negroes were now taught by "men as ignorant as themselves—'blind leaders of the blind.'" The black preachers were said to be too often venal, ignorant, licentious and unworthy of their offices. The General Assembly of the Southern Presbyterian church in 1874 observed that blacks needed a good dose of sound Presbyterian doctrine to counterbalance "the mere frenzy of the emotions," while the Episcopal *Southern Churchman* in 1911 suggested that Negroes needed "the moral leaven," which, incidentally, was "just exactly the thing our Church has the history and genius to give."[15]

While believing in the moral retrogression of blacks, many ministers of the Lost Cause did not see a hopeless situation. They were paternalists, searching for a substitute for slavery, which would restore what they thought was the moral discipline of the peculiar institution. Episcopal Bishop Thomas Dudley, for example, represented a moderate racial position, and he was a prominent minister of the Lost Cause. Born and raised in Richmond, Virginia, Dudley served as a major in the Confederate army in his home state, and after the war he became an Episcopal bishop in Kentucky and an active member of the veterans' groups. He later became vice-chancellor at a leading Lost Cause college, the University of the South. With a strong identity as a defender of the old order, he had been able to propose in a national magazine a more liberal racial policy than most Southerners favored. In "How Shall We Help the Negro," which appeared in *Century Magazine* in June, 1885, Dudley opposed rigid segregation, especially in church work. Like all Lost Cause ministers, Dudley accepted the doctrine of black moral retrogression after emancipation, but he argued that this decline was not inevitable and that it could be halted by contact with "individuals of the higher race." For this reason he openly opposed segregation in churches and schools. His position was that white religious leaders still had the same Christian responsibilities toward blacks as the prewar ministers and planters had had toward slaves. Although his opposition to segregation was atypical, his belief in white responsibility toward blacks was a key assumption shared by Lost Cause preachers.[16]

By the 1890s segregation had become the accepted substitute for slavery. The ministers of the Lost Cause saw the institution as a paternalistic one. Methodist Bishop Charles B. Galloway of Mississippi was perhaps the best-known Lost Cause paternalist in the post-1900 period. Born to pious Mississippi parents, he reached adolescence during the Civil War, and he always remembered that the Southern preachers he had heard when young had "expounded the old prophecies and proved to my perfect satisfaction that the South was bound to win." He later became one of the most prominent second-generation ministers of the Lost Cause. Unlike Dudley, Galloway was a segregationist. In "The Negro and the South," an address delivered at the Seventh Annual Conference for Education in the South, he outlined his white supremacist views, advancing four principles for race relations: no social mixing, separate schools and churches, white control of politics, and opposition to the colonization of blacks. Galloway claimed that whites still had a paternalistic responsibility to halt black decline, although (in contrast to Dudley) he had retreated on the issue of segregated churches. Galloway absolutely refused, though, to justify or to condone the lynchings that plagued racial relations after 1900. He blamed the resort to lynch law on political demagoguery and the sensation-seeking press. While these institutions had failed the South, he noted approvingly in 1904 that a Confederate veterans' camp in Mississippi had again provided the moral leadership for the South. These "heroic men, who feared not the wild shock of battle in contending for what they believed to be right, recently passed some vigorous resolutions against this spirit of lawlessness." He insisted after 1900 that blacks were impotent and "the old cry that 'white supremacy' may be imperiled is a travesty on Anglo-Saxon chivalry."[17]

Like Galloway, Episcopal Bishop Theodore DuBose Brattan was a child of the Lost Cause, and a spokesman on racial matters for his denomination. He advanced the idea of Negro education as a way to substitute self-discipline for the vanished discipline of slavery. In a 1908 address in Memphis before the Conference for Education in the South, Brattan pointed out that disfranchisement of Negroes had correctly settled the political aspect of the racial relationship, but he insisted that any permanent solution required Negro education. He claimed that blacks were unable to direct that education and thus needed "white guidance and white leadership." As on the antebellum plantation, supervision of blacks was "the duty of the Christian South," although, unlike earlier, education was now a duty, as was evangelism.[18]

While the paternalists thus looked for moderate means to insure a moral black population, the Ku Klux Klan saw only a violent and harsh solution to the problem of perceived black moral retrogression. The ministers stressed the background of the development of the Klan and its inevitability. The myth of Reconstruction was an integral part of the Klan story. Southern religious leaders believed that black virtue had reached its height during the Civil War, but that moral decline had accompanied freedom. In Reconstruction blacks, aided by Yankee carpetbaggers and Southern scalawags, began using freedom as license; they soon were threatening the civilization of the South. Ignorance and corruption were said to have dominated politics under black rule, the indolence of Negro workers hampered the economic system, and black crime and brutality threatened society itself. Without the bonds of slavery, the primitive nature of the blacks was emerging.[19] Into this situation, "this condition of total lawlessness," as James Gambrell phrased it, came the savior of the South—the Ku Klux Klan. "Christianity and civilization lay in the balance," said one pastor, and the Klan was simply one more illustration of how "the mighty Anglo-Saxon race on this continent" had always met the challenges to it. The Reverend John Paris remembered that "disorder sprang up in communities" during Reconstruction, a state which inevitably gave rise to the Klan. James McNeilly wrote that Northerners used the Klan "to show the lawless spirit of the South, yet that mysterious organization arose only when the outrages of carpetbag rule became unbearable." The Klan was needed to deliver the South from "that wild orgy of corruption, graft, thievery, and lust miscalled Reconstruction." The Nashville *Christian Advocate* in 1889 concisely summed up the Klan's emergence as a desperate attempt to restore "good morals and civil order."[20]

As the defenders of the old order had it, the main characteristic of the Klan seemed to be its lack of violence. As defenders of the concept of an orderly, moral society, the preachers were aware of the dangers in extralegal activities. The Episcopal theologian William P. DuBose argued that the Klansmen did not desire to be violent; besides, the presence of Northern troops in the South would have prevented any violence. He used the word "discreet" to describe the Klan's handling of the situation. That violence had occurred, though, could not really be denied. One justification was to suggest that any Klan violence had prevented greater bloodshed in the lawless, disordered world of Reconstruction. Other clergymen tried to divert the blame for violence from the Klan. The *Christian Advocate* in 1889 admitted that "excesses" had existed in the name of the Klan, but it added that these were rare instances when individuals used the Klan to gratify "brutal instincts or personal grudges." When this began happening, the leaders disbanded this "extraordinary agency." The Klan was thus essentially a nonviolent organization, so most of the violence attributed to the Klan was said to be really the fault of other groups. As the Texas Baptist preacher W. T. Tardy wrote, "a kind of bastard Ku Klux organization" functioned in his area long after the Klan officially dissolved. He admitted that it had suppressed the lawlessness of blacks, but he believed it created a lawless spirit among "irresponsible whites." John L. Underwood agreed, asserting that "rowdy imitators" of the Klan did much harm.[21]

The Klan, in truth, was a vital organization of the religion of the Lost Cause. Southerners romanticized it as a chivalrous extension of the Confederacy. The original Klan began as a social fraternity among six bored young ex-Confederates, all of good family, educated, and active church laymen. Like a college fraternity, they took the name of their group from a Greek word *kuklos*, meaning circle or band. The organization began in Pulaski, Tennessee, site of the wartime hanging of the Confederate hero Sam Davis; it spread throughout the state as an aggressive opponent of the Northern-sponsored Union League, the Republican party, and the congressional Reconstruction policy. Because of its growth, the Klan reorganized in Nashville in 1867, formulating as its objectives to protect Southern whites from indignities, to aid the impoverished families of dead Confederates, and to defend the American Constitution and legitimate laws. It then became the "Invisible Empire of the South," ruled by a Grand Wizard. A Grand Dragon supervised each state, or realm; a Grand Titan directed each dominion, or county; and a Grand Cyclops dominated each den, or local group. In the first four months of 1868 the Klan expanded from its base in central Tennessee into every Southern state. Republican Governor William Brownlow bitterly opposed the Klan and its violence, and in February, 1869, he proclaimed martial law in east Tennessee. By this time the Klan had clearly become a terrorist group, with an important political function, supporting the Democratic party. It was on a vigilante crusade for white supremacy. The organization was officially dissolved in 1869, because of growing opposition and because its leaders had difficulty controlling the vigilante impulse. Despite this formal action, the Klan continued in effective existence, and other secret bands emerged in imitation of it. Congress launched an investigation of the Klan conspiracy, and it passed anti-Klan laws in 1871.[22]

The Ku Klux Klan had crucial Confederate connections that made it a part of the religion of the Lost Cause. The first and only Grand Wizard was Nathan Bedford Forrest, the chivalric Confederate general from Tennessee; many other former Confederate officers also participated. John B. Gordon, the popular first commander of the United Confederate Veterans in the 1890s, was the Grand Dragon of the Georgia Klan, and George W. Gordon, also a leader in veterans' activities, was active in the Tennessee Klan. Father Abram Ryan may have served as a chaplain. Confederates used their wartime military connections to spread the Klan's influence. Klansmen frequently bypassed established political leaders, who might be suspicious of extralegal activities, so the Confederate link was a vital organizational factor. It was a natural step for the rank-and-file Confederate soldiers to become rank-and-file Klansmen. One old Confederate veteran put it colorfully on his tombstone: "An unreconstructed Johnnie, who never repented, who fought for what he knew to be right from '61 to '65 and received one Mexican dollar for two years' service. Belonged to the Ku Klux Klan, a deacon in the Baptist Church and a Master

Mason for forty years."[23] In the Reconstruction years, before the Confederate organizations had emerged, the prominence of Confederates in the Klan kept alive the holy memory and tied it to the Klan's racial approach.

The Klan's religious orientation reflected the mystical Celtic roots of early Scotch, Irish, and Scotch-Irish Southern settlers. To be sure, ministers of the mainline Southern Protestant churches were more middle class than mystical. The local Klans apparently included many community leaders, but, in contrast to the second Klan, little direct evidence existed to indicate that Southern ministers were Klan members. In the testimony before a congressional committee, only one incident involving a cleric as Klansman was identified. More important than direct ministerial responsibility for Klan activities was the mystical, religious tone to the Klan. Its members cultivated a mysterious appearance, dressing like medieval penitents in robes, usually ghostly white or demonic black. They also wore conical headpieces, decorated with devilish horns, beards, and sometimes long red tongues sticking out. The organization used phrases to evoke the images of darkness, graveyards, and ghosts. The Klansmen worked at night, said the Presbyterian clergyman Walter Capers, so that "the mystery and fear of the unseen" would aid them. As a result, the Klan "became a terror to the guilty. Their imagination became invested with the grim images of retribution." The Klan left as its calling card such delightful warnings as gallows or miniature coffins. The Reverend James McNeilly played down any Klan violence, emphasizing instead that the Klansmen, with "their ghostly apparel, their mysterious movements, their dread warnings in the sepulchral tones of the dead" frightened superstitious blacks into submission. In 1917, at the unveiling in Pulaski of a bronze tablet commemorating the birth of the Klan, a local pastor evoked the religious nature of the organization in his prayer honoring the men "who came from dens and caves in the weird mystery of nightfall to the defense of our rights and homes." The Klan was thus "an army of defense, a safeguard of virtue, and a victory for the right. Thine be the glory, Almighty God." The ceremony ended with the singing of the hymn "How Firm a Foundation."[24]

The Klan thus entered Southern mythology. The Southerner who most sensationally explored in fiction this relationship between the

Klan, blacks, religion, and the Confederacy was a minister, Thomas
Dixon, Jr., of North Carolina. Born in 1864 in Shelby, North Carolina, Dixon grew up during the turmoil of Reconstruction; one of his
strongest recollections was a nighttime Klan parade that frightened
him in 1869. His mother quieted his fears, telling him that the Klansmen were "our people," who were "guarding us from harm." Dixon's
uncle, Colonel Leroy McAfee, was the leader of the Klan Den in Piedmont, North Carolina, and his colorful tales and romantic example
stimulated the youngster's imagination. Thomas was equally affected
by his father, the Reverend Thomas Dixon, a prominent North Carolina Baptist cleric. An 1883 graduate of Wake Forest, a North Carolina Baptist college, Dixon went to graduate school and was an actor,
a lawyer, and a state legislator before becoming a Baptist preacher.[25]

Dixon's ambitions prevented him from being a typical minister of
the Lost Cause, since his career took him into the North. Indeed, before 1900 he wrote little in justification of the South or in con-
demnation of the Negro, and he never mourned the passing of the
slaveholding class. He seemed to have deserted his Lost Cause
heritage. Around 1900, however, he reassessed his values in response
to nationwide developments. Dixon approved America's new overseas
involvement; he came to believe that, just as the "inferior" peoples of
the Philippines and Puerto Rico did not deserve equality with Anglo-
Saxons, so America's blacks did not deserve equality. When he came
to view the threat of blacks to American democracy as being immediate and apocalyptic, he began a nationwide crusade against Negroes.
Dixon's actions were thus part of a national movement toward racism,
but he soon used his Southern past to embroider his views.[26]

Dixon became a popular novelist and two of his novels, *The Leopard's Spots* (1902) and *The Clansman* (1905), dealt especially with
black decline in the Reconstruction era. By showing how Reconstruction had turned the Negro into "a possible beast to be feared and
guarded," Dixon represented Southern negrophobia at its peak. He
portrayed the black as an animal who "roams at night and sleeps in the
day, whose speech knows no word of love, whose passions, once
aroused, are as the fury of the tiger." During Reconstruction, black ter-
rorism represented "a veritable Black Death for the land and its people." Dixon praised the Ku Klux Klan, noting that its purpose was "to

bring order out of chaos, protect the weak and defenceless, the widows
and orphans of brave men who had died for their country, to drive
from power the thieves who were robbing the people, redeem the
commonwealth from infamy, and reestablish civilisation."[27] Dixon's
portrait of the Klan especially stressed its religious nature. An important character in The Clansman was the Reverend Hugh McAlpine, a
Presbyterian preacher and the chaplain of the local Klan. McAlpine's
prayer at a Klan meeting held to avenge the rape of a Southern white
girl expressed Dixon's view of the Klan's religious orientation:

Lord God of our Fathers, as in times past thy children, fleeing from the op-
pressor found refuge beneath the earth until once more the sun of righteousness rose, so are we met to-night. As we wrestle with the powers of darkness
now strangling our life, give to our souls to endure as seeing the invisible, and
to our right arms the strength of the martyred dead of our people. . . . While
heathen walks his native heath unharmed and unafraid, in this fair Christian
Southland, our sisters, wives, and daughters dare not stroll at twilight
through the streets, or step beyond the highway at noon.[28]

Dixon's novel was made into one of the most popular movies of all
time, The Birth of a Nation, by another Southerner, D. W. Griffith.
After seeing the film, Southern-born President Woodrow Wilson said
it was like "writing history with lightning." The Reverend A. J. Emerson, undoubtedly representative of countless others, expressed approval of it in the pages of the Confederate Veteran magazine, further
using the occasion to reassert the Klan's worth. He claimed that
between 1868 and 1872 a war had been fought against Negro domination, and that through the efforts of the Klan an unwritten amend-
ment was added to the American Constitution: "The American
nation shall forever have a white man's government." Emerson concluded that the Klan celebrated by Griffith "was one of the most remarkable and successful armies that ever campaigned in any age or
nation. They were good men and true."[29]

The movie was so powerful and so popular that it encouraged the
formation of a second Ku Klux Klan in 1915. The Birth of a Nation pre-
miered in New York City in March, 1915, and on Thanksgiving night
of that year, before its Atlanta premiere, the Klan was born again.
William J. Simmons, an Alabama native and a former Methodist cir-

cuit rider, led a contingent of fifteen followers, including two members of the original Klan, to the top of Stone Mountain, a huge granite slab east of Atlanta. It became a Confederate monument in the 1920s, with the figures of Lost Cause heroes carved in the granite. Simmons and his disciples gathered stones on that Thanksgiving night to make an altar, on which they placed an American flag, an unsheathed sword, a canteen of initiation water, and a Bible open to the book of Romans, chapter 12. In this resurrection of the Klan, its leader made a striking ritualistic advance. The burning of crosses was an ancient practice in the Scottish highlands, and the ceremony was dramatically recalled to Americans through the novels of Thomas Dixon, Jr. On that November night in 1915, Simmons lighted a cross of pine boards padded with excelsior and doused with kerosene, thus making cross burning the central Klan ceremony.[30]

The week after this ritual Simmons, whose father had been a member of the first Klan, incorporated the group in Atlanta. Like its Reconstruction predecessors, Simmons's group began as a fraternal club; however, it cultivated publicity, rather than secrecy. Simmons had a talent for ritual and an understanding of fraternalism, which he blended with the new Klan's white supremacist philosophy. The modern Klan knight had mass initiations and rallies, parades, picnics, midnight cross-burnings, ceremonial greetings and liturgies, masks and robes. The Klan grew slowly, though, and by early 1917 it had less than 2,000 members, mostly in Georgia and Alabama. With strong Confederate roots, the Klan marched in the 1917 reunion parade of the United Confederate Veterans. When the United States entered World War I in April, 1917, the Klan began a new phase, with a new purpose of representing an endangered "Americanism." In 1920 it entered an even more aggressive period, when Simmons allowed the Southern Publicity Association to direct the expansion of the group. At this point vigilante violence became an integral part of the Klan's promotion of what it defined as "Americanism." An intolerant inquisition resulted. By 1921 Klan membership rolls included 100,000 dues-paying members, and its influence was even greater in the Midwest than in the South of its birth.[31]

By this time the reconciliation process with the North had matured to the point where the Lost Cause virtually stood for the same old-fashioned, rural-based values that "Americanism" represented. As earlier, white supremacy was a vital part of the second Klan's outlook, especially in the South, but the Klansmen directed much of their ugly vigilante actions less at blacks than at Jews, Catholics, foreigners, and those Protestants who were deemed moral degenerates. The Klan's crucial value, which united "Americanism" and the Confederate outlook, was Protestantism, so that it became above all a defense of Protestant morality. Even more thoroughly than in the first Klan, white supremacy and Protestant morality became interfused. Baptist, Methodist, and Disciples of Christ congregations provided the rank and file of the Klan, and their preachers gave it leadership and respectability. The First Grand Dragon of the Texas Klan was A. D. Ellis, an Episcopal prelate from Beaumont; a Baptist pastor named L. A. Nalls was a leader of the Alabama Klan. Most Klan lecturers were Protestant clerics, and many local cyclopses were from small rural churches. Whenever the Klan appeared in an area, it worked to gain the support of clergymen by giving them free membership, leadership positions, and financial contributions for their churches. The Klan leadership promoted the unification of Protestant denominations and even proposed the creation of a Klan church itself. The symbolism, membership, and organization thus reflected the organization's Christian roots.[32]

By the 1920s, then, differences had appeared between the first and second Klans. What had begun in the Reconstruction period as a secret Southern white supremacist cadre was now a national, highly organized group, dedicated above all to preserving morality through vigilante actions. But, as earlier, this simply testified to the close link between racial and moral issues in the minds of Southern whites. Like the more moderate Lost Cause paternalists, the Klansmen feared the threat that blacks represented to their vision of a virtuous society. While Klansmen took the fear to a harsh extreme, they, like the paternalists, were essentially moralists. In the tightly knit Southern small towns, the Klan's contribution to the religion of the Lost Cause was in its symbolism, ritual, and organization. The second Klan was less Confederate and more Christian in its symbolism than the earlier group, but both organizations united the two themes. Confederate organizations endorsed and publicized the Klan's work. The mainstream philosophy of the Lost Cause did not focus on race, however, and when Southerners met to celebrate their Lost Cause religion in its non-Klan rituals and organizations, they did not frequently talk about blacks and racial questions. The ministers of the Lost Cause accepted segregation as a substitute for the discipline of slavery, but their vision of the Southern identity did not hinge only on race. Although racial superiority was assumed, the religion of the Lost Cause taught that the two fundamentals of the Southern identity were religion and regional history. It thus provided a foundation for the Southern identity that was related to, but separate from, race. Nevertheless, the white supremacist outlook was so pervasive in Southern society and was perceived as being so synonymous with Southern tradition that most Southerners must have seen the caste system as visible evidence that the Lost Cause still lived. The post–Civil War Klan had linked the Confederacy to a white supremacist philosophy in a way that Southerners would never forget.

Chapter Six

J. WILLIAM JONES ✝ EVANGELIST OF THE LOST CAUSE

IN ADDITION to its prophetic function, the Southern civil religion, like the American civil religion, had a priestly function. While the ministers feared that the defeated South would abandon its traditional values, many of them tried to prevent this, not by castigating their brothers with jeremiads for their failures, but by celebrating the virtues of the Southern Way of Life. By affirming the tenets of the Southern creed and evoking the memory of past sacrifices, Southerners could be made to realize their place in a distinctive culture and to understand the need for continued commitment to it. A peculiarly Southern aspect of the priestly function was the role of evangelist. Growing out of a prewar evangelical orthodoxy and developing at a time when a prevalent postbellum Southern religious trend was revivalism, the Lost Cause, in the hands of many preachers, took on an evangelical dimension that apparently has not been well defined in the American civil religion.

The supreme exponent of this tendency was the Reverend Mr. John William Jones, a Virginia Baptist who was known as J. William Jones. The catchwords, phrases, appeals, and techniques of Southern evangelical religion reverberated in his career as a spokesman for the Lost Cause and for his own denomination. He was of special interest also because he was the most influential and well-known clergyman in the cult of the Lost Cause; as one of the most popular Southerners in late nineteenth-century Dixie, Jones is a man worth examining. Through his involvement in the religion of the Lost Cause, one can observe its organization and channels of communication. He explored several themes of the movement—the primary focus on virtue, the use of Confederates as moral exemplars, the ecumenical nature of the Lost

. Cause, and the importance of education to it—but he added a distinctive evangelical angle. He represented those preachers who used the Lost Cause to teach Southerners about the importance of conversion to Christianity, as well as about virtue. The Confederate religious experience was for him a paradigm of the old-time religion.

Jones was born on September 25, 1836, in Louisa County, in the piedmont country of Virginia. He attended preparatory academies in Louisa and nearby Orange counties, was converted to Christianity in a camp meeting, and then went to the University of Virginia, where he participated in numerous religious activities. One of the first college Young Men's Christian Associations in the world was nearby, and Jones was its first treasurer. He walked five miles into the mountains every Sunday to teach, took an active part in the Negro Sunday school run by the YMCA, and participated in a protracted revival in his dormitory that resulted in the conversion of all of its residents. Even at this age he had shown that he was an evangelist at heart; it was also significant that his religious endeavors centered on the non-denominational YMCA. After graduation Jones went south, to Greenville, South Carolina, where he became the first member of the first class of the Southern Baptist Theological Seminary. In June, 1860, the church ordained him as a Baptist minister; in July the Foreign Mission Board approved his request to do missionary work in China; in December he married Judith Page Helm. He soon began as a rural pastor at the Little River Baptist Church, in Louisa County.[1]

To this point Jones had shown unswerving interest in religion; the Civil War then intervened to deflect his missionary hopes. A part of Lee's Army of Northern Virginia from the hopeful beginning to the bleak end, he was in many battles, first as a private in the ranks and then, after the first year of the war, as a chaplain. In November, 1863, he accepted the position of evangelist to General A. P. Hill's corps. The war provided "the fighting parson," as he came to be known, with crucial Confederate contacts and a degree of fame for the vigor of his religious work. Jones helped form the Chaplains' Association of the Army of Northern Virginia, and while representing the group he had his first occasion to meet Robert E. Lee, beginning a relationship which later developed into an intimate friendship. Jones worked even more closely with Stonewall Jackson, since he was under the Gener al's command. In addition, Jones became instrumental in promoting the revivals that occurred in the Confederate army, after the battle of Fredericksburg in the winter of 1862–63. Jones cooperated with preachers of other denominations, worked at the hospitals, distributed religious tracts and Bibles, sent letters to denominational journals pleading for more chaplains, and—most important—he preached. He preached in the rain, at sunrise as the troops prepared for battle, and at night to thousands of men sitting on logs before campfires. The fighting parson made a notable record in baptizing soldiers. Once, he cut the ice on a millpond and baptized several soldiers; he later immersed twelve young converts in the swollen, rampaging Rapidan River; twice he baptized Confederates in full view of Union sentries, who did not interfere. He baptized 222 men in one year.[2]

Jones's religious work could not prevent Confederate defeat. In the first months after surrender, he farmed briefly and then served as an evangelist in the coastal area of Virginia. Southern Baptist missionary work was in disarray, and Jones himself had apparently conceived a stronger vision than even foreign evangelism. The rest of his life was devoted to preaching a potent Confederate-Christian doctrine to his fellow Southerners. He picked the right place to begin. In the late fall of 1865 he started work as pastor of the Goshen Bridge and Lexington Baptist churches in Rockbridge County, Virginia. A year later he abandoned work with the rural church at Goshen Bridge and concentrated his energies at Lexington. He had arrived there in November, 1865, one month after Robert E. Lee began his duties as the new president of Lexington's Washington College. During the war Jones had known Lee only casually, but at Lexington he was thrown into frequent contact with the general, who appreciated the parson's Confederate record and his evangelistic talents. Jones quickly joined the list of clergymen conducting the daily chapel services at Lee's school, and he became an early supporter of the Friends of Temperance, a non-sectarian group which received the approval of denominational assemblies and Robert E. Lee.[3]

Moreover, Jones held a "protracted meeting" at his own church shortly after assuming the Baptist pastorate, and after only two years in Lexington his church had added eighty-four new members, including blacks as well as whites. However, the blacks soon withdrew from his congregation and, with his aid, set up their own church. In addition, with Lee's assistance Jones formed a Lexington chapter of the YMCA, which he utilized to promote his evangelical work. In addition to the revival at his own church, Jones promoted one among students at Washington College and at the adjoining Virginia Military Institute. He led nightly prayer meetings, attended and spoke at YMCA meetings, and used the daily chapel services to create conditions for a revival. At Washington College he preached a sermon on the need for "a genuine 'God-sent revival,' not one that man might manipulate and 'get up,' but such a one as 'God alone could send down.'" He insisted that only "the Holy Spirit" could inspire such a revival, and he urged Lexington Christians "to repent of our sins, come back from our wanderings, reconsecrate ourselves to the service of the Lord, and besiege the 'blood-bought mercy-seat' for the presence and the power of the Holy Spirit." The result of this appeal was the "season of refreshing" Jones had prayed for, "a general and all-pervasive revival" in which 110 cadets at V.M.I. and 40 students at the college were eventually converted. He claimed that 35 of these men later became preachers. The revival did affect Washington College, but it centered on the V.M.I. campus, where Jones taught a religion class in New Testament Greek.[4]

When General Lee died in October, 1870, Jones did not tarry in the village. Five months later he resigned his pastorate and became an agent for the Southern Baptist Theological Seminary, and in September, 1873, he accepted another position, as general superintendent of the Sunday School and Bible Board of the Baptist General Association of Virginia. In this position he referred to himself as a "Sunday-school missionary"; his work took him into rural areas, as well as to towns and cities, giving him wide-ranging personal contacts. Meanwhile, he was not ignoring his Confederate work. Upon General Lee's death, his family turned over to Jones the material for a memorial volume, and in 1874 Jones produced his first book, *Personal Reminiscences, Anecdotes, and Letters of R. E. Lee*, which sold 20,000 copies.[5]

Lee had clearly been the central figure in the cult of the Lost Cause immediately after the war. Martin E. Marty has argued that the supreme priestly celebrant of the American civil religion has usually been the President, but until his death General Lee probably filled this role in the Southern civil religion.[6] Jones's intimate association with Lee at Lexington, his almost immediate departure upon Lee's death, his numerous writings about the general, and the wide range of his later services to the Lost Cause symbolically suggested that Jones was an apostle of Lee, who had laid hands on the parson in order that the tradition might be continued. The later achievements of the Reverend Mr. Jones as an organizer and promoter of the Lost Cause indicate that, if Lee was the Christ figure, Jones was his Apostle Paul.

In any event, at the same time that he was working in church agencies, Jones had become involved in an organization that dominated his most productive years. He attended and became temporary secretary of the first convention of the Southern Historical Society in August, 1873; in January, 1875, he became permanent secretary-treasurer, a position which he held until 1887. Under his direction the *Southern Historical Society Papers* appeared in January, 1876, and he eventually edited fourteen volumes. In the late 1870s and 1880s this was the most important publication of the Lost Cause, and Jones's position enabled him to control much of its shape by controlling the dissemination of its ideas. Jones allowed a wide range of Confederate opinion in his Richmond-based publication, thus facilitating much of the postwar bickering among generals in regard to actions and mistakes in battle. In addition to publishing the *Papers* under his guidance, the Society became the focus for efforts to assemble and preserve Confederate history. It helped gather a large Confederate archive, with Jones negotiating the exchange of material between his society and the War Department in Washington.[7]

Jones possessed a wondrous ability to maintain, amid great pitfalls, good relations with his fellow Southerners. A pleasant, social man of usually even temper, the stocky, stylishly goateed, impeccably dressed Jones cultivated the friendship of the prominent. Although in one article he mentioned that he had personally known nineteen Confederate generals in the war, most of these he did not know well. After the war, however, he did indeed know and maintain contacts with more famous Confederate military and civil leaders than probably any other Southerner.[8] Because of background, temperament, position, and inclination he was privy to the broad range of Southern efforts to preserve the Confederate past. If something went awry, former Confederates usually wrote him to straighten it out, or at least to explain their positions. Jones became a celebrity because of his position. Although a brave soldier and chaplain, his greatest fame as a Confederate did not come until after the war, when he became such a prominent preserver of sacred traditions. His frequent contacts with famed generals added luster to his own name.

In his work with the Southern Historical Society, Jones clearly promoted Virginia as the focal point for the Lost Cause. His attitude toward his home state appeared in a toast he made in 1892 to the "'Old Virginia Brag'. Sometimes fervent, always overdone, but ever excusable, because we have something to brag on in the hallowed traditions, glorious history, grand men, and noble women of the peerless old Commonwealth." Having served in Lee's Army of Northern Virginia, his reminiscences in the *Papers* naturally focused on its experiences; he clearly skewed his publication by printing more material on the Virginians than on any other branch of the Southern army. While he believed that the tasks and achievements of Lee's command warranted such an emphasis, he refused to grant that he distorted the Confederate story in any way by focusing on Virginia.[9]

Jones was not afraid to use the Confederate past, or his ministerial office, for political purposes. In 1879 he praised the South for honoring Confederates as "our Governors, our Judges, our Legislators, our State and county officers, our Senators and Congressmen," and he warned that the day should never come "when the voters of the South shall neglect to put the survivors into the high places within their gift." While other such appeals undoubtedly appeared, most of the ministers of the Lost Cause were not so blatant in urging election of their heroes. He even went so far as to support a Lost Cause candidate, General Fitzhugh Lee, for governor of Virginia in 1885. Jones wrote a small campaign promotional book summarizing the General's war record, discussing his political views, and suggesting that Lee's moral courage shown in the war was exactly what Virginia needed in the 1880s. The voters approved Jones's recommendation.[10]

Despite his maintenance of good relations with prominent Confederates, controversies permeated Jones's career. He was happy to respond when his South was attacked. He castigated "the cringing, crawling, dirt-eating spirit" of George Washington Cable, who in

1885 published an appeal for a desegregated South and who questioned
the wisdom of the Confederate effort. Jones became indignant in the
1890s over the Northern use of the word "rebellion" to describe the
Confederate effort. "It was not a rebellion and we were not rebels or
traitors," Jones insisted. The parson helped to create two especially
heated controversies. He devoted seven issues of the *Southern Historical Society Papers* to examining the reasons for Confederate defeat at
the battle of Gettysburg. The officers involved contributed articles,
and Jones himself wrote an 1895 statement summarizing the disagreement. He also precipitated an uproar over the issue of the treatment of
Northern prisoners of war in Southern prisons. In the March and April, 1876, issues of the *Papers* Jones published material for a defense of
the South and an incrimination of the North. While admitting that
cases of cruelty and neglect occurred, he maintained that "the Confederate authorities *always* ordered the kind treatment of prisoners of
war," and that any suffering was caused by Union restrictions on the
flow of non-contraband supplies. A good debater, he counterattacked
by indicting the Union government for deliberately mistreating
Southern prisoners of war.[11]

As a popular historian of the South in a particularly sensitive era,
Jones's interest in history was inherently and intentionally controversial. He became something of a self-appointed truth squad, a regulator
especially of textbooks used in the South, and in this role he verbally
flailed Yankee authors for their ignorance. When the Charlotte,
North Carolina, school board adopted a book by a Northern author,
Jones gave speeches and organized protests by veterans' groups. He
called it "a Yankee book that is utterly untruthful," one written "with
all of the prejudices and stupendous ignorance of a conceited Yankee."
The jaunty minister made a list of the fallacies in the book and said he
would "want no better fun than to meet on any fair platform the author, the publishers, or any of their many high-salaried agents" and
dissect the book. "We should *demand* the abolition of this and of all
other Yankee school histories from our schools. And if they force the
issue, we should squarely meet it and fight for *a change in our school
authorities*, if they persist in using Yankee school histories." Earlier, in
reviewing a textbook entitled the *Eclectic History of the United States*,
he characterized it as "so utterly unfit to be used in our schools that it

is a great outrage for school boards (from whatever motives) to intro-
duce it into our schools." He said that teachers should protest it *"and
parents should absolutely refuse to allow their children to study that part of it
pertaining to the war."* Jones demonstrated his talent for dramatizing the
issue when he reported to the 1905 veterans' reunion that his son had
recently brought home a schoolbook which "only a glance" showed
"was not the truth," and which therefore was unfit for the schools. "I
took my knife and cut out all the pages of that book which treated of
the war. I said to him: 'Give my love to your teacher, and say to him if
it is necessary for you to study that book you can quit that school.'"[12]

Jones was also hard on Southerners who wrote false history. In an
1871 letter to the Atlanta *Christian Index*, he warned that many histories by Southerners were no more accurate and fair than Northern accounts of the past. He singled out the works of Edward A. Pollard,
charging that they were "not worth the paper they are printed on,"
accusing him of plagiarism and of "malignant slanders" in treating
Jefferson Davis. Jones recommended that all Southerners "drive his
books from our libraries." In their desire for peace and fraternity, other
Southerners, he complained, tended to "smooth over the matter" and
to suggest that both sides were cruel in the war. He proposed that
Southern historians correct this mistake by showing that only Union
troops were consistently brutal.[13]

Although Jones himself published many volumes, all on Southern
history and none on purely religious matters, his most influential book
was his 1895 textbook, *School History of the United States*. "I have tried
to avoid sectional and partisan bias, and to do justice to all sections of
our common country," he said, "but writing as a Southerner, and for
Southern schools, I have treated more fully than I have seen elsewhere
many matters which will be of especial interest to the South." In this
volume and in other writings Jones sketched a view of the war that was
partly realistic history and partly mythology. Some of his writing epitomized romantic themes, as when he pictured Generals Turner Ashby
and J. E. B. Stuart as dashing heroes, and when he used sentimen-
talized, flowery language. But Jones could also be realistic in describing the war, and, since he had served as a private and a chaplain with
the infantry, he saw the war from the trenches and gave the common
man's experience. Jones developed a popular lecture about the average

soldier, entitled "The Boys in Gray, or the Confederate Soldier as I Saw Him," which he delivered across the South. Jones even suggested half-humorously that the Confederates found that one of them could not really whip ten Yankees; indeed, they could not handle more than four to one odds. Jones's view of the army was not simply a homogenized portrait of saintly, gallant Confederate heroes, although one should bear in mind that his realism and his humorous stories did not necessarily detract from that overall picture. His evaluation was that the Army of Northern Virginia in which he served was "the noblest army . . . that ever marched under any banner or fought for any cause in all the tide of time." Jones affirmed that the average soldier was a committed Christian, and, more specifically, an evangelical Christian. "No army in all history—not even Cromwell's 'Roundheads'— had in it as much of real evangelical religion and devout piety as the Army of Northern Virginia," he said. Religion in Lee's army was "not a myth, but a blessed reality."[14]

Although he focused attention on the holiness of the average soldier, Jones devoted even more of his writing to the legendary leaders of the Lost Cause. One of his heroes was Stonewall Jackson, whom he first met in June, 1861. He pictured Jackson as a potent combination of morality and evangelism, a man of prayer, a Bible reader, a staunch Calvinist, and even "an able theologian." "Jackson took Jesus as his Saviour, his guide, his great exemplar, 'the Captain of his Salvation,' whom he followed with the unquestioning obedience of the true soldier." Jones's view of Stonewall was distinctive because he stressed the General's morality less than the purely Christian dimensions of his religious character, so that Jackson emerged less as an Old Testament figure and more as a New Testament Christian. One of Jones's articles, aptly subtitled "How a Poor Orphan Boy Became One of the Immortals," depicted Jackson as a Horatio Alger figure who was redeemed in this world by his Christian faith. Jones wrote that, when Jackson lay dying, he proved "that he had been taught by God's spirit how to die, as well as how to live." Preacher Jones closed the article with the following sentence which recurred throughout his discussion of the Confederates: "Be ye followers of him, even as he also was of Christ." Jones used this biblical passage to exhort Southerners to join their Confederate heroes in the ranks of the Christian righteous. In an article about the unveiling of a Jackson statue in Lexington, Virginia, Jones used this same message to implore the assembled veterans to become Christians. "God grant that one and all of them may hear the voice of the glorious and glorified leader calling to them in trumpet tones: 'BE YE FOLLOWERS OF ME, EVEN AS I ALSO AM OF CHRIST!'" Conversion could bring an ultimate spiritual victory that would counterbalance all earthly defeats. When Jackson died, Jones said, he "went to wear his 'crown of rejoicing,' his fadeless laurels of honor, and heaven and earth alike have echoed the plaudit: 'Servant of God, well done; / Rest from thy loved employ, / The battle's fought, the victory's won, / Enter thy Master's joy!'"[15]

Jones also wrote of his Lexington, Virginia, colleague, Robert E. Lee, whom he had first met in February, 1864. In his 1900 article, "The Inner Life of Robert Edward Lee," Jones pointed out that he could speak of the general "as a model man," an example of correct moral behavior, but that instead he would confine himself to "the Christian character of this military chieftain. I think that I can show that he was a humble, devout Christian who trusted in Christ as his personal Savior and tried to follow with firm tread the 'Captain of our salvation.'" The general's Christianity displayed lessons on denominationalism and theological bickering that Jones wanted to teach. Lee was a committed Episcopalian, and Jones admitted that he "was sincerely attached to the Church of his choice." Jones added, however, that Lee's large heart took in "Christians of every name." Jones recalled that Lee dismissed theological questions as secondary. The general supported Jones's efforts to promote revivals at Lexington; after one particular meeting, "Lee came across the chapel to take me warmly by the hand and say, 'I want to thank you for your talk, sir. You struck the very key-note of our wants. We poor sinners need to come back from our wanderings to seek pardon through the all-sufficient merits of our Redeemer. And we need to pray earnestly for the power of the Holy Spirit to give us a precious revival in our own hearts, and among the unconverted.'" Like a character from a novel Jones could have written, Lee had expressed the precise message that the minister wanted to deliver. Jones insisted that "I have never known a man who more fully realized that he was 'a sinner saved by grace,' a sinner cleansed in the atoning blood of Christ, a sinner whose only hope of salvation was built on 'the Rock of Ages.'" He closed his 1874 biography of Lee by noting that Lee "lived the life of a faithful soldier of the Cross—he fell at the post of duty with the harness on—he died in the full assurance of faith in Jesus, and now wears the Christian's 'crown of rejoicing'—'That crown with peerless glories bright, / Which shall new lustre boast, / When victors' wreaths and monarchs' gems / Shall blend in common dust.'" In his 1906 biography of Lee, Jones observed that the general's "whole life had been 'a living epistle, known and read of men,' and there came from his silent form a voice more eloquent than the tongue of man can utter saying, 'Be ye followers of me even as I, also, was of Christ.'"[16]

Jones also wrote of Jefferson Davis—in fact, he took the lead in trying to change the Confederate president's negative wartime image into a positive one. In the 1880s he called Davis "the greatest living American." As with the other Confederate leaders, Jones stressed Davis's religious character, calling him "one of the humblest, most intelligent, most decided evangelical Christians whom I have ever known." As Confederate president, Davis was "always outspoken and decided on the side of evangelical religion and his fast-day and thanksgiving-day proclamations . . . breathed a spirit of humble, devout piety, which was not perfunctory, but welled up from a sincere and honest heart." Like Lee, Davis was an Episcopalian, but he had converted to his faith late in life, while serving as Confederate president. Before that he was a Baptist, like Jones, and in the minister's interpretation he still seemed like a Baptist. "He rested," said the preacher, "with child-like trust in the grand old doctrines of salvation by grace, justification by faith, and . . . he rejoiced in the sweet comforts and precious hope of the Gospel." When Davis died, Jones prayed that the controversial leader would "rest in peace, wear 'the fadeless crown of victory,' and rejoice in the plaudit of the Great Captain—'Well done good and faithful servant'—when he shall join Lee and Jackson and others of our Christian soldiers in that bright land where 'war's rude alarms' are never heard." The year after Davis's death, Jones edited the family-approved *Davis Memorial Volume.*[17]

The key document in Jones's portrait of the war and its leaders was *Christ in the Camp; or Religion in Lee's Army* (1886), which exhibited his talents as a collector of the primary sources of history. The book consisted of long quotes from wartime published materials and from letters and reminiscences of ministers involved in religious work in the Confederate ranks. It especially focused on the revivals in the army in the last two years of the war. Aside from assembling these materials, Jones's contribution to the book was to recall his role in the revivals, which made it somewhat autobiographical. Moreover, his comments tying everything together revealed that he conceived the volume not just as a record of religion in the Confederate army, but as a collection of parables about morality and religion. In case after case Jones wrote about an incident and drew a conclusion, a moral, directed toward his contemporaries. While other clergymen used the Confederate example to teach purely moral lessons, Jones's contribution was to explore most fully the peculiarly religious—in this case, the evangelical—dimensions of the Confederate past. That Jones had a broader purpose than simply recounting past greatness was evident in his expressed hope that the book would "be useful in leading men to Christ and in strengthening the faith and brightening the hope of true children of our loving father."[18]

Jones asked John C. Granberry, a bishop in the Southern Methodist church, to write a foreword to the book, noting that the Bishop's wide influence with "evangelical Christians of every name" gave his words "peculiar weight." In this way Jones made clear the book's acceptability to all evangelical denominations. Granberry himself put the book in a broad framework, suggesting that it had "a theme of deep, thrilling, world-wide significance. The only triumphs the author records are the triumphs of the Cross." When Jones used the Confederates as moral and religious exemplars, he made clear their relevance to the postwar South. For example, Jones learned from the Confederates the right way to conduct religious services, and he contrasted their attitudes with those of his contemporaries. While waiting for a worship service to begin back in early 1863, the soldiers did not waste time "in idle gossip, or a listless staring at every new comer"; instead someone began "some familiar hymn, around which cluster hallowed memories of home, and of the dear old church far away." The "whole congregation" soon joined in the singing. When the hymn ended, one of the men prayed. "*And he prays.* He does not tell the Lord the news of the day, or recount to him the history of the

country." In those holy days of war, the preacher would arise; "who-
ever it is, *he preaches the Gospel.* . . . He has no use for any theology
that is *newer than the New Testament,* and he indulges in no fierce polemics against Christians of other denominations." Jones recalled
that, when preaching to soldiers at the battlefront, his "soul was
stirred within him, and he 'determined to know nothing among them
save Jesus Christ and Him crucified.'"[19]

Jones reported that the soldiers spent much time building rustic
chapels, structures which, he admitted, could not compare "in archi-
tectural design or finish to the splendid edifices of some of our city
churches." The Confederate chapel had "no frescoed ceilings," "no
brilliant gas-jets," and "no lofty spire"; "no clear-sounding-bell summoned to cushioned seats elegantly attired ladies or fashionably
dressed men," and "no pealing notes of the grand organ led the music." An undertone of disdain ran through his account of these city
churches, reflecting his belief that the old-time religion did not need
fancy adornments and that indeed it might be best preached without
them. While admitting that he might be an "old fogy" he still confessed to prefer "those old songs which 'the boys' used to sing 'with the
spirit and the understanding,' and into which they threw their souls,"
to "all of the 'classic music' which grand organ and 'quartette choir'
ever rendered." Jones also used the Confederate religious experience
to chide the attendance patterns of his contemporaries. After telling
of Southern soldiers listening to him preach in the rain, Jones said,
"Our brethren who in these days are accustomed to stay from church if
it rains or snows, *or looks like it might do so in the course of a week,* would
do well to study the example and catch the spirit of these soldiers."[20]

The heart of Jones's book was a re-creation of the revivals in the
Confederate army. Focusing on the Army of Northern Virginia, he
discussed the widespread revivals that began in the winter of 1862–63.
Jones insisted, however, that the revivals of the last year of the war
"were as general and as powerful as any we had at all, and only ceased
when the army was disbanded." He reported at the time that in the
last year of the war "many souls" were "being 'born again' in the
trenches." He did not think this great awakening really ended with
Appomattox, since "in the great revivals with which our Churches in
Virginia and the South were blessed during the summer and autumn of

1865 a very large proportion of the converts were from among our returned soldiers." Jones understood that much of the remarkable postwar strength of the Southern churches stemmed from the impact of
the wartime revivals; he estimated that in Lee's army alone at least
15,000 and possibly as many as 50,000 were born again amid the destruction of war. He argued "that a very large proportion of our church
members within the past twenty years have been those who found
'Christ in the camp,' or had the pure gold of their Christian character
refined and purified by the fiery trials through which they were called
to pass."[21]

Jones identified an important element of his own religious creed
when he stressed the interdenominational quality of the Confederate
revivals. He pointed out that one reason for the success of the revivals
was the cooperation "of all Christian workers of the evangelical denominations," and he excluded very few Southern clergymen from
these ranks. No clergyman had to compromise the creed of his church
"but instead of spending our time in fierce polemics over disputed
points, we found common ground upon which we could stand shoulder to shoulder and labor for the cause of our common Master." As a
result, "we mingled together in freest intercourse . . . and formed ties
of friendship—nay, of brotherhood—which time can never sever, and
which, we firmly believe, eternity will only purify and strengthen."
Jones again saw that the wartime events had profound postwar religious effects, concluding "that the fraternal spirit which has so
largely prevailed for some years among evangelical Christians at the
South is in no small degree due to the habit of co-operation which so
generally prevailed during the war." He retained this ecumenical spirit
that had grown out of the war, frequently preaching in the pulpits of
wartime colleagues and delivering eulogies to preachers of all denominations.[22] To Jones, the "crown of rejoicing" was not limited to
Baptists.

Jones made a powerful contribution to the Lost Cause through his
writings, but he also took a vigorous role in the activities of the Confederate veterans' groups, particularly the Association of the Army of
Northern Virginia and the United Confederate Veterans, which he
served for almost nineteen years as chaplain-general. The Dixie divine
was a celebrity at the annual reunions, riding in an honored place

with the famous generals in the processions and appearing regularly on the platform. Old comrades he did not even remember came up and told him he had baptized them before a battle, or had given them still-cherished Bibles, or had saved their lives in battle by pulling them to safety. His ability as a promoter at the veterans' meetings was visible at the 1895 reunion, when he gave a rousing speech urging support for a Jefferson Davis monument in Richmond. He engineered a subscription for the monument amounting to over $10,000, with pledges from the local Confederate camps.[23]

Jones exploited public prayer fully to disseminate his evangelistic Lost Cause message. Typically his prayers began, "Oh, God! Our God, our help in years gone by, our hope for years to come—God of Abraham, Isaac and Jacob, God of Israel, God of the centuries, God of our fathers, God of Jefferson Davis, Robert Edward Lee, and Stonewall Jackson, Lord of hosts and King of kings. . . ." Sometimes his prayers were those of reconciliation, peace, and prosperity, but frequently he could not resist adding that the "glorious prosperity which we enjoy in the Southland" was "largely due to" the Southerner's "own effort." In 1901, at the veterans' reunion, he turned his prayer into a sermon, beseeching Confederate veterans never to "forget the hallowed memories of the past or fail to teach their children the great principles of constitutional freedom which our fathers established and for which we fought in the brave old days of '61–'65." When Jones was a chaplain at the University of North Carolina at Chapel Hill, he once gave the following prayer, which must surely have been the apogee of his unreconstructed preaching in prayer form:

Lord we acknowledge Thee as the all-wise author of every good and perfect gift. We recognize Thy presence and wisdom in the healing shower. We acknowledge Thou had a divine plan when Thou made the rattle-snake, as well as the song bird, and this was without help from Charles Darwin. But we believe Thou will admit the grave mistake in giving the decision to the wrong side in eighteen hundred and sixty-five.[24]

Jones also developed the evangelistic elements of the Lost Cause to their fullest at veterans' reunions. He used his fame and position as chaplain-general to try to convert every veteran, and as he and his comrades grew older he seemed more intent on achieving this goal.

His sermons before veterans also taught how to die a Christian death. In developing these two themes of conversion and Christian death, Jones used the Confederates as models for his points. In closing a 1902 memorial sermon, he told the old soldiers that "it will not be long before all of us who are here to-day shall have passed away." He continued:

> Are we ready for our summons? Are we "soldiers of the cross?" Are we trusting in Christ alone for salvation? When the roll is called up yonder will we be able to answer, "I am here?"
>
> God bless you, my comrades, guide you and help you, that you may heed the lesson of this hour, heed the voice of Davis, Lee and Jackson, and Christian comrades gone before. "Be ye followers of me, even as I, also, am of Christ." God help you to bear the cross now that you may wear the crown "over there"![25]

The biblical sentence that he quoted was the same one he had used much earlier in his writings, when symbolically extending to his readers the invitation to accept the Gospel after learning of the Confederate saints. Implicit in all of the religious exploration of the Lost Cause was the idea of following the Confederate-Christians into conversion, but most ministers had talked of virtue and morality, rather than fully developing the evangelical aspect. Jones was a Baptist revivalist in a great age of widespread Southern, as well as national, revivalism, and he grasped the utility of the Lost Cause for his religious concerns. His work in this regard had two implications that epitomized the meaning of the entire Southern civil religion: on the one hand he showed adeptness in exploiting the Confederate past to add converts to Christianity, and at the same time he cemented the ties between the dominant postwar religious happenings in the South and the Confederate past.

His most revealing sermon in this regard came in 1900, on the ninety-second anniversary of the birth of Jefferson Davis. His text was Hebrews 12:1–2, and his son, the Reverend Carter Helm Jones, read the Scriptures before his father spoke. Jones began by taking off from the biblical passage and asking, "Are we not compassed about with a great cloud of witnesses, and do not voices more eloquent than the tongue of man can utter ring in our ears to-day and call upon us to run with patience the race set before us, looking unto Jesus, the author and finisher of our faith?" The witnesses, of course, were wearing Confederate gray, and he knew that his audience was haunted by them. The dead Confederates testified to their faith through Jones. He praised the Confederate army as the most holy in the world's history, and he condensed for his listeners his conclusions on religion in the army. As the sermon neared an end, Jones carefully established his respect for the old soldiers, but this presaged the real message Jones wanted to deliver. "Will you, then, old comrades, suffer one who respects, honors, and loves you to say this faithful word? *Patriotism is not religion, and to have been a true soldier of your country does not constitute you a soldier of the Cross.*"[26] The stress he put on the last sentence indicated that, for Jones, the Lost Cause and Christianity were not simply a blurred composite. To be sure, the point can be pushed too far; but it is a healthy reminder that the Southern ministers were aware of the seriousness of the issues involved. In this context, the real point was that, for Jones, the difference between the two faiths was the redeeming power of Christ. While Lee, Jackson, Davis, and others were Southern saints, Christ was the son of God. The saints could witness for their Savior; in doing so they linked the rich symbolism and meaning of the Southern Way of Life to that of the Christian tradition.

"As I stand to-day amid these hallowed memories that come trooping up from the past, and look into the eyes of loved comrades," Jones continued in his 1900 sermon, "I but echo the voice of the 'so great cloud of witnesses' as I appeal tenderly, and earnestly to you to enlist under the banner of the Cross—to pay now unto the Lord the vows you made amid the iron and leaden hail of battle—to be true servants of the Lord." By doing so, Jones said, the old veterans would one day "join Christian leaders and comrades gone before, and wear with them the crown of victory."[27] Jones offered the hope of eternal life, and his starting point was the limited life of the Confederacy. Though the old soldiers had known defeat in this life, they could know eternal victory. When addressing such a veterans' reunion, Jones obviously addressed his words primarily though not exclusively to the old soldiers. Family and friends also heard his plea, and, indeed, his lesson was intended for all Southerners. A converted Confederate could then testify to the respectful Southern community and spread Jones's message abroad.

Jones's connection to his own denomination provided a resonance to his work as a Lost Cause evangelist. He always took an active role in church work, and to ignore this would be to underestimate his role as the single most important link between Southern religion and the Lost Cause. While editing the *Southern Historical Society Papers* in Richmond, he at the same time preached at the Ashland Baptist Church. In the early 1880s the vibrant Jones worked part time for the Home Mission Board of the Southern Baptist Convention, becoming a member of the board of managers of the Foreign Mission Board in Richmond in 1883. A year later, when he left his position with the Southern Historical Society, he began full-time work in Atlanta as assistant corresponding secretary of the Home Mission Board, a position which he filled through 1893. In addition, Jones regularly attended the annual Southern Baptist Convention and zealously participated in its sessions, suggesting moralistic resolutions, such as those he introduced on temperance and the Sabbath. Sometimes he even asked for special prayers for his own evangelistic efforts. Jones was among the most conservative men of his denomination on the issue of women's rights in the church, and he vigorously opposed an 1883 resolution to allow a woman to serve as an officer of the Home Mission Board. Jones was a popular figure at the Baptist conventions, as at the Confederate reunions. A prominent and appealing leader of his church, he had ready access to Baptist periodicals, in which he published many columns, some on evangelism and morality and some with the related focus of Confederate activities. Baptist editors reviewed his books, thus giving him valuable publicity. [28]

Jones spent his last years working at a variety of educational, church, and Confederate activities. For two years he was chaplain at the University of Virginia, served in the same position at the Miller Manual School, Albemarle County, Virginia, and he then spent several years as chaplain at the University of North Carolina. In 1903 he left Chapel Hill to become secretary and superintendent of the Confederate Memorial Institute in Richmond. A former Confederate veteran, Charles Broadway Rouse, a private who had made a fortune after the war from retail clothing stores in Richmond and New York City, had offered $100,000 to build this Institute, provided the South would contribute an equal sum. A former Confederate general, John C. Underwood, first assumed the position that Jones later occupied; however, his questionable financial activities brought on his ouster and made Jones's work that much more difficult. The pastor worked six years without much progress, then made an appeal to the wealthy citizens of Richmond and managed to scrape together $50,000, only half of the needed amount. Jones then persuaded the Richmond city government to provide the remainder, so that the Institute was able to launch its work as a museum and archive. Jones also worked hard to raise money for a Jefferson Davis monument on Monument Boulevard in Richmond, which was erected in 1907, and he finished work on his last book, *Life and Letters of R. E. Lee* (1906). His last years were also marked by much lecturing, which made him an even better-known figure and added to his reputation as a popular historian in the North as well as the South. He published articles on Jackson's and Lee's religion in a Northern magazine, and he received an enthusiastic reception when he lectured on Jackson in Boston in March, 1907.[29]

Like a biblical patriarch, Jones had five hardy sons, four of whom became Baptist preachers and one of whom, Carter Helm Jones of Louisville, was especially active in the work of the Confederate organizations. "The Jones Boys," as the father and his sons were affectionately known, attended the Southern Baptist Convention and enlivened the scene with their camaraderie and energy. Jones's wife made her own contribution to tying religion to the Lost Cause with her numerous poems honoring the Confederate cause. Her husband dedicated his last book to her.[30]

Jones died in Columbus, Georgia, on March 17, 1909, at the home of a son. His body was taken to Richmond, where he was laid to rest in Hollywood Cemetery, the resting place for many prominent Confederates. A writer for the Virginia Historical Society noted that "the bluff and cheery 'Dominie'" had died, a man "who was never 'reconstructed,' and who, worshipping Lee and Jackson next to his God, devoted his whole life to defending by tongue and pen the eternal righteousness of the 'Lost Cause,' after it went down in defeat, and who at the last died not only in the 'faith once delivered to the saints,' but in the good old Confederate faith." A representative of the Confederate Memorial Institute noted that "to chronicle the deeds of its mighty men, was the chief inspiration and joy of his life."[31] In fact, his greatest achievements had come in service to the Lost Cause, rather than in service to his denomination, although the two were not sharply distinguished in his own mind. As a soldier, he had served God by serving the Confederacy; after defeat he served God by celebrating the mysteries of the Lost Cause. He did continue to insist, though, that a baptism of blood was not a baptism of water, and that only the latter could bring ultimate redemption. Jones showed talents as an administrator, promoter, publicist, lecturer, historian, archivist, and orator. His talents exemplified those of an expansive evangelistic movement in the South, and he used them to convert his brethren to Christianity and the Lost Cause. He was only the most prominent of the clergymen who provided the crucial link between the Southern civil religion and Christianity. While remaining unreconstructed, Jones was not embittered by defeat, as some other clerics had been. The latter feared that a Southern Way of Life could not survive without a separate political existence. Jones more perceptively understood that a separate culture, with religion at its heart, could thrive within the boundaries of the nation.

Chapter Seven

SCHOOLED IN TRADITION ✝ A LOST CAUSE EDUCATION

SOUTHERNERS REALIZED that ultimately the Southern Way of Life could not survive if their children rejected the Confederacy. The Lost Cause movement helped Southerners to retain their identity in light of the crushing defeat and poverty that war had brought. But Southerners especially wanted their descendants to understand that defeat had not destroyed the relevance of the Southern resistance to that identity. Southern ministers played a large role in this phase, as in the other aspects of the Lost Cause. They supervised and institutionalized the teaching of a "correct" interpretation of Southern history. Clergymen led the call for textbooks and historical monographs suitable for use by Southern children, served on committees to canvass the books and determine their acceptability, and wrote history books themselves. In addition, the preachers promoted the link between the Confederacy and Christianity by founding and serving at educational institutions which taught Southern and Christian values. Denominational colleges provided a postwar home for large numbers of former Confederates, and the schools thus became museums of living models of virtue for the students. A few religious schools so strongly cultivated the Confederate-Christian connection that they became among the South's most important Lost Cause institutions, a fact often overlooked by historians.[1] These Lost Cause denominational colleges continued to educate an elite, as antebellum schools had done. While the trend in the nation and indeed in the South was toward the state university and away from classical education, the schools of Southern tradition continued to educate gentlemen on the prewar pattern.

Throughout the 1870s and 1880s Southerners organized local historical societies and launched magazines to promote the assembly, preservation, and study of materials on Southern history. The formation of the Southern Historical Society in 1869, its reorganization in 1873, and the launching of the *Southern Historical Society Papers* marked the most important institutionalization of this trend. The establishment in 1892 of a permanent Historical Committee of the United Confederate Veterans was another important landmark. As a result of its efforts, the first chair of American history in the South was set up at Peabody Normal College in Nashville; the committee complained in 1899, however, that few other schools had followed Peabody's lead. After 1900 Southern women directed many of these historical activities. The United Daughters of the Confederacy was even more aggressive and single-minded than Southern men. In 1912 the "U.D.C. Catechism for Children" appeared, with historical facts about the war and Reconstruction arranged in dogmatic question-answer form. The historical interpretation was belligerently pro-Southern. The women appeared before state textbook commissions and pressed for adoption of books they approved. In 1901 the Daughters' historical committee urged the examination not just of histories, but also of "readers, biographical sketches, poems for recitation, songs, and even geographies." [2]

The denominations, especially the Southern Baptists, even believed Northern prejudices affected Sunday school materials. "They tell of the noble boys and girls of the North, and of their gallant soldiers," said Jeremiah Bell Jeter, editor of Richmond's *Religious Herald*, in 1866, "laying all upon the altar of country, and then, on the next page, of the cruel fiendish 'rebels.'" In that same year, the official "Report of the Sunday School and Publication Board" of the Southern Baptist Convention complained that its survey of new religious material uncovered in many books allusions to the war "made in accordance with the views and feelings of the Northern people." The report concluded that Southern Baptists would not order library books or even hymnals from the North because they might contain insulting comments on the war. The Baptists in particular, and all the churches to some extent, continued throughout Reconstruction to express wariness over Northern Sunday school materials, and the concern over prejudiced Northern historical accounts even survived Reconstruction. What disturbed Southern clergymen about Northern histories

was the attack on Southern virtue, which was, of course, the key concept in the ministerial view of the Confederacy. The editor of the
Central Presbyterian identified the crucial issue in 1868, when he wrote
that Northern writers were bringing "an indictment against the humanity, the morality, the *Christianity* of the South," hoping to "degrade and injure her people in the opinion of Christendom." James
McNeilly observed that Northern distortions represented "the most
deliberate, stupendous, and malignant system of falsehood ever de-
vised by fanaticism." Fanaticism, of course, had always marked Yankee
tradition.[3]

Given this situation, Southerners expressed special interest in
school textbooks. The two most popular texts among followers of the
Lost Cause were J. William Jones's *School History of the United States*
(1896) and Susan Pendleton Lee's *A School History of the United States*
(1895). Both authors had strong religious ties: Jones was a prominent
Baptist preacher, while Susan Lee was the daughter of Brigadier General William Nelson Pendleton, an Episcopal priest. Their books were
similar in approach, form, orientation, and organization. They gave
more space to the settlement of Virginia than of New England, and
they stressed the South's crucial role in the American Revolution. In
Lee's book, the entries under "slavery" in the index were revealing of
her argument: "introduction of, throughout the world, in all the colonies, opposition to, Southern view of, guaranteed by Constitution,
continued agitation, difficulty of abolishing, under Southern Confederacy." Both writers had more photographs of Confederate than
of Union generals, and Lieutenant General Leonidas Polk received
much more attention than a modern textbook would give.[4]

In addition to authentic textbooks, several clergymen made notable
contributions to the assembling and writing of Confederate history,
and their works were on the official lists approved by Confederate
groups. Howard M. Hamill's small book entitled *The Old South* was
approved, as was Henry M. Wharton's collection of *War Songs and
Poems of the Southern Confederacy, 1861–1865*. Albert T. Bledsoe in
1866 published the most important constitutional defense of the
South's right to secede, *Is Jefferson Davis a Traitor?*; in 1915 a Virginia
chapter of the United Daughters of the Confederacy republished his
book as *The War Between the States*. Southern schools quickly adopted

it for use. The Presbyterian theologian Robert L. Dabney also contributed to the constitutional defense of the South, with his *A Defence of
Virginia and Through Her of the South* (1867), and he inaugurated another trend of the writing of Confederate history with his 1866 biography of Stonewall Jackson. More than just a biography, the book was a
religious document containing moral lessons, a Presbyterian theology,
and a judgment of the North. The Reverend John R. Deering, of Lexington, Kentucky, became chairman of the United Confederate Veterans' historical committee in 1914; earlier he had published *Lee and
His Cause* (1907), a collection of historical addresses which broke no
new ground but instead gave a popularized account of the themes of
Confederate history.[5]

Two ministers with Confederate backgrounds were especially important. Like a character in a Tolstoy novel, Brigadier General Clement
A. Evans was so profoundly moved by the suffering he saw on the battlefield at Fredericksburg, Virginia, that he swore to devote his life to
brotherhood if he survived the war. In 1866 he began a quarter-
century career as a Methodist circuit rider in northern Georgia. He
served as chairman of the veterans' historical committee, later acted
as commander-in-chief of that group, and was president of the Confederate Memorial Institute in Richmond. His greatest historical
contribution was in editing and contributing to the twelve-volume
Confederate Military History (1899). A politician, diplomat, and educator, J. L. M. Curry had preached to Confederate soldiers and became a Baptist minister at war's end. As administrator of the Peabody
and Slater funds, Americans identified him as the educational leader
of the South. While Curry was influential with exponents of a New
South, he devoted much energy to honoring the Confederate past. He
published historical monographs and essays which once again explored
the constitutional justification of secession. Advocates of a New
South approved of Curry's efforts to expand vocational training in the
public schools, but he was careful to explain that the schools should
also be a force for preserving Southern tradition. Ultimately, he recognized, the virtue of Southern youth was the best protection of Southern liberty.[6]

In addition to the writing of history, Southerners related the Lost
Cause to their young through teaching. Confederate veterans served

as superintendents, principals, and teachers in private academies and public schools. In addition, many of the impoverished daughters of the prewar planter families went into teaching, and by the 1880s they dominated the lower grades of Southern education. Because they retained their Old South–Confederate values, their presence in the classroom was a potent influence for tradition on another generation of Southerners. One Southern woman, Mrs. Eugenia Hill Arnold, who studied Robert E. Lee's postwar career at Washington College in Lexington, Virginia, proposed the establishment "in the sin-darkened land of China or India a great university like that he built up in Lexington and inscribed upon it in letters of gold [should be], 'Sacred to the memory of Robert E. Lee.'" She also had a home mission plan of locating a "Stonewall Jackson Sunday School" in every hamlet in the South. Southern women also directed the activities of the Children of the Confederacy, the organization for youngsters of at least nine or ten years of age.[7]

The most direct religious-Confederate connections occurred not in the public schools but in the private academies and colleges, and especially in the religious schools. Methodist Bishop Warren A. Candler, among others, argued that the teachers who had been Confederate officers "carried into the institutions they served the most pronounced religious spirit," while the Confederate students were serious "crusaders for culture." The ministerial view of the role of the ex-Confederates in education thus became part of the legend of Confederate virtue. Typical of the Lost Cause denominational secondary schools was the Episcopal High School of Alexandria, Virginia. Founded before the Civil War, at war's end the school reopened under the leadership of the Reverend William F. Gardner, whose war record, said Bishop Arthur Kinsolving, "attracted our admiration and regard." The key figure at the school, though, was Confederate Colonel Llewellyn Haxton, who in 1870 became associate principal and mathematics teacher. Kinsolving praised his "gallant career in the western army." "The very embodiment of truth, honor and chivalrous fidelity to duty, in him the boys had before them a Christian knight," said the bishop. "Who can tell the wide-reaching influence of this man upon the lives of the hundreds of youths who, at their most susceptible age, came under the power of his pure and single-minded example?" Kinsolving added that Lee and Stonewall Jackson represented the explicit models of character for the students.[8]

Several colleges for young ladies were established to teach the values of the Old South and the Confederacy. The administrators of Carr-Burdette College in Sherman, Texas, advertised their school with photographs of sweet-looking little girls lined up in Confederate outfits, holding rifles at parade rest. Mrs. O. A. Carr, described as "a true Daughter of the Confederacy," founded the school for "the higher education of Southern girls." The Blue Mountain Female Institute, a Mississippi Baptist college founded in 1873, received much of its Lost Cause tone from its founder, thin-faced, goateed Brigadier General Mark P. Lowery, a Baptist preacher before and after the war. A more important example of Lost Cause education was the Stonewall Jackson Institute, a Presbyterian college founded in 1886 in Abingdon, Virginia. The Reverend C. D. Waller called the school "a living monument" to Jackson, "where that type of piety which was his might be instilled in the hearts of the youth of the land." In advertisements for the school, the young girls sometimes appeared in their Confederate military uniforms; other times they were portrayed dressed in white, holding bouquets of roses, with smiling mothers nearby. The text for one advertisement was a vignette of an Old South lady, written by the great romanticizer of the plantation, Thomas Nelson Page. The Institute, like others, obviously exploited the Southern past, in order to persuade parents to educate their children at the school. In November, 1914, the Stonewall Jackson Institute burned down but was rebuilt, opening as Stonewall Jackson College in September, 1917. The United Daughters of the Confederacy encouraged the rebuilding of the school and provided thirty-three scholarships to encourage attendance. The new college was even more evocative of the Lost Cause than the old school had been. The rotunda housed a statue of General Jackson, and the names of those serving under him adorned the walls. The school wanted to serve as a museum for Jackson memorabilia, and even the building materials of the rotunda were symbolic: blocks of granite symbolized Confederate victories, bronze tablets represented battlefields, and marble blocks symbolized burial places of Confederate dead. As a writer in *Confederate Veteran* magazine noted, young women at the school would "gaze upon these testimonials of purity, courage, devotion, sacrifice, and suffering until the transforming power of that influence has helped to mold into shape and quicken into life characters that are to grow brighter and brighter throughout eternity and to stand forever as true emblems of virtue." The college continued producing emblems of virtue until the Great Depression, when rising debts led to its closing.[9]

While few denominational colleges were as blatantly Confederate in spirit as the Stonewall Jackson Institute, the destruction of the war, the shared Confederate experience, and the chaos of Southern defeat shaped their postwar experiences. The war destroyed endowments and thinned the ranks of professors and students. After the war, most of the students at the religious colleges were Confederate veterans. The Georgia legislature went so far as to pay the tuition of disabled veterans at the Methodists' Emory College, which helped save the institution. The Lost Cause was preserved on such campuses by the influence of prominent Confederates like Richard McIlwaine, president of Hampden Sydney College, and James Boyce, John Broadus, and Crawford H. Toy at the Southern Baptist Theological Seminary. McIlwaine, for instance, once held a three-hour class session with students, finally persuading them to reject the abolitionists' view of the ethics of slavery. His students came "to an understanding and adoption" of the Southern point of view. In addition, these colleges were sometimes the focus for Southern ritual—as when, on Confederate Memorial Day, 1897, Warren A. Candler gave a Lost Cause address during the dedication of Emory College's new library.[10]

Two religious schools existed as major institutional shrines to the Lost Cause. The first was the University of the South, located like an isolated retreat in the mountains at Sewanee, Tennessee, sometimes called the "stronghold of the Southern aristocracy." Leonidas Polk, the Episcopal bishop of the Southwest, issued a call in 1856 for the founding of a church school to be supported by the ten Southern dioceses. The first meeting of the Board of Trustees was held on July 4, 1857, and five temporary buildings stood in October, 1860, when 5,000 people attended the ceremonies for the laying of the cornerstone. From its inception in the sectionally divided 1850s, the institution had sectional dimensions. One minister, the Reverend John Fulton, later remembered that Polk's plan for the school had a direct "relation to his political principles." The chief historian of the university, Arthur Ben Chitty, wrote that much of the support for it "had been for the glory of the South. The idea was a natural concomitant of the growing southern self-consciousness of the 1850s." Bishop Richard Wilmer observed that the sectional conflict of the 1850s was "at first a conflict of ideas, and ideas could only be met by ideas." Sewanee was to "educate in harmony with Southern ideas."[11]

After an encouraging beginning, the war intervened to disrupt the progress of the institution. The Unionist mountain people harassed the budding university by burning buildings, and a few minor engagements occurred on the school's property. Union soldiers blew up the six-ton marble cornerstone laid in 1860 and used the fragments to make small trinkets. (This was done without the approval of the commander of the local Union forces, an Episcopalian who was furious over the destruction. He took one of the marble fragments from the cornerstone, had it cut into the form and shape of a Bible, and carried the relic with him until 1902, when he donated it to the university. It still rests in the All Saints Chapel at Sewanee.) After the war, the endowment was gone, as were the temporary buildings that had been constructed. Leonidas Polk was a battle victim, and the University of the South seemed dead. Charles Quintard resurrected it. Of Northern vintage, the son of a wealthy Connecticut family, Quintard had a successful career as a physician before he became an Episcopal priest in Tennessee in 1856. When the war commenced, the previously Unionist Quintard saw the error of his ways and became a Confederate chaplain and surgeon. Despite his Northern ancestry, education, and prewar Unionist sentiment, the war made Quintard a staunch Confederate, and he became an enthusiastic participant in postwar veteran activities.[12]

Quintard, nonetheless, became an important symbol of the reconciliation of Northern and Southern Episcopalians after the war. His confirmation as bishop of the Tennessee Diocese by Northern and Southern bishops assembled in Philadelphia for the 1865 convention was a sign of sectional reconciliation. With the symbolic act completed, he began efforts to save the Sewanee school. In March, 1866, accompanied by two area Episcopal rectors and Major George Fairbanks, Quintard journeyed to what was then known as University

Place, where he selected the locations for a chapel and a diocesan training school. That evening Quintard erected a twelve-foot-high cross of freshly cut trees from the adjacent woods; surrounded by a caretaker and his family, a few mountaineers, and a black workman, he recited the Nicene Creed, prayed for the success of the endeavor, and led everyone in singing "Gloria in Excelsis" in the Tennessee mountains. As his biographer Arthur Noll wrote, "It was a scene worthy of association with those of the sixteenth century, where discoverers and Conquistadores preempted new lands by planting a cross and claiming the territory for their king and for the Church. Thus was the domain at Sewanee reclaimed for the King of Kings and for the cause of Christian education."[13]

Quintard gained for Sewanee the approval of Northern bishops, but he avoided the North in his fund-raising activities. He turned instead to England for support, making five trips there and raising tens of thousands of dollars, including a contribution for a new theological seminary from an expatriate South Carolina widow. With his associates Quintard, a nervous, impulsive, energetic man, patiently but relentlessly made Sewanee a unique Southern institution, with a peculiar mixture of British, Episcopal, and Southern elements. As Quintard revived it, the University of the South rejected Northern university experience in favor of British models. The campus architecture was Gothic, with some features being replicas of those at Oxford and Cambridge. Sewanee established, on the British plan, a formal collegiate ceremony, and the Sewanee preparatory schools cultivated the spirit and the forms of the British grammar school. Oxford and Cambridge contributed books for Sewanee's library, and they officially honored its vice-chancellor. Religion was also essential. Chapel services were held twice daily, with required attendance. One of the South's greatest theologians, William P. DuBose, spent his productive years here; unlike most Southern Episcopalians, the bishop himself was a High Church mystic, interested in the ritualistic Oxford movement. The school was also Southern and especially Confederate, with all university and preparatory school students required until 1892 to wear their Confederate gray uniforms and to participate in drills under the command of former Confederate officers. Students came to Sewanee from all states in the South, and prominent Southern Episcopalians built summer homes on the mountain. Quintard wrote letters urging young Southerners to attend Sewanee, rather than venturing into the alien North for an education.[14]

The most potent Confederate influence came from the faculty. Although Robert E. Lee turned down the school's vice-chancellorship, Sewanee still provided a home for more prominent Confederate officers than any other Southern university. They were "a body of noble men," said Sarah Elliott in 1909, "with the training, education, and traditions of the Old South and whose like we shall never see again." They included William P. DuBose, a captain in the Army of Northern Virginia, who was characterized by Sydney Ahlstrom as "one of the most profound American theologians of the period"; Major George Rainsford Fairbanks, the grizzled veteran known as "the patriarch of Sewanee," who built his log cabin "Rebel's Rest" after the war; Colonel Frank R. Sevier, a Tennessee Confederate who, as drillmaster of university students, brought a rigid military discipline to the campus before his forced resignation in 1877; Brigadier General Francis Asbury Shoup, who had been baptized on a Civil War battlefield and then took orders in the Episcopal ministry when peace came; and Brigadier General Josiah Gorgas, the Confederacy's chief of ordnance, who became vice-chancellor in 1872.[15]

In terms of influence on the students, few of Sewanee's faculty members could rival General Edmund Kirby Smith. He had the honor of being known among Southerners as the last Confederate general to surrender. Kirby Smith briefly became an exile in Mexico and Cuba after the war; he later returned to the South, to serve as president of two unsuccessful businesses. Active in the Episcopal church, he was pleased with the move to Sewanee in 1875. His home, Powhatan Hall, with his wife, eleven children, dozen boarding students, countless dogs, and a horse named George, was famed for its hospitality. He hosted many visiting army friends, captivated his Sewanee neighbors with war stories, and lectured his students on the meaning of the Confederacy—although he ostensibly taught mathematics. Astride his horse, the tall, long-bearded, graying general was a familiar figure in the woods around Sewanee, leading one ex-student to write a poem re-creating the heroic model he made, galloping through the woodlands and campus, as if going into battle. When the Confederate veterans organized in 1889, Kirby Smith became prominent in the organization, and in 1892 he was named chairman of its historical committee. In early March, 1893, he attended the annual veterans' reunion in New Orleans; during that convention General P. G. T. Beauregard died, making Smith the only surviving full Confederate general. Ironically, returning from the funeral he became ill and died at age sixty-nine on March 28. The Kirby-Smith Chapter of the United Daughters of the Confederacy at Sewanee thereafter honored the general's birthdate, May 16, as their Decoration Day.[16]

The women on the Sewanee campus were crucial to the preservation of Lost Cause values. The university gave free tuition to the children of Confederate widows in exchange for their boarding students. The Sewanee matrons purposely chose names to connect their abodes to the South; one could thus find a Palmetto Hall, a Magnolia Hall, and an Alabama Hall. They re-created and fostered the gentility and culture of the Old South. To complete the mountain environment, two Mississippi widows, assisted by DuBose, in 1873 launched Fairmont, a school for girls in nearby Monteagle, which supplied many Sewanee men with wives trained in Southern tradition.[17]

The student body itself contributed to the Lost Cause environment and was a fitting product of the faculty. It was, in the early years, a noticeable mix of unruly younger students and older Confederate veterans. The only organized sport among the first student body was baseball; the name of the team was, naturally, the R. E. Lees. (One need not ask the color of the uniforms.) At least one Northern student somehow was in the early class, and he testified to the strong sectional orientation of the school in those years. In a letter to his parents in New York, he complained that he was among "rebels" who were "only overcome and not subdued." He reported that Northerners were labeled as "infidels, Mercenary Vandals, Scum of the Earth"; he himself characterized his Southern teachers as "Bombastic, ignorant, lazy and defiant" and the Southern woman as "the very personification of His Satanic Majesty." For some reason, he did not stay long in Sewanee. Even the land itself was a continual reminder of the Confederate past. Writing in the school's 1883 yearbook, the *Cap and Gown*, a student told of reliving the war while riding to the nearby town of Monteagle: "We traced in the imagination the march of the armies in '62 and heard the rumble of artillery and the voices of angry men."[18]

In addition to all this, the University of the South was an institutional focus for Lost Cause orations, dedications, and other ritualistic activities. Such events usually adapted Lost Cause themes to the student audience. When Robert E. Lee died in 1870, for example, the Episcopal bishop of Louisiana, J. P. B. Wilmer, preached a sermon on Lee's life, intended for the edification of the students. Praising Lee's "heroic virtues," his "brilliant deeds," and his "example of moderation," Wilmer especially lauded the general for his last years, which gave "august testimony to the importance of Christian education." If Christian education was important enough for Lee's attention, could Sewanee boys ignore their responsibilities? Wilmer noted that the general's profound faith "was not a creedless religion. His faith embraced all the doctrines of a pure and primitive Christianity. He was a communicant of this Church." Lest they were obtuse, Wilmer pointed out "for the encouragement of the young men assembled before me" that the Episcopal church "sheltered his early youth as it shelters you. He was a good boy before he was a good man."[19]

The Lost Cause spirit was also rekindled when one of the local heroes died, an event which focused regional attention on the campus and prompted the appearance of all the ritualistic trappings of the movement. When General Kirby Smith died in 1893, a special six-coach train came from Nashville for the funeral. St. Augustine's Chapel was filled with veterans seated behind the mourning family. The day's eulogist, Vice-Chancellor Thomas Gailor of Sewanee, honored the brave general's simplicity of faith, and observed that his death symbolically "closed another generation of men." Southern women placed a tall memorial shaft on the campus as an inspiration for students and visitors. In 1903 the school dedicated a granite monument to General Shoup; Gailor gave another Lost Cause oration, recalling that the general's qualities affected him "like a breath of air from the Elysian fields." Sewanee's cemetery became sacred Lost Cause ground.[20]

Despite the passage of time, the University of the South retained its distinctive qualities. With the founding of the *Sewanee Review* in

1892, the school seemed to affirm its commitment to a Southern education grounded in classical liberal arts values. In an article entitled
"The Romance and Genius of a University," DuBose expressed Sewanee's desire to remain a school educating a Southern elite to be gentlemen. It was no wonder, then, that the writer Charles Dudley
Warner called the University of the South a "mill for the manufacture
of gentlemen." Sewanee's semi-centennial came in 1907; the celebration took place in June at the still uncompleted All Saints Chapel,
which one day would display Confederate battle flags from every state
in Dixie. In poems and addresses, speakers paid tribute to the founders
of Sewanee and to the school for, as Bishop David Sessums put it, producing in Southern men a "righteous conservatism." At the same
time, the post-1900 trend toward North-South reconciliation affected
Sewanee. During the 1907 ceremonies President Theodore Roosevelt
sent a message praising the school as "a University of all America,"
and in 1913 the Carnegie Science Hall opened, symbolically bringing
to the campus the forces of Northern industrialism and science.[21]

The changes should not be exaggerated. In a 1920 pamphlet, Sarah
Elliott, the daughter of Bishop Stephen Elliott, made clear that the
Confederate past had not been forgotten at Sewanee. She praised the
Confederate professors who realized that education should produce
gentlemen, adding that "this standard has been, and is being pre-
served." She then proposed that the university become even more of a
Lost Cause religious shrine:

And thus the University of the South at Sewanee is the fit Representative—
the Child and Heir—of the Old South, worthy to be the Custodian and the
Conservator of all Southern Relics, of all Southern Literature of any shape or
kind,—Books, Pamphlets, Diaries, Manuscripts, old Letters, Clippings,—
anything belonging to the South, to be kept here safe and sacred. Gather
them, send them to us, you who fought that sacred War,—send us those relics of our beloved Country, so that the future historian can here read and
study the truth about us.

She noted that a Confederate battle flag was displayed in the All
Saints Chapel, and she urged Southerners to "send us others—the
Flags of our glorious past—to hang where our prayers will hover."[22]

Washington and Lee University reflected a different aspect of the

Southern civil religion than the University of the South. Located at Lexington in the Virginia valley, it was more Virginian in its Confederate orientation, and its Christian influence was predominantly Presbyterian. Its attitudes continued to reflect the Scotch-Irish immigration that had occurred in the area in the late colonial period. Originally known as the Augusta Academy and then renamed Liberty Hall in the patriotic year of 1776, it was renamed Washington College in light of George Washington's financial contributions to the school. Stonewall Jackson had taught in Lexington at the Virginia Military Institute, and when the Civil War began, the town provided recruits for his famed Stonewall Brigade. In June, 1865, the college was on the brink of dissolution, with her endowment unproductive and her educational materials damaged or destroyed. "Her sons, where were they?" asked Henry A. White. "A hundred battle-fields gave answer. Scores of them had baptized the cause of their fathers in their life-blood." In August, 1865, the trustees made a shrewd move, unanimously electing Robert E. Lee as their new president. Accepting the offer, Lee was inaugurated president on October 2, 1865, and the fall session opened with fifty students, four professors, and one instructor. By the end of Lee's third year at Lexington, the school's enrollment had risen to 410.[23]

With the selection of Lee, the college earned a reputation as the home of the Lost Cause. An outcry from the North accompanied the news that Lee was to be the new college president. Wendell Phillips sarcastically observed in New York "that if it were fitting for General Lee to head a college, then it would be equally appropriate to appoint Wirtz, late Commandant at Andersonville, to the chair of 'humanities.'" The Chicago *Daily Tribune* in the same year accused Washington College of being "one of the most virulent rebel institutions in the land . . . a school run principally for the propagation of hatred to the Union. The faculty, tutors and all, are thoroughly rebel in sentiment and inculcate their doctrines on all occasions." Nevertheless, as time went on the outcry diminished, and the college was even able to raise funds in the North. Lee himself wrote letters for the drive. Among the Northerners to contribute were Henry Ward Beecher, Samuel Tilden, and Thomas A. Scott, president of the Pennsylvania Railroad. Most important, the Yankee inventor Cyrus McCormick had contributed $20,000 by his death in 1884, and George Peabody eventually donated $250,000. Speaking in terms of a "R. E. Lee Endowment," the agents appealed to Southern expatriates and Confederate sympathizers in England.[24]

The school richly deserved its reputation as a Lost Cause denominational institution. As Randolph Preston wrote, the campus was "a picture which represents what the South has always stood for." In a sermon, the Baptist preacher Edwin T. Winkler described the sacred atmosphere in evocative phrases: "Lexington is the parable of the great Virginian soldiers. In that quiet scholastic retreat, in that city set upon a hill and crowned with martial trophies, they, being dead, yet speak. . . ." Winkler added that "in the quiet hall of the lecturer and professor," Lee "renewed the war, transferring it to the sphere of mind!" Episcopal Rector William Nelson Pendleton argued that no "other centre of influence at the South" could match Lexington "by reason of the mighty effect of Genl. Lee's presence and example."[25]

As at Sewanee, the presence of prominent Confederates was the key factor fostering a Lost Cause atmosphere in Lexington. A former professor remembered that it was known as the "Headquarters of the Southern Confederacy." Among the residents of the town were John Letcher, the wartime governor of Virginia; Confederate Judge John W. Brockenbrough, who became dean of the law school and a trustee of Washington and Lee; Colonel William Preston Johnston, the son of Albert Sydney Johnston, himself a war hero, and professor of history and literature until 1878; Colonel William Nelson, chief ordnance officer for Stonewall Jackson's command; John Randolph Tucker, attorney general of Virginia during the war, postwar congressman, and a dean of the Washington and Lee law school; Colonel J. T. L. Preston, who directed the black Sunday school that General Jackson had founded; General William A. Anderson, town lawyer, known as "the lame lion of Lexington" because of a crippling war injury; General Francis H. Smith, superintendent of the Virginia Military Institute, the "West Point of the South"; Colonel John M. Brooks, builder of the *Merrimac*; and Commander Matthew Fontaine Maury, famed geographer who represented the Confederacy in Europe and came to the Virginia Military Institute as professor of meteorology. Next to Lee, the greatest Lost Cause hero in Lexington was Brigadier General

William Nelson Pendleton, chief of artillery in the Army of Northern Virginia and pastor after the war of Grace Memorial Church, where Lee worshipped.[26]

Despite the presence of Confederates like Pendleton, the Lost Cause religious values of Washington College flowed from the influence of one man. As well as being a part of the legend of the Lost Cause, Robert E. Lee was important for his own religious views and the contribution he made in his last five years to tying the Confederate memory to religion. While the American president has usually been the chief symbolic figure of the American civil religion, Lee filled that position in the Southern civil religion until his death. Lee, an Episcopalian, traced his family's Anglicanism back to the Reformation; during his own childhood his parents were communicants at Christ Church in Alexandria, where George Washington worshipped. Lee was taught the catechism by William Meade, who later became bishop of Virginia. Despite his Episcopal heritage, Lee had much of the ascetic Calvinist in him, even before the Civil War. During the conflict, and especially as defeat became more apparent, these tendencies intensified. He repudiated drinking, gambling, and profanity, and he blamed Confederate setbacks on Southern sins and himself. He approved fast days, days of humiliation, revivals, and the honoring of the Sabbath. As Marshall Fishwick observed, "he de-emphasized denominational preferences and respected non-Christians." Although he retained his Confederate ideals, he clearly separated his religion from everything else. One anecdote in particular was suggestive. Some Lexington veterans became embroiled in a street-corner argument that mixed war memories and religion. One veteran insisted that any good Confederate soldier would have an entrance pass to heaven. Just then General Lee came along, and the veteran asked him to confirm this interpretation. "No, my good friend," Lee replied. "I'm afraid not. That may be good Confederacy, but it's poor theology!"[27]

When the war ended, Lee stoutly refused to capitalize on his fame. He turned down lucrative business offers and rejected any plan for one day entering politics. Instead, he chose to work as an unglamorous educator. He modernized Washington College, broadening its curriculum and instituting the elective system in advance of most American colleges. He also did everything he could to create a religious environment on campus. Lee frequently dispensed moral and spiritual encouragement to students; one former student admitted typically that he trusted in the general's words "just as much as I do in the gospel." Lee helped launch Lexington's YMCA, and the first building erected under his directorship was a chapel, a Gothic structure on the edge of a gently sloping hill. He allowed the clergymen from Lexington's churches to conduct the daily devotionals on campus, encouraged the local ministers to oversee and counsel the students, and invited preachers of differing denominations across the South to give baccalaureate sermons. Lee was an avid Bible reader and revivalist. In 1869 Lexington's Baptist pastor, J. William Jones, preached a sermon at the Virginia Military Institute on the need for a revival, and it resulted in over a hundred conversions. Lee said this was "the best news I have heard since I have been in Lexington. Would that we could have such a revival in our college, and in all of the colleges."[28]

The Confederate-Christian atmosphere remained even after the General's death in 1870. His son, Major General George Washington Custis Lee, who had been a professor of civil and military engineering at the Virginia Military Institute, was appointed in February, 1871, to succeed his father as president of Washington College, which was soon renamed Washington and Lee. Until 1878 students at the college stood watch each day, in alphabetical order, at Lee's tomb. Beginning on January 19, 1871, three months after the hero's death, Lee's birthday has been celebrated every year with an appropriate ceremony. The Reverend C. C. Brown, a Baptist preacher who graduated from the college and became a pastor in Sumter, South Carolina, remembered that after Lee's death he often went to the grave beneath the chapel to sit and brood upon the general's holiness.[29]

The students perceived Lee as such a presence that in 1895 and again in 1907 they dedicated their school yearbook to him. On the former occasion they dedicated it to "the Man whose noble Christian character is the most perfect human model for the young men of the land"; on the latter they said that "the character of Lee" was the school's "greatest endowment." Randolph Preston, who entered Washington and Lee in 1897, testified to the abiding spirit of the institution. He remembered that the students were "practically all from the South and of Confederate ancestry. For the magic of Gen. Lee's name still had great drawing power." "We were all hot Southerners and Confederates," he recalled, "for the lengthening and depressing shadows of the War between the States still hung over us. If anyone had presumed to doubt the justice of the South's cause or the supreme military genius of Gen. Lee and Gen. Jackson he would certainly have had an argument and probably a fist fight on his hands." The United Daughters of the Confederacy continued to approve of the work at Lexington, and after the turn of the century they contributed scholarships to the college.[30]

After General Lee's death, many schemes were advanced for the development of Washington and Lee College, with most of them attempting to exploit the general's name. On October 15, 1870, the day of Lee's funeral, Virginians formed the Lee Memorial Association with William Nelson Pendleton as chairman of the Executive Committee. He journeyed south shortly thereafter, trying to raise funds for a memorial to Lee in the campus chapel, but he had difficulty raising money because of competition from Richmond money-raisers, who also wanted to build a memorial to the general. The still-poor Southerners responded to the appeal, though, as women held fairs and bazaars and prominent leaders contributed the proceeds from speeches and books to the Lexington organization. Pendleton solicited contributions from the North and Europe as well. However, the undertaking was divisive. General Joseph E. Johnston charged that many Southerners resented "that the people of Lexington are disposed to use the prestige of General Lee's name to build up their local interests." This was a direct hit at Pendleton, who was gathering money for a Lee Memorial Church, as well as for the campus memorial. He refused, however, to admit "any idea of rivalry between them."[31]

At any rate, work progressed toward completion of the campus monument. The general's widow chose the sculptor Edward C. Valentine to execute a white marble statue recumbent on a sarcophagus. Valentine finished in April, 1875, a decade after Appomattox; students from the Baptists' Richmond College transported the statue to Lexington, to await the construction of a limestone mausoleum, which took another eight years. The monument was unveiled on June 28, 1883, in a major Lost Cause ceremony. Early in the morning, a large contingent of Maryland veterans arrived by train and marched to the cemetery to the sound of the band playing "Dixie." At the cemetery gates, the veterans entered to the roll of muffled drums, decorated the graves of certain Confederate soldiers, and placed near Stonewall Jackson's grave a five-foot-high bronze memorial tablet. At 9:30 that morning another procession, headed by General Wade Hampton, arrived at the cemetery and covered Jackson's grave with flowers. After the cemetery observance, the group marched to the Washington and Lee campus, where almost ten thousand people gathered for the outdoor event. At noon the ceremonies began, including Abram Ryan's reading of his poem "The Sword of Lee," the day's oration by Major John W. Daniel, and the unveiling of the Lee mausoleum and recumbent statue by Julia Jackson, daughter of General Jackson. In his prayer the Reverend R. J. McBryde, Pendleton's successor as rector of the Grace Memorial Church, urged Southerners to follow Lee's Christian example. "He was not ashamed to confess the faith of Christ crucified and manfully to fight under His banner against sin, the world, and the devil, and to be Christ's faithful soldier and servant. And we pray Thee that the influence of his life and the power of his example may never die out in the land."[32]

Stonewall Jackson was an equally real presence in Lexington, and he also became the focus for Lost Cause ritual. He had been buried in the cemetery of the Presbyterian church after his death in 1863, but in 1891 he was disinterred and moved to a burial plot beneath a new statue honoring him. The new statue was unveiled in the Lexington cemetery on July 21, 1891—thirty years to the day since the first battle of Bull Run, where he earned his fame as Stonewall. With General Wade Hampton presiding and General Jubal A. Early delivering the day's oration, almost 30,000 people gathered for the day's events. After the main ceremonies on the campus the group proceeded to the graveyard, where Jackson's widow, dressed in black, and her two granddaughters, dressed in white, ascended a platform near the new monument; one of the children, Julia Jackson Christian, unveiled the eight-foot bronze memorial, atop a ten-and-a-half-foot, fifteen-ton granite pedestal. The figure faced the southwest, along the line of the Virginia valley where Jackson had gained his greatest battle triumphs.[33] As with the burial grounds at Sewanee, the Lexington cemetery was a melancholy focus for the Lost Cause.

In addition to ceremonial funeral rites, Washington and Lee College was the center for Lost Cause orations. Benjamin Morgan Palmer delivered one of the more noteworthy addresses, "The Present Crisis and Its Issue," on June 27, 1872, two years after Lee's death. Palmer acknowledged that the invitation to speak at the college "touched me with the solemnity of a call from the grave. I felt as I turned my steps hither, that I was making a pilgrimage to my country's shrine." He urged the students to preserve the "gentlemanly instincts which have hitherto characterized our people," because without them "there is no longer the possibility of virtue." He foresaw future problems for the nation, so the Southern young had to be prepared to save "our an-cestral faith." In fulfilling this charge they were to draw upon the Southern experience, "born of adversity and trial." Thomas Nelson Page, himself a Washington College graduate, similarly tailored his address, "The Old South," to his student listeners. Lauding the Southern past, Page encouraged the students to chronicle its story. If "there be any young son of the South in whose veins there beats the blood of a soldier who perilled his life for that civilization which has been so inadequately outlined . . . he has before him a work not less noble, a career not less glorious" than his Confederate father. The young Washington and Lee historian could thus fulfill his destiny and live up to the legacy of the past by preserving the story of his father's war. For such an aspiring scholar, Page said, "there can be no fitter place for his sacrament than these hallowed walls—no better time than the present."[34]

Despite the passage of time, the school continued serving as a cen-ter of the Lost Cause. The year of the centennial of Lee's birth, 1907, was an important one for Washington and Lee. Although attempts to gain material improvements for the school failed, the celebration of the event was a major commemoration of the Lost Cause. With the South and the nation looking toward Lexington as Lee's shrine, the campus chapel filled with Confederate veterans and other celebrities. Confederate, United States, and Virginia flags hung placidly from the platform, which was also decorated with flowers. The Reverend G. B. Strickler, captain of the Liberty Hall Volunteers, offered the invoca-tion, and the assembly sang "How Firm a Foundation," the general's favorite hymn. In a splendidly ironic and richly symbolic act, the day's main orator was Charles Francis Adams, Jr., a New Englander who commanded a Union regiment in the Civil War, but who in 1906 had defended Lee's decision to join the Confederacy. Acknowledging that his appearance at the ceremony was a novelty, Adams went on to praise Lee as an unselfish, honest man of character who reflected "honor on our American manhood."[35]

By 1920 the school clearly reflected the movement toward reconciliation with the North. The college's effort, beginning in 1919, to increase its endowment encouraged this tendency. A *Confederate Veteran* article reported that "while we claim it proudly as a part of this Southern country, its history identifies it with the whole country, and its influence has been national in extent." Robert E. Lee had become a national hero by 1920, and his name was saleable in the North. The author of the article insisted that the campus had "become a meeting ground" for all regions. Its service as a base hospital during World War I and the large number of its sons who had served on European battlefields had, moreover, brought national honor to Washington and Lee.[36]

In the educational aspect of the religion of the Lost Cause, one could see the best and the worst elements of the overall religious effort to honor the Confederate past. On the positive side, it fostered a worthwhile sense of continuity with the past, preserving for the Southern young an awareness of their origins and preventing the sense of rootlessness and alienation that might have resulted from Confederate defeat. It nurtured among the young, who in many societies are apathetic toward the past, the renowned Southern respect for history. But this suggests the negative implications of the attempt to teach Confederate truths to the young. The effort resulted in discouraging a truly objective view of the past, and thus of contemporary Southern society. Since they were so closely aligned with Southern tradition, the writers of history and the teachers at Southern schools had difficulty separating themselves from it. One must insist on the difference between history and mythology. The latter undoubtedly helped Southerners to recover from serious postwar psychological and cultural problems and embodied its own truths; however, the South also needed a critical examination of the past to meet other needs. Not until well into the twentieth century would Southern history lose its polemical tone. In particular, the interweaving of two such powerful influences as a distinct Southern history and a distinct Southern religion made criticism of the South more difficult.

As in the antebellum period, the postwar South was suspicious of intellectual speculation. The Lost Cause colleges reflected this spirit. William P. Trent was a case in point; a born-and-bred Virginian from a gray-blooded Southern family, he had received graduate training at Johns Hopkins, and in 1888 he began teaching at Sewanee. While there he criticized the South, especially in his biography of the antebellum novelist William Gilmore Simms. Southerners were outraged with the book and with Trent's subsequent scholarship. He complained that at Sewanee he was "continually made the object of prayers and other pietistic propaganda for my spiritual regeneration." Trent fled in 1900 to Columbia University, with its modern graduate school.[37] Heretics were not welcome in the Lost Cause South.

Whatever the positive and negative dimensions of the attempt to relate the Southern past to the young, one must affirm the importance of the denominational school in the undertaking. Each of the two most prominent institutions provided a specific denominational linkage to the Lost Cause. The Confederate-Christian theme was interdenominational, and on most ritualistic occasions in the South one heard generalized Christian themes, rather than distinct, well-developed sectarian influences. Similarly, although they identified with Southern tradition in general, religious assemblies and conventions seldom directly validated the Confederacy. This made the spirit at the denominational colleges even more significant in assessing the religious connection to the Lost Cause. At these colleges the specific creeds of the sects became, more closely than elsewhere, intertwined with the teachings of Southern tradition. Sewanee's Episcopalianism and Lexington's Presbyterianism fostered the growth of the Lost Cause and gave it a peculiar shape. As the home for veterans and clergymen, and as a focus for ceremony, these institutions were major components of the Lost Cause religion.

Chapter Eight

A HARVEST OF HEROES

RECONCILIATION AND VINDICATION

THE LOST CAUSE provided the rationale for Southerners maintaining a culture separate from the rest of the nation's. Nonetheless, Southerners eventually regained pride in being Americans, as well as citizens of Dixie. The dream of a separate political nation died among most Southerners with Confederate defeat, even though it died hard. Gradually replacing the political dream was the cultural dream, and as the latter took hold Southerners found that they could honor the American political nation if it honored the Southern civilization, including a degree of local self-government.

Reconciliation with the North did not, of course, happen overnight.[1] While reunification had progressed by 1890, perhaps the key period of reconciliation, judging by ministerial attitudes, was after 1890 and especially after 1900. The Spanish-American War and World War I provided the perfect context for Southern ministers to identify again with the values of the American nation. After 1900 the American civil religion began fully functioning in the South for the first time since the Civil War. At the same time, the Southern civil religion continued as the dominant value system of the region. Despite marked evidence of sectional reconciliation, the Southern churches in 1920 remained among the South's most distinctly sectional institutions. Although Southern Episcopalians reunited with Northerners, their pastors still embodied sectional values as faithfully as preachers in the popular churches. The Baptists, the Methodists, and the Presbyterians all retained a sectional structure and influence. The period from around 1900 to 1920 is therefore essential for understanding the peculiar situation in the South—the interaction of two well-developed civil religions.

The Lost Cause entered its most highly organized and institution-alized phase after 1890, with the United Confederate Veterans, the United Daughters of the Confederacy, and the United Sons of the Confederacy all launching their activities. Paradoxically, this inten-sification of memory did not signal increased Southern isolation from the nation. War had been the occasion of national division; appropri-ately, it provided the crucial context for the promotion of North-South reconciliation. J. L. M. Curry, speaking before the veterans' reunion in 1896, had pledged that if a war came in the future, South-erners would stand up for their country. When war did break out in April, 1898, Southerners, including the regional churches, supported it. While Northern Christians also supported the Spanish-American War, Southerners had a special need to relate the conflict to their own past and to the question of nationalism. Bishop Warren A. Candler insisted, for example, that the sight of Southern youth marching en-thusiastically to fight in the war would

have been impossible, if Confederate memories had been despised and Con-federate history spat upon during all the years since 1865. Visions of heroic sires inflamed the courage of gallant sons. Men who since the war between the States have struggled through orphanage and poverty inflicted by Federal arms looked on faded gray jackets pierced by minie-balls, gazed on dented swords and rusted muskets, and were fired to patriotism by those holy relics of illustrious fathers. They dared not be less than brave men in the presence of such sacred treasures.

Candler thus believed that Confederate virtue had inspired the South-ern young to endorse national virtue.[2]

The Reverend A. N. Jackson pondered how Southerners could "honor the Union that our fathers combated," and yet honor South-ern heroes in the Spanish-American War. He came back again to the mysteries of the Lost Cause. "Here is the South's holy of holies. The veil is not rent, and only they can know what is within whose own have been to the sacrifice. And they are legion. The blood of our fa-thers are on the lintels and doorposts of thousands of these Southern homes where death passed not by; what boots it if we linger under the inspiration of the incense so long as the sons go bravely up to new baptisms of blood?" The Lost Cause was thus an inspiration for Southern youth who had partaken of its sacraments and participated in its ceremonies.[3]

While Candler and Jackson stressed the effect of the Lost Cause as an inspirational force on the young, other preachers emphasized the related point that the Spanish-American War marked an end to sectionalism. The Methodist *Christian Advocate* of Nashville argued that the events of 1898 had destroyed "the lingering remnants of sectional prejudice in every part of the land," and a contributor to the Baptist *Christian Index* of Atlanta concluded that the war proclaimed that Appomattox "was a reality and that the Civil War is really at an end!" The Reverend B. A. Owen of Kentucky believed that the war was providential, arguing that "the destiny to which we have arrived as a united people" could never have been achieved "by a divided country." Together, Americans had "brought liberty to the captives of" Cuba, so the South was again participating in the saving work of a successful Redeemer Nation. The preachers accordingly paid homage to the preeminent symbol of nationalism—the American flag.[4]

While the Spanish-American War was an important milestone of reconciliation, that did not mean that the Lost Cause disappeared. Not all symbols of nationalism were acceptable. For instance, Sumner Cunningham, editor of the *Confederate Veteran* magazine, led a movement to let Southern soldiers in the United States army wear brown (rather than blue) uniforms. "Many a noble Confederate who is in blue uniform to-day does not feel as comfortable in it as if he did not remember the bitter experiences of 1861–65, and no good can come from continuing to use that color." Cunningham's Nashville friend, James McNeilly, represented the unreconstructed minister's view of the Spanish-American War. Some Southerners pointed out that Southern enlistments in the American army proved the region's loyalty to the nation, but by implying past disloyalty this argument enraged McNeilly. "This is accompanied by the usual flood of gush about the blue and the gray marching shoulder to shoulder and keeping step to the music of the Union." He pointed out that when Southerners accepted "the new order" after Appomattox they were "duty bound to strive to make it a benefit and a blessing to all the people." Their role in the Spanish-American War simply was a fulfillment of that duty.[5]

The Spanish-American War, then, was one stop on the road to rec-

onciliation, but it was not the final one. After 1900 Lost Cause devotees increasingly speculated on the role their values and traditions
would play in the nation. Southern clergymen in these years articulated their interpretation of the South's part in the nation; in particular, they explained how their region was the most American of all
areas of the country. They revealed their view of what the American
civil religion should be, and what the Lost Cause values and traditions
could contribute to it. They showed a new confidence that virtue was
again attainable within the confines of the American nation. At
times, Dixie's denizens committed themselves to a typically American
outlook of optimism, belief in progress, the goal of material prosperity,
moral innocence, and the dream of success; more often, however, this
was not the Southern definition of "Americanism." It certainly was
not the definition given by clergymen. Southerners came to believe
that they were to serve a prophetic function within the nation—a part
of it, and yet not fully of it. They argued that Southern values were
really original American values, consecrated by Revolutionary and
Confederate blood. They warned Americans that these values were
endangered by change, and that they must be preserved. The result,
though, was that in this ministerial examination of national and regional values, the Lost Cause itself was transformed. The preachers
now saw it as precariously triumphant.

Above all, the ministers now stressed that the Lost Cause had been
concerned, in essence, with liberty. As the Reverend H. D. C. Maclachlin said in a 1909 sermon in Richmond, secession was "a sacred
duty" because it involved "a question of fundamental human right, or
the liberty for which the blood of the Anglo-Saxon had been spilled
from the days of the Magna Charta until their own." The Confederacy
had thus been a legitimate part of a long and glorious tradition of freedom. Most typically, this interpretation of liberty had certain narrow
limits to it. Randolph McKim, who had served in the Army of Northern Virginia as a private, a staff officer, and a chaplain attached to a
cavalry unit, suggested that the establishment of the Confederacy had
been only the means to an end, namely "the sacred right of self-government," which the states' rights philosophy was still protecting in
his own age. He contended that over the previous forty years the concept of local self-government, once only Southern, had become more

accepted throughout the United States. His conclusion was that the Northern armies saved the Union, while "the armies of the South saved the rights of the States within the Union."[6] McKim's argument did not do an injustice to the ministerial interpretation of the Lost Cause before 1900; rather, it gave it a different configuration. Clerics had earlier taught that the Confederacy stood above all for virtue, morality, and essentially religious principles. This did not preclude concern for freedom (the idea of liberty had been an ingredient of virtue since the days of the ancient Greeks, not to mention the American Revolutionaries), but it had not been the essential focus of the earlier ministerial view.

The developing transformation was seen more clearly when the idea of liberty was given a broader definition than simply states' rights. The Reverend P. D. Stephenson, speaking in 1909 in Richmond, claimed that the Confederacy should be viewed in terms of its worldwide influence. The failed Southern independence movement had ignited "a wave of popular uprisings that for the half century since intervening has been sweeping over the world." France, the South American nations, and the English colonies had all known the birth or extension of liberty; news of impending disturbances in Russia and "the petrified East" also showed the repercussions, said Stephenson, of the Confederate war for freedom. In the history of the previous half-century, then, in terms of influence, "the typical Confederate soldier was one of the forces of the world."[7] This was doubtful history but revealing rhetoric. When Stephenson preached the sermon, the ghosts of Robert Lewis Dabney, Albert Taylor Bledsoe, and others must have stirred perceptibly, because these men would have been outraged at the simplified argument linking the Confederacy to revolution for the idea of liberty. They had argued that the nation's problems in the Civil War era were the result of the North's unbridled liberty, and they spoke derisively of reformers concerned with abstract "liberty." Their message had been that men must understand the limits of liberty and the need for authority; Stephenson, on the other hand, seemed to ignore it.

Another element of the Lost Cause at the turn of the century was a belief in a special Southern destiny. This converged with the idea of an American destiny. "My brethren, what thoughtful man can fail to see that God is in the history of our country, and that this people has a great part to play in the onward march of the events of the world," reflected R. A. Goodwin, rector of the historic St. John's Episcopal Church in Richmond, in a 1909 sermon. "He is leading the nations to the light of liberty, so that His truth may make them free, and in a marvelous way He has used, and is using, our country to enlighten the world." He dwelled on the South's role in this American mission. Like the Israelites, Southerners should remember their forty years in the wilderness of defeat, and he believed that they could now understand God's purpose. In 1861 Americans "were going after other gods," but the Southern concern for liberty, constitutional rights, and its willingness to fight and sacrifice for them insured that the nation's traditional values would survive. According to Goodwin, the South still had that function to serve in his own age, but it could fulfill its destiny only by retaining the abiding "principles of self-government, self-defense, self-respect and loyalty to our traditions for which we have contended ever since Appomattox."[8]

The ministers believed the South had a redemptive history that solidified the section and taught it spiritual and moral lessons. Victor I. Masters eloquently conveyed this idea, noting that the South's experiences had been "deep and poignant. And the children of those who drank to the dregs her cup of greatest woe make up practically the entire population of the South of the present." This legacy was fundamental to the belief in a special Southern destiny within the confines of the American nation. Masters concluded that the South's

consciousness of its own pains and sorrows, of the gallantry and chivalry of its sons, of its mistakes and sufferings, of its superiority to the worst calamities which came to it, of its ability to build a civilization out of ashes, makes the present South worth far more both to the nation and to itself. Having had such experiences, it has become not merely a loyal part of the nation, but something more. That something more is the wisdom and the strength and a certain depth of soul which the South has acquired through the bitterness of trials which purged it of dross and have healed without hate. We do well to treasure the lessons of the history of our section.

This, then, was the burden of Southern history as perceived by a Southern minister in 1918. Warren A. Candler claimed that the

South was solidified more by the impact of "glorious memories and the influence of epic history" than by the race issue. The people of his region were bound together "as a great family," and the Confederates were the continual reminder of Southerners' cultural kinship. "The blood of our slain on a thousand fields is the cement which holds the living together in bonds too dear to be easily forgotten or heedlessly broken." He insisted that the Union would profit from the "heroic conservatism" of a solid South.[9]

Because of its historical experience, the preachers suggested that the South was quintessentially American. As the rest of the nation had changed because of industrialism, urbanization, immigration, and other forces of modern America, the South had remained most like the nation of the Founding Fathers. Another facet of this belief involved the purity of Southern blood. "The South above any other section represents Anglo-Saxon, native-born America," claimed Episcopal Bishop Theodore DuBose Bratton. "No race ever had more passion for liberty than the Anglo-Saxon," said Victor I. Masters. "In America the love for freedom of this race found its fullest expression, and in the South their blood has remained freest from mixture with other strains." And the Reverend R. Lin Cave noted in 1896, "The preservation of the American government is in the hands of the South, because Southern blood is purely American." At the same time, Southern religious leaders after 1900 increasingly feared that this pure blood was being contaminated. As the Southern Presbyterian Assembly noted in 1918, the post-1900 arrival of European immigrants in Southern cities "had almost overnight changed the complexion of our people and modified our claim to Anglo-Saxon exclusiveness."[10]

Anglo-Saxonism was linked to another element of the Southern definition of Americanism—evangelical religion. As Victor I. Masters noted, in the South, "the Anglo-Saxon's devotion to evangelical religion has been less interfered with than in other sections." Masters was a Baptist, but Episcopal Bishop Brattan also affirmed that the South above everything else was "the Christian South." "Should this great body of Anglo-Americans ever cease to be Christian," he continued, "or become less Christian than it is, the effect upon our entire nation would be disastrous beyond the power of thought to conceive." James McNeilly agreed with his colleagues on the South's religious character. "Each one of the great denominations has done a noble part in giving inspiration and direction to the activities of our life. Each has its own distinct ideas for the formation of character, and all combined have impressed on the South a high type of religious and biblical character." An additional benefit was the high moral tone of the South. The church and the home—institutions of morality—were said to be in decline in the North but thriving in Dixie.[11]

The attitudes of the sons of Confederate veterans were especially revealing as to these prevailing developments in the Lost Cause sentiment. Although the organization would never rival the United Confederate Veterans in importance, the Southern heirs did found their own United Sons of Confederate Veterans in July 1896, in Richmond. The group's members paid proud homage to their fathers and made clear that they would pass the Lost Cause memory on to future generations. At the same time, they were even more attuned than their fathers to the spirit of reconciliation. The Reverend Carter Helm Jones of Louisville, son of John William Jones and a chaplain of the USCV, said in a 1907 sermon that the Confederate cause was no longer a lost cause. "Every principle for which you fought, every obligation that sent you to the rostrum of comrades have been achieved." He made clear that the victory had come within the bounds of the American nation: "The United States could not be today what it is if you had not been true to trusts and true to faith and true to duty." Similarly, B. A. Owen, assistant chaplain of the same group, speaking at the end of World War I, explained Confederate defeat as God's way of preparing the nation for "her manifest destiny" as "the champion of the moral forces of the universe." This was clearly a destiny that Southerners wanted to participate in, but it could never have "been achieved by a divided country."[12]

The most influential ministerial son of a veteran was probably Thomas Frank Gailor. His life and ideas made him one of the most important interpreters of the Lost Cause. In background, he was thoroughly Southern; indeed, his boyhood would have made Scarlett O'Hara envious. When only six years old, he was caught up in General Sherman's capture of Memphis in 1862. He did his part for the cause, carrying baskets of food to Confederate soldiers in a Memphis prison. In October, 1862, his father, a Confederate major, was killed at the battle of Perryville, Kentucky. His strong-willed mother went to the battlefield because she believed her husband had to have a Christian burial, but she could not find his body. When Mrs. Gailor returned, she and young Thomas went to Jackson, Mississippi. On the trip the six-year-old cavalier had to sleep on the coffin of a dead Confederate colonel, being taken to Jackson for burial. After a fiery stay in the besieged city, he and his mother returned to Memphis, where they remained until the end of the war.[13]

Gailor, a somewhat pudgy, beardless, cherubic-faced man, with short hair and big eyes, passed on his Confederate values to his children and friends. Family legends about the war were passed down from generation to generation and are still cherished today. Gailor kept his father's sword and spurs hanging in his library, teaching their own lessons to those who saw them. Gailor was also a public participant in the Lost Cause. Active in the Nathan Bedford Forrest Camp of the USCV, he took special interest in trying to resurrect the historical reputation of General Forrest, one of the fiercest Confederates. When he died, the United Daughters of the Confederacy praised him as "a staunch friend and co-worker," and the *Southern Churchman* called him "a Chevalier Bayard," just like a Confederate.[14]

Appropriately, this important interpreter of the Lost Cause was an Episcopal bishop, belonging to the church of the Old South aristocracy. Most of his life's work was devoted to the University of the South, which he served as chaplain, professor, vice-chancellor, and chancellor (1908–35). He was profoundly shaped by, as well as contributing to, the sacred Southern spirit at Sewanee; nevertheless, his church experiences had national dimensions. He had studied in the North, and for six years he served in high church office, as the first president of the National Council of the Episcopal Church. In addition, he was Sewanee's leading fund-raiser, successfully garnering contributions from J. P. Morgan and Andrew Carnegie, and he counted Theodore Roosevelt as a friend.[15]

In a series of orations from 1890 to 1920, Gailor drew on his own and his region's background to express cogently the evolved meaning of the Lost Cause. In his 1902 address to the USCV reunion, he affirmed that the organization was "the splendid witness" to the fact that "our children shall not be educated to depreciate and discredit our fathers' patriotism and our fathers' faith." Insisting that "the virtue of filial loyalty" was the most deeply felt of human virtues, Gailor explained his affection for the Confederates. "To some of us," he said, "from the misty past, from blood-stained battlefields, from acrid deathbeds, the whisper comes, 'Well done, my son,' and through that vast and pleading bond of blood and birth wells up the interest, the love for those who endured the same experience and who are with us here to-day."[16]

Gailor was also, though, attuned to the new power of nationalism. He suggested that Southerners now viewed the Civil War as "an epoch in the process of the evolution of the nation, and we welcome the results." Affirming that "the nation is greater than any section, than any class, than any generation," he was confident that "the nation, under God," would live long after "we are in the dust." In a 1903 address in the North, Gailor urged Americans to embody the spirit of "altruism, unselfish thought for others than ourselves," which was "God's law of true happiness and true prosperity for peoples as for individuals." The infusion of this ideal of altruism into Americans would be "the safeguard against that canker of selfishness which ultimately destroyed every republic that heretofore has been attempted on earth." In idealism and "not in material prosperity alone, rests the safety of the republic." Gailor conceived of the challenge to American virtue as an internal challenge of individualistic materialism, but he seemed hopeful in 1903 that the nation had awakened to the threat.[17]

At this point, his view of the relevancy of the Lost Cause to the nation became apparent, because the Confederates were among America's preeminent examples of virtue. He had elaborated on this idea at the dedication of a Confederate monument in 1899 in Shelbyville, Tennessee, pointing out that the Confederates had willingly surrendered "everything for that which they believed to be the cause of righteousness." A nation could not last without "the virtue and loyalty of its citizens," and the Lost Cause activities were, he maintained, dedicated to that end. This communal sacrificial spirit must "be built into the permanent and abiding life of our people," "woven into the fair tapestry of our civilization." This spirit promoted love of nation, he believed, because "the surest love of country begins with love of one's native place," and "loyalty to one's section is the mother of that loyalty that feels for the whole country."[18]

By the second decade of the twentieth century, Southern ministers who believed in the Lost Cause had thus taken immense strides in reincorporating themselves into the American nation. World War I was the key event that crystallized these sentiments and gave an impressive demonstration of the way Southern clergymen combined belief in the Southern civil religion with acceptance of the American civil religion. When the United States entered the war, the Southern churches gave their full approval to the endeavor, blessing it, cooperating in war relief work, and supporting the chaplain program. The Southern denominations welcomed the war for the spiritual and moral effects they anticipated from it. This attitude was an outgrowth of the repeated warnings from Southern clergymen on the dangers of materialism, a fear shared by Northern clerics as well. Many ministers looked upon Germany's empire as simply an exaggeration of materialistic values pervasive in Western civilization. War would be, in the words of the Dallas *Baptist Standard*, "an antidote for the effeminacy and decay of luxury." The Southern preachers also were happy because, said Baptist pastor J. F. Love, "the spell of German rationalism" would be ended. No longer would an admired higher education include a Ph.D. from a godless German university.[19]

In Randolph McKim, the Lost Cause produced perhaps America's fiercest, most militant ministerial advocate of a holy World War I. Speaking at a Palm Sunday evening service on April 1, 1917, the day before assembly of the Congress that on April 6 (Good Friday) would declare war, he preached on "America Summoned to a Holy War." For over two years he had used his pulpit for unqualified calls for American assistance of the European Allies. In this sermon he compared himself to a biblical prophet, and then he begged for war:

Let me say then, as plainly and as strongly as I can, speaking as a minister of Christ, speaking as a messenger of God, speaking with a solemn sense of the obligations of my sacred office, speaking in the sanctuary of Christ, and with a full sense of my accountability for every word I utter in this holy place,— that it is the high and sacred duty of the American people to take up the gage of battle which Germany has thrown down to us and to persecute the war against her with all our energy and with every resource at our command—not hesitatingly, not half-heartedly, but with all our hearts and with every pound of energy at our command, realizing the vast interests at stake, the tremendous consequences for weal or woe dependent upon its issue.[20]

McKim insisted that Germany "must be beaten to its knees; it must be crushed, if civilization is to be saved—if the world is to be made safe for Democracy." Seeing the coming war as more significant than the Crusades of the Middle Ages, he predicted that the war itself would be a crusade. "This conflict is indeed a Crusade. The greatest in history—the holiest. It is in the profoundest and truest sense a Holy War." He discussed the Old and New Testament holy warriors, including his old commander Robert E. Lee in the charmed circle. He savagely attacked pacifists as "weak-kneed, chicken-hearted, white livered individuals." "If the pacifists' theory be correct," he asked, "how could Robert E. Lee have been such a saint as he was?"[21]

When war began, Southern preachers like McKim again brought out the Confederate example to inspire the young. For a half-century, in their sacred ceremonies and elsewhere, they had told the young of the importance of maintaining virtue, and to the older clergymen the Great War provided the greatest testing ground for Southern virtue, which would have to be proven now in the national context. Their eyes turned to the days of their warring youth, and they urged their contemporaries to study the noble Confederates. The Reverend Joseph Packard, for example, began his article on "The Manly and Christian Attitude Toward War" with appropriate words from Stonewall Jackson. McKim made clear that his 1917 book *The Soul of Lee* was intended as an inspiration for "our young men" who were "offering their strength and their lives in the greatest struggle for liberty and democracy the world has ever seen." Thomas F. Gailor said, in a 1917 monument dedication at Shiloh, that in Lost Cause ceremonies "we are sending a message to all our young men, not only in the south, but throughout the United States, to rejoice that they are Americans and to be proud of the opportunity to render service to their country and maintain its liberties." Gailor went on in this wartime Lost Cause oration to endorse the new draft laws. James Gambrell, the grizzled veteran who was president of the Southern Baptist Convention in 1917, was especially attuned to the Confederate religious experience and wanted it to be a model for World War I. He recalled that "the strong, evangelistic spirit running through General Lee's army, had a great deal to do with maintaining the spirit of the army," and he hoped for the same result in the Great War.[22]

Southern clergymen also argued that World War I was a vindication of the Lost Cause. In the first place, World War I was the occasion for Southern youth to prove its virtue; in doing so, the young would validate the Lost Cause. "I am my father's son, and for that reason one may see / That something noble and heroic is expected now of me," said D. G. Bickers, in a 1918 poem in the *Confederate Veteran*. He added that his Confederate father had "left a precious legacy into my keeping; now / I am responsible for this, its safety." Littell M'Clung's poem, "Old Virginia, Once Again," had the same message, although less personal: "What a legacy to carry to the battle fields of France! / O Virginia, old Virginia, let your shadows point the way / To immortal paths of honor for the children of the gray!"[23]

At war's end, the former Confederates affirmed that their sons had indeed been true to their heritage. Baptist preacher George McDaniel lavishly praised these "knight-errants of the holy grail—these young crusadors who rescued the tomb of France's freedom from the unspeakable Turk and heartless Hun." In "Heroes of the World War," a poem written and read by the Reverend J. W. Bachman at the 1920 United Daughters of the Confederacy meeting, the traditional rhetoric of virtue had a new focus. The "cross of wood" marking the grave of a Southern hero in World War I was the "patent of nobility and badge of patriotism." The faith of the new heroes "cried out, 'Noblesse oblige,' and they met the challenge at the front with the shout of victory." "We thank God they belong to us, that they are our crowns of rejoicing."[24]

World War I also vindicated the Lost Cause, the ministers said, because American participation in it had validated the same principles the Confederacy had fought for: belief in liberty and democracy. The Southern churches and preachers committed themselves to Woodrow Wilson's definition of the war as a holy crusade. "This is not a war of conquest or of retaliation," said the *Baptist Standard*. "It is a conflict between liberty and autocracy—between democracy and monarchism, a protest against the spirit of despotism and militarism." In the struggle, "we hear the summons to a new crusade." The Southern Baptist Convention affirmed that "the issues involved in the great war concern fundamental human rights and liberties. The cause of democracy is at stake." The 1918 Bishop's Address of the Southern Methodist General Conference concluded that the war was for "the glorious cause of freedom." The Southern Presbyterian General Assembly argued that the war was for "the 'righteousness that exalteth a nation.'"[25]

As seen earlier in this chapter, Southern clergymen had, from the late 1890s, redefined the Lost Cause as a crusade for liberty, as well as for morality and religion, so that the way had been prepared for linking the Lost Cause with the American cause in World War I. A spate of poems appeared during the war making this connection. The most cogent was Mrs. C. G. Bierbower's "The Cause Triumphant," published in *Confederate Veteran* magazine in March, 1918:

> The cause of Lee and Jackson, though 'twas trampled in the dust
> By overwhelming odds, has risen, commanding world-wide trust;
> 'Tis now the cause of Pershing and our brave boys o'er the sea,
> The cause upheld by Dixie's knights with Jackson and with Lee.
> Yes, Dixie's cause triumphant is the South's "lost cause" no more;
> Speak not of it as "lost," for it gleams out as ne'er before.[26]

George McDaniel, a Richmond Baptist preacher, had grown up in Texas on reunions of Hood's Brigade and images of far-away Richmond as "in my boyish imagination a sort of shrine." He also saw the cause of World War I as a validation of the Confederate cause. "In other words, gentlemen," he told a Confederate gathering, "the moral strength of the Allies' cause to-day . . . is in essence the same as that for which you contended nearly sixty years ago." Not content with making this connection, he elaborated on it, portraying the Confederate South, and especially Virginia, as the embodiment of all Allied virtue in World War I:

Your actions, my fathers, combined the virtues of little Belgium, who made her bosom a battle ground rather than break her word; of Great Britain, who risked her hegemony to protect a small nation; of heroic France, who bled to repel invasion; and of the United States, who unsheathed her shining sword to make obligatory an international compact on sea and land. What if you did lose? You saved your honor and preserved your star from tarnish. The principles you cherished are the hope of all democracies and the dread of all autocracies the world around.[27]

The Confederate–World War I connection was partly a response to the tendency of Northerners to compare Germany and the Confederacy. A comparison of Dixie with the militaristic, rationalistic, materialistic Germans was unthinkable to Southerners, and the Reverend Mr. McKim typically protested that such arguments represented "a contradiction of the facts of history" and "a cruel slander against a brave and noble people." He turned the charge around and pointed it north, suggesting that if Yankees wanted to find a parallel to the German spirit they would "find it in the record of the pillage and rapine and the desolation inflicted by the soldiers of the Union and their camp followers in the Shenandoah Valley of Virginia under Sheridan's orders and in the States of South Carolina and Georgia under the orders of General Sherman." A problem that could not be ignored was the fundamental one of slavery. When Northerners impolitely asked how a Southern war for slavery could be compared to an American war for liberty and democracy, McKim met the issue squarely with conventional Southern wisdom, arguing that Southerners had not fought for slaves, "but for the right of self-government, for the principle lately asserted by President Wilson, that 'governments derive their just powers from the consent of the governed.'" This polarizing disagreement was not settled by these arguments. It represented a major flaw in the wartime movement toward reconciliation.[28]

World War I also provided the context for symbolic cultural reconciliation with the American civil religion. Southerners increasingly paid homage to the rituals, ceremonies, symbols, and images, as well as the values of the American nation. The churches and the Confederate groups conveyed the emblems of reconciliation to their members. Denominational periodicals published the words and music to "The Star-Spangled Banner," presidential speeches and proclamations, reports of war work, and advertisements for Liberty Bonds. Church assemblies showed off their new patriotic spirit. Secretary of the Navy Josephus Daniels, himself a Southerner and a symbolic representative of the federal government, addressed the 1918 Southern

Methodist Assembly. Observing that the war had demonstrated "the cementing of the patriotism of the whole republic in the struggle to preserve for mankind the principles incarnated in the national air and in the waving Stars and Stripes," he went on to urge the reuniting of Northern and Southern Methodists. The 1917 Southern Baptist Convention, meeting in New Orleans, began its initial session by singing "My Country, 'Tis of Thee" and then "How Firm a Foundation." (In 1915 the convention had begun with the singing of only "How Firm a Foundation.") At a session of the 1918 convention, President James B. Gambrell welcomed to the platform a contingent of soldiers from Camp Pike, Arkansas, who led the group in the singing of "America" and "Nearer, My God, to Thee." Hymns, in fact, were prime tokens of the Southern reconciliation. To be sure, young Albert Carlyle Mitchell of Atlanta composed a new song, "The Dixie Division," for the soldiers; but most songs were national, not sectional, such as "America to France" and Captain E. F. Fenton's poem entitled "The Star-Spangled Banner." The *Confederate Veteran* even performed the unlikely feat of praising the spiritual qualities of Julia Ward Howe's "Battle Hymn of the Republic," noting that originally it had not been an anthem of anti-Southern hate.[29]

Ritual days were also occasions for reconciliation. Although Southerners had not celebrated Thanksgiving Day with relish after the Civil War, by the time of World War I they were taking comfort and reflection from it. For several years before 1917 McKim had used the day to preach sermons in his Church of the Epiphany in Washington, D.C., urging and justifying American preparation for entrance into the European war. Southerners were enthusiastically celebrating the Fourth of July as well. The denominational periodicals especially praised Woodrow Wilson's 1918 Independence Day speech at George Washington's Mount Vernon. The war saw the reemergence of special days of reflection; the South honored these too, including the national Memorial Day. On these ritual occasions one could see that the South had reconciled itself to the national flag. In 1917 the raising of Old Glory on Jefferson Davis Parkway in New Orleans became a symbolic event marking renewed patriotism. Ministers even wrote poems praising the flag, although acceptance of the prime symbol of national unity created a tension with continuing adoration for the equally potent Confederate Battleflag. Randolph McKim suggested that Southerners should still "consecrate in our hearts our old battle flag of the Southern Cross," but he added that it should be honored not as "a political symbol, but as the consecrated emblem of an heroic epoch."[30]

Of special importance was acceptance by Southerners of the symbolic figure of the American president, who has usually been the prime interpreter of the American civil religion. From the perspective of the Lost Cause, it was an extraordinary coincidence, at least, that Woodrow Wilson was president during World War I. Born the son of a prominent Presbyterian minister in Virginia, raised in parsonages across the South, nurtured by the strict moral and spiritual creed of the Southern Presbyterian church, educated at the University of Virginia and Johns Hopkins, a young lawyer in Atlanta—Wilson was a product of the South, especially of its pervasive religious atmosphere and tradition. One biographer of Wilson entitled his opening chapter "A Boy Finds God Amidst Civil Strife."[31]

All of the Southern denominations believed they had a friend in the White House. The 1918 Southern Methodist General Conference referred to Wilson as "our great leader"; the 1917 Southern Baptist Convention, through its president, James B. Gambrell, called Wilson a man "whom Providence has thrust into the leadership of advancing civilization." The Southern Presbyterians believed they had a special relationship to him, and they rarely mentioned his name without noting that his "honored and venerable father" had been one of their own. In an official wartime telegram to the president, the Assembly said that "in this crucial hour of Christian civilization . . . we are confidently relying upon you, as the spokesman for the moral forces of the world, to carry on your gigantic task to a righteous consummation."[32]

To be sure, the Northern churches came to have an equally providential view of Wilson's wartime role, but Southerners believed his regional background had itself been providential. In May, 1917, the Reverend Peyton Hoge, son of Richmond's famed Moses Drury Hoge, gave an address at the centennial celebration of the First Presbyterian Church in Wilmington, North Carolina; in it he noted that Wilson—whose father had preached there—had been planning to attend. With America in a wartime crisis, this was not to be, but he noted that Wilson "sought to rule and lead according to the principles of

Jesus Christ. And it will be to the perpetual honor of this church that in this high endeavor he was guided by the teachings received from this pulpit, and in the home of a pastor of this church." Wilson thus took honor and idealism from the South to the nation, and in so doing he contributed further glory to the region. In an address before the 1917 Southern Baptist Convention, the Reverend W. J. McGlothlin of Louisville argued that Southern sectionalism was disappearing. "To-day a Southern man sits in the White House. He is one of the greatest of our presidents." McGlothlin insisted that Wilson would surpass even the great earlier Southern presidents. "It is Woodrow Wilson, a Southern man, who will be the principal factor in using this nation for the emancipation of other nations."[33] All along, then, God's destiny for the South included providing the nation with leaders, and Wilson was the most important of them all. Through him, the South's destiny and the nation's symbolically were one.

The World War I era thus had a profound impact on the Lost Cause, transforming its tragic meaning, which had emphasized suffering, failure, and defeat, into a more typically American success story. From one perspective, the ministers of the Lost Cause had played a prophetic function, insuring that the United States would continue to stand for traditional American values. From a more profound view-point, though, the Lost Cause had failed in its prophetic aspect. Rather than standing in judgment of the American civil religion from the perspective of defeated, chastened holy warriors, the Lost Cause civil religion had linked itself with the national faith. As it had un-questioningly defended the inherent virtue of the Confederacy, the ministers of the Lost Cause now almost blindly endorsed the sanctity of the American mission in World War I.

These developments had an ironic meaning. While Southerners looked upon the war as a vindication of what the Confederacy had fought for, the war nevertheless ushered in a new era. It was a landmark in the vanishing of an older American civilization. As Southerners took an important step in reconciling themselves to the American nation, the rural-based Americanism they believed in was ebbing away. The Lost Cause, originally the rationale for a provincial culture, during World War I was reinterpreted to justify international warfare by the American nation. The Lost Cause thus took on international dimensions. But the postwar era was one of disillusionment through-out much of Western society, as the world was not made safe for de-mocracy or the Lost Cause. Southerners had identified with a winning cause and noble ideals, but even that could not prevent frustration. After the disillusionment with World War I, the Lost Cause would re-turn to its earlier regional orientation, albeit without the vigor it had once had. The real impact of the Lost Cause after World War I was as a counterpoint to American progress. Its literary configurations in the 1920s and 1930s gave it a new profundity, one that drew heavily on the region's conservative religious heritage. Novelists of the Southern Lit-erary Renaissance explored the tragic meanings of the Southern expe-rience that the Lost Cause religion had apparently forgotten during the war.

Although the rhetoric of the Lost Cause religion had shifted, in the ritualistic aspect of the movement one could still observe during the World War I period the embodiment of profound spiritual lessons. One wartime ceremony in particular seemed to epitomize the de-velopments after 1900, and at the same time to suggest the timeless meaning of a religion built on ruins. The 1917 Confederate Veterans' reunion, held in Washington, D.C., marked an especially symbolic point of reconciliation to the national faith. This was the first reunion held outside the geographical boundaries of the Confederacy, and the selection of Washington was especially meaningful. Columbus Park, fronting Union Station, was turned into a tented field, with a thou-sand tents providing bivouac facilities for the old soldiers. The re-union did not begin until Tuesday, June 5, but on the previous Sunday a memorial service was held in Arlington National Cemetery, at-tended by President Wilson and his wife. Special services were held at the Tomb of the Unknown Soldier and at the grave of General Joe Wheeler, hero of the Confederacy and of the Spanish-American War. Flowers were strewn on the graves encircling the Confederate monument.[34]

President Wilson spoke to the convention at its opening session, on Tuesday morning at the Arcade Auditorium. The place was packed, the rebel yell greeted him as he came to the platform, and his speech was interrupted by repeated cheers and applause. Wilson drew on the ideas of reconciliation that ministers and others had been developing for several decades. He first paid poignant tribute to the gathering and its "days of memory," but added that "the world does not live on memories." Noting that, in the days of the Civil War, "there was one common passion among us, and that was the passion for human freedom," Wilson the Presbyterian then explained that God's mysterious ways with the South were becoming clearer. The South was to be part of "the great world purpose" which the United States was meant to fulfill. Southerners were now "part of a nation united, powerful, great in spirit and in purpose," and "we are to be an instrument in the hands of God to see that liberty is made secure for mankind." Wilson pointed out that the day of his address marked the beginning of registration for the new draft law, and he saw "some significance in this coincidence" of his appearance before old veterans and the registration day for future soldiers. Confederate veterans knew, said the President, that "there comes a time when it is good for a nation to know that it must sacrifice, if need be, everything that it has to vindicate the principles which it possesses." The American reputation "as a trading and money-getting people" was a false one; Americans themselves "know the ideals with which the hearts of this people have thrilled." The Confederate reunion, then, was an opportunity for Americans to recall their dedication to ideals, and to pledge themselves to fulfill the future promise of the nation. After Wilson's address General George P. Harrison, commander-in-chief of the veterans, appealed to Americans to stand by the president in the time of crisis. He closed his comments by reading Anne Bachman Hyde's poem "The Crisis," which linked the ideals of World War I with those of the Confederacy. Music was then provided by the Marine Band, hymns were sung by the Confederate Choir, and "The Star-Spangled Banner" was sung by Miss Mamie Harrison, daughter of the commander-in-chief.[35]

Another memorial service was held Wednesday afternoon at Arlington Cemetery. The principal oration was by the Methodist Bishop Collins Denny of Richmond, a thin, short-haired man with wire glasses that made him look like Woodrow Wilson. Arguing that the Civil War had been inevitable because of ambiguities in the Constitution, he suggested that only "the red blood of hearts, precious alike in the North and in the South, could fill the crevice left in the foundation of our government." The existence of the Confederate monument in the national cemetery was proof "of a country genuinely reunited" and evidence that the glory of the Civil War era was "now the common heritage of all Americans." "This monument is not the memorial of a bloody division," he said; "it is the seal of a fraternal union."[36]

Denny then turned his attention to the present war. His discussion evoked the rhythms and phrases of Abraham Lincoln, which were those of the Bible. While gathered at Arlington, he said,

the storm of another war breaks on us. We did not want this war; honestly and patiently we tried to avoid it. Long time we bore abundant tribulation, submitted to unprovoked wrong. Ardently we hoped, eagerly we worked, fervently we prayed that this cup might pass from us. A righteous and merciful God, our God and the God of our fathers, saw it was not wise to indulge our longing for peace and permitted the Scourge of Europe to make war on us.

He speculated that the war might be a punishment for sins, a discipline to teach the need for "service and sacrifice," or a test to show present and future generations their potential greatness. In any event, as Americans marched off to battle, they should pause and draw strength from the Lost Cause.

Standing beside this monument, so full of significance, surrounded by our immortal dead, in the presence of our living heroes, now grown gray, we renew the vow of our fathers and mutually pledge to each other our lives, our fortunes, and our sacred honor, that, by the blessing of God, our land shall not furnish the grave for the liberty they so hardly won; that, having lived upon the heritage they left us, we will not shirk the responsibility its possession inevitably entails.[37]

After Bishop Denny's sermon, Chaplain General W. J. Bachman gave the benediction; the group gathered around the monument, as a bugler played the mournful taps. Later that day, near twilight, the Marine Band played an outdoor concert for the veterans on the grounds of the Washington Monument, and a thousand school children formed a human flag of red, white, and blue.[38]

The reunion closed with the traditional parade, and the 1917 march was perhaps the grandest veterans' parade ever. It came down Pennsylvania Avenue, where, more than fifty years before, Lincoln had reviewed the victorious army shortly before his assassination. At the front of the marchers waved the Confederate Stars and Bars, alongside the Stars and Stripes. To the tune of "Dixie" the old veterans marched, or rode on horseback, or rode in that token of time's changes, the automobile. Seated on a float, the Confederate Choir sang patriotic songs and tunes of the Southland. The Children's Choir occupied another float, with the smiling little girls in red, white, and blue dresses. On the reviewing stand above the parade stood Woodrow Wilson, reviewing the troops. He smiled as some of the Confederate veterans yelled out their offers to go to France and whip the Germans. At one point Supreme Court Chief Justice Edward White, a Louisiana Confederate veteran and Ku Klux Klan member in his youth, left the reviewing stand to march in the parade. It rained during the march, a downpour. But the parade continued to its conclusion, and President Wilson remained until the last veteran had passed by.[39]

NOTES

INTRODUCTION

1. The preceding is based on Samuel S. Hill, Jr., *Southern Churches in Crisis* (New York, 1966), pp. 12–14, 52, 56–59; John Boles, *The Great Revival, 1787–1805: The Origins of the Southern Evangelical Mind* (Lexington, Ky., 1972); Walter B. Posey, "The Protestant Episcopal Church: An American Adaptation," in George B. Tindall, ed., *The Pursuit of Southern History: Presidential Addresses of the Southern Historical Association 1935–1963* (Baton Rouge, 1964), pp. 377–97; Clement A. Eaton, "The Ebb of the Great Revival," *North Carolina Historical Review* 23 (January, 1946): 1–12.

2. Richard M. Weaver, "The Older Religiousness in the South," *Sewanee Review* 51 (Spring, 1943): 238, 241–43, 248; Hill, *Southern Churches*, p. 12; John B. Boles, *Religion in Antebellum Kentucky* (Lexington, Ky., 1976), pp. 123–45; Donald Mathews, *Religion in the Old South* (Chicago, 1977); Posey, "Episcopal Church," pp. 385, 387, 397; Edwin M. Poteat, Jr., "Religion in the South," in W. T. Couch, ed., *Culture in the South* (Chapel Hill, 1935), pp. 248–69; Dickson D. Bruce, Jr., "Religion, Society and Culture in the Old South: A Comparative View," *American Quarterly* 26 (October, 1974): 399–416.

3. The preceding is based on Rollin G. Osterweis, *Romanticism and Nationalism in the Old South* (New Haven, 1949), pp. vii, 87, 104, 109, 133–35; William R. Taylor, *Cavalier and Yankee: The Old South and American National Character* (New York, 1961), pp. 146, 148, 263, 328, 333–34; Clement Eaton, *The Growth of Southern Civilization, 1790–1860* (New York, 1961), pp. 318–22, 296.

4. Sydney Ahlstrom, *A Religious History of the American People* (New Haven, 1972), ch. 40.

5. Eaton, *Growth of Southern Civilization*, pp. 298–99, 303–5.

6. James W. Silver, *Confederate Morale and Church Propaganda* (Tuscaloosa, Ala., 1957), pp. 15–24, 30–31; W. Harrison Daniel, "Southern Baptists in the Confederacy," *Civil War History* 6 (December, 1960): 391; Haskell Monroe, "Southern Presbyterians and the Secession Crisis," *Civil War History*

6 (December, 1960): 357–58, 360; Willard E. Wight, "The Churches and the Confederate Cause," *Civil War History* 6 (December, 1960): 362; A. D. Cummings, "The Southern Ministry and Secession" (Master's thesis, University of Texas, 1938); John William Jones, *Christ in the Camp; or, Religion in Lee's Army* (Richmond, 1887), p. 239; Fred T. Wooten, Jr., "Religious Activities in Civil War Memphis," *Tennessee Historical Quarterly* 3 (June, 1944): 131–49, and 3 (September, 1944): 248–72; William Edward Dunstan III, "The Episcopal Church in the Confederacy," *Virginia Cavalcade* 19 (Spring, 1970): 5–15; Robert E. L. Bearden, Jr., "The Episcopal Church in the Confederate States," *Arkansas Historical Quarterly* 4 (Winter, 1945): 269–75; Joseph D. Cushman, Jr., "The Episcopal Church in Florida During the Civil War," *Florida Historical Quarterly* 38 (April, 1960): 294–301; T. Conn Bryan, "The Churches in Georgia During the Civil War," *Georgia Historical Quarterly* 33 (December, 1949): 283–302.

7. Silver, *Confederate Morale*, pp. 15, 53–55, 60, 62–64, 93–94; W. Harrison Daniel, "Southern Baptists," pp. 393–97.

8. Herman Norton, *Rebel Religion: The Story of the Confederate Chaplains* (St. Louis, 1961), p. 97; Charles F. Pitts, *Chaplains in Gray: The Confederate Chaplains' Story* (Nashville, 1957); James W. Silver, "The Confederate Preacher Goes to War," *North Carolina Historical Review* 33 (October, 1956): 499–509; Sidney J. Romero, "The Confederate Chaplain," *Civil War History* 1 (June, 1955): 127–40; E. M. Boswell, "Rebel Religion," *Civil War Times Illustrated* 11 (October, 1972): 26–33; Arthur L. Walker, "Three Alabama Baptist Chaplains, 1861–1865," *Alabama Review* 16 (July, 1963): 174–84; Edgar L. Pennington, "The Church in the Confederate States," *Historical Magazine of the Protestant Episcopal Church* 17 (December, 1948): 308–448; W. Harrison Daniel, "An Aspect of Church and State Relations in the Confederacy: Southern Protestantism and the Office of Army Chaplain," *North Carolina Historical Review* 35 (January, 1959): 47–71.

9. John Shepard, Jr., "Religion in the Army of Northern Virginia," *North Carolina Historical Review* 25 (July, 1948): 341–76; Herman Norton, "Revivalism in the Confederate Armies," *Civil War History* 6 (December, 1960): 410–24; Boswell, "Rebel Religion," p. 33.

10. "Three Victories," *Christian Index*, March 15, 1866, p. 46; Samuel S. Hill, Jr., "The South's Two Cultures," in *Religion and the Solid South* (Nashville, 1972), p. 36; Hill, "Epilogue," in John Lee Eighmy, *Churches in Cultural Captivity: A History of the Social Attitudes of Southern Baptists* (Knoxville, 1972), p. 202; Edward A. Pollard, *The Lost Cause: A New Southern History of the War of the Confederates* (New York, 1866), pp. 750–52.

11. Hill, "South's Two Cultures," pp. 36–37; Rollin G. Osterweis, in *The*

Myth of the Lost Cause, 1865–1900 (Hamden, Conn., 1972), pp. x, 6, stresses that after the war the Lost Cause no longer sanctioned "hopes for a new nation" but did sanction "the hope of achieving the life of the country gentleman."

12. Hill, "South's Two Cultures," pp. 26–28, 36; Hill, *Southern Churches,* pp. 18, 201.

13. Kenneth K. Bailey, *Southern White Protestantism in the Twentieth Century* (New York, 1964), pp. 2–3; Hill, *Religion,* pp. 18–19; Hill, *Southern Churches,* p. xvii. See also Wallace M. Alston, Jr., and Wayne Flynt, "Religion in the Land of Cotton," in H. Brandt Ayers and Thomas N. Naylor, eds., *You Can't Eat Magnolias* (New York, 1972), pp. 99–123.

14. Eighmy, *Churches,* pp. 75, 94.

15. Anthony F. C. Wallace, *Religion: An Anthropological View* (New York, 1966), pp. 30, 102; Clifford Geertz, "Religion as a Cultural System," in Michael Banton, ed., *Anthropological Approaches to the Study of Religion* (New York, 1966), pp. 4, 8–12, 14, 23, 28. See also Andrew M. Greeley, *The Denominational Society: A Sociological Approach to Religion in America* (Glenview, Ill., 1972), p. 28; Mircea Eliade, *Myth and Reality* (New York, 1963), pp. 8, 17–18.

16. Wallace, *Religion,* pp. 30–165.

17. Hill, "South's Two Cultures," p. 24.

18. Robert N. Bellah, "Civil Religion in America," Sidney E. Mead, "The 'Nation with the Soul of a Church,'" Will Herberg, "America's Civil Religion: What It Is and Whence It Comes," all in Russell E. Richey and Donald G. Jones, eds., *American Civil Religion* (New York, 1974), pp. 21–44, 45–75, 76–88; Bellah, *The Broken Covenant: American Civil Religion in Time of Trial* (New York, 1975); Will Herberg, *Protestant, Catholic, Jew: An Essay in American Religious Sociology* (Garden City, N.Y., 1960); Catherine L. Albanese, *Sons of the Fathers: The Civil Religion and the American Revolution* (Philadelphia, 1976); James H. Moorhead, *American Apocalypse: Yankee Protestants and the Civil War, 1860–1869* (New Haven, 1978).

19. In his *Public Religion in American Culture* (Philadelphia, 1979), esp. chs. 6 and 7, John F. Wilson skillfully clarifies the conceptual problems of the civil religion.

20. Emile Durkheim, *The Elementary Forms of the Religious Life* (New York, 1965), 52, 56, 59, 261; Wilson, *Public Religion,* 153–59; Lloyd A. Hunter, "The Sacred South: Postwar Confederates and the Sacralization of Southern Culture" (Ph.D. dissertation, St. Louis University, 1978), 12–15. The latter study deals with many of the same phenomena that the present volume does, but is an attempt at, in the author's words, "a theological interpretation of

the Lost Cause myth." Unaccountably, he overlooks the role of ministers in this and does not use church records.

21. Hill, "Toward a Charter for a Southern Theology," in *Religion*, pp. 182–4.

22. Robert Penn Warren, *The Legacy of the Civil War: Meditations on the Centennial* (New York, 1961), pp. 108–9.

CHAPTER 1: SACRED SOUTHERN CEREMONIES

1. The quoted phrase appeared in *Confederate Veteran*, 16 (April, 1906): 175. *Confederate Veteran* will hereafter be cited as CV.

2. See Mrs. B. A. C. Emerson, comp., *Historic Southern Monuments: Representative Memorials of the Heroic Dead of the Southern Confederacy* (New York, 1911).

3. Reverend J. William Jones collected documents relating to the dedication in an appendix to John Esten Cooke, *Stonewall Jackson: A Military Biography* (New York, 1876).

4. Ibid., pp. 514–22.

5. Ibid., pp. 514, 570, 574–77.

6. Ibid., pp. 537–41, 574; W. Asbury Christian, *Richmond: Her Past and Present* (Richmond, 1912), pp. 347–49. Richmond's *Religious Herald*, a Baptist newspaper, reported that a contingent of blacks had wanted to march in the procession but after complaints by a few whites they withdrew. "The Last Week," *Religious Herald*, November 4, 1875, p. 174.

7. Cooke, *Jackson*, pp. 543–47.

8. Henry Alexander White had a sketch of Hoge in *Southern Presbyterian Leaders* (New York, 1911), pp. 426–45; see also Peyton Hoge, *Moses Drury Hoge: Life and Letters* (Richmond, 1899), which contains the address, pp. 147–52, 168–97, 235, 425–47, 463–66, 497, 560. For Hoge's role as a Bible-runner, see W. Harrison Daniel, "Bible Publication and Procurement in the Confederacy," *Journal of Southern History* 24 (May, 1958): 198–99.

9. Cooke, *Jackson*, pp. 548–50.

10. Ibid., pp. 551–55, 557–59.

11. Ibid., pp. 560–66.

12. Ibid., pp. 567–68. The religious press praised Hoge's oration and the day's events. The Episcopal *Southern Churchman* insisted that the statue would eternally teach one idea: "that duty to Christ and our fellow-men to be done at any personal cost, is the grandest feeling that can take possession of any human being. So let it speak; and it will not be in vain that Jackson lived." The *Central Presbyterian* stated that all true Southerners endorsed

Hoge's remarks. It printed the oration because of its moral lessons, and urged that it be placed in textbooks used by Southern children. It observed that the crowd in Richmond had been like "a congregation of worshipers in the sanctuary" (ibid., pp. 579–81).

13. Wallace, *Religion*, pp. 30, 102, 238; Geertz, "Religion as a Cultural System," in Banton, *Anthropological Approaches*, pp. 4, 8–12, 14, 23, 28.

14. Eliade, *Myth and Reality*, p. 17; United Daughters of the Confederacy, *Minutes of the Fourteenth Annual Meeting of the UDC . . . 1907* (Opelika, Ala., 1908), p. 6; *Minutes of the Twenty-second Annual Meeting of the UDC . . . 1915* (Charlotte, N.C., n.d.), p. 357; Kate Coles Donegan, "Personal Reminiscences of Father Ryan," *Alabama Historical Quarterly* 7 (Fall, 1945): 450; "The South's Tribute to General Lee," *CV* 22 (February, 1914): 62.

15. "The Memorial Window in Trinity Church, Portsmouth, Va., to the Confederate Dead of Its Congregation," *Southern Historical Society Papers* (hereafter cited as *SHSP*) 19 (January, 1891): 207–12; "Pegram Battalion Association," *SHSP* 16 (January–December, 1888): 194–206; J. William Jones, "The Career of General Jackson," *SHSP* 35 (January–December, 1907): 97; "A Memorial Chapel at Fort Donelson," *CV* 5 (September, 1897): 461; Elizabeth W. Weddell, *St. Paul's Church, Richmond, Virginia: Its Historic Years and Memorials* (Richmond, 1931), I, frontispiece, pp. 224–25.

16. "Sermons Before the Reunion," *CV* 5 (July, 1897): 351; *CV* 22 (May, 1914): 194; and Herbert and Marjorie Katz, *Museums, U.S.A.: A History and Guide* (Garden City, N.Y., 1965), p. 181.

17. United Confederate Veterans, *Minutes of the Ninth Annual Meeting and Reunion of the UCV . . . 1899* (New Orleans, 1900), pp. 17, 32; *Minutes of the Twenty-first Annual Meeting and Reunion of the UCV . . . 1911* (New Orleans, n.d.), p. 111; *Minutes of the Nineteenth Annual Meeting and Reunion of the UCV . . . 1909* (New Orleans, n.d.), p. 64; United Daughters of the Confederacy, *Minutes of the Nineteenth Annual Meeting of the UDC . . . 1912* (Jackson, Tenn., n.d.), pp. 321, 407; *Minutes of the Twenty-first Annual Meeting of the UDC . . . 1914* (Raleigh, N.C., 1915), p. 406; *Ritual of the United Daughters of the Confederacy* (Austin, n.d.); "Burial of Margaret Davis Hayes," *CV* 17 (December, 1909): 612.

18. "Old Time Confederates," *CV* 8 (July, 1900): 298; M. B. Wharton, "A New Version of Dixie," *CV* 12 (September, 1904): 431–32; "Reunion of Tennessee Division," *CV* 8 (October, 1900): 434–35; Mrs. Flora M'Donald Williams, "The Words of 'Dixie,'" *CV* 12 (February, 1904): 66; and Joseph M. Brown, *CV* 12 (March, 1904): 134; and "Memorial Ode," *CV* 9 (December, 1901): 567.

19. *CV* 9 (April, 1901): 147; United Daughters of the Confederacy, *Min-*

utes of the Sixteenth Annual Meeting of the UDC . . . 1909 (Opelika, Ala., 1909), p. 56. See also C. H. Scott, "The Hymn of Robert E. Lee," *SHSP*, n.s. 2 (September, 1915): 322; "The Burial of Lieutenant-General Jackson: A Dirge," a wartime hymn reprinted in the Baltimore periodical *The New Eclectic* 5 (November, 1869): 611; CV 26 (August, 1918): 368; Harold B. Simpson, *Hood's Texas Brigade in Reunion and Memory* (Hillsboro, Tex., 1974), p. 76; "The Confederate Choir No. 1," CV 15 (April, 1907): 154–55; "United Confederate Choirs of America," CV 15 (July, 1907): 304; "Stonewall Jackson's Way," CV 25 (November, 1917): 528–29; "Our Confederate Veterans," CV 5 (August, 1897): 439; CV 6 (November, 1898): cover.

20. See Southern Presbyterian General Assembly, *Minutes of the General Assembly of the Presbyterian Church in the United States* (Columbia, S.C., 1867), p. 137; Stephen Elliott, "Forty-fifth Sermon: On the State Fast-day," in *Sermons by Stephen Elliott* (New York, 1867), pp. 497, 505, 507; and "Day of Fasting, Humiliation and Prayer," Atlanta *Christian Index*, March 9, 1865, p. 3.

21. "Thanksgiving Day: Its Afterclaps," Atlanta *Christian Index*, December 16, 1869, p. 2. See also "Day of Thanksgiving," Columbia (S.C.) *Southern Presbyterian*, November 14, 1872, p. 2; "The Two Proclamations," Atlanta *Christian Index*, November 22, 1866, p. 1; and Elliott's sermon "On the National Thanksgiving-day," in his *Sermons*, pp. 514–15.

22. James H. McNeilly, "Jefferson Davis: Gentleman, Patriot, Christian," CV 24 (June, 1916): 248; "Our Memorial Day," CV 22 (May, 1914): 195; Mrs. A. M'D. Wilson, "Memorial Day," CV 17 (April, 1919): 156; UDC, Lizzie Rutherford Chapter, *A History of the Origin of Memorial Day* (Columbus, Ga., 1898); UDC, *Minutes of the Eighteenth Annual Meeting of the UDC . . . 1901* (Nashville, 1902), p. 112.

23. United Confederate Veterans, Texas Division, Jas. J. A. Barker Camp, no. 1555, *Burial Ritual* (n.p., n.d.); "Burial Ritual for Veterans," CV 3 (February, 1895): 43; "Burial Ritual: Suitable for Confederates Everywhere," CV 17 (May, 1909): 214; Arthur B. Kinsolving, *Texas George: The Life of George Herbert Kinsolving* (Milwaukee, 1932), p. 130; James H. McNeilly, comp., *Memorial: Colonel John Overton and Mrs. Harriet Maxwell Overton* (n.p., 1899?), p. 124; "Rev. Romulus Morris Tuttle," CV 12 (June, 1904): 296–97; and "Sumner Archibald Cunningham," CV 22 (January, 1914): 6–8.

24. "The Monumental Spirit of the South," CV 22 (August, 1914): 344; Confederate Monumental Association, *Tennessee Confederate Memorial* (Nashville, n.d.), p. 44; "Dedicatory Prayer of Monument," CV 9 (January, 1901): 38; "Confederate Monument at San Antonio," CV 7 (September, 1899): 399; "Confederate Monument at Bolivar, Tenn.," CV 8 (August,

1900): 353; UCV, "Fourth Report of Monumental Committee," *Minutes of the Twenty-first Reunion*, p. 52; Emerson, *Historic Southern Monuments*, pp. 53–54, 133, 265, 426–27; UCV, *Minutes of the Seventeenth Annual Meeting and Reunion of the UCV . . . 1907* (Richmond, 1907), pp. 118–27; Mary B. Poppenheim et al., *The History of the United Daughters of the Confederacy* (Richmond, 1938), pp. 49–51. For the significance of stone markers as religious signs, see Mircea Eliade, *Patterns in Comparative Religion* (New York, 1958), pp. 216–35.

25. W. Lloyd Warner, *The Living and the Dead: A Study of the Symbolic Life of Americans* (New Haven, 1959), p. 280. See also Claude Lévi-Strauss, *The Savage Mind* (Chicago, 1962), p. 236; W. Lloyd Warner, "An American Sacred Ceremony," in Richey and Jones, *American Civil Religion*, pp. 89–111; Catherine Albanese, "Requiem for Memorial Day: Dissent in the Redeemer Nation," *American Quarterly* 26 (October, 1974): 386–98; Conrad Cherry, "Two American Sacred Ceremonies: Their Implications for the Study of Religion in America," *American Quarterly* 21 (Winter, 1969): 739–54.

26. In addition to the two institutions discussed in this chapter, two other organizations embodied the religion of the Lost Cause. The Ku Klux Klan is discussed in ch. V, and the contribution of Southern Schools is assessed in ch. VII. The Democratic party also promoted the Lost Cause, but its role was political, not religious. In states like Virginia and Georgia especially, but throughout the South, former Confederates cultivated the wartime memory in order to win election from grateful Southerners. Orators used their rhetoric at monument dedications to further their own cause. In truth, virtually all postwar institutions nurtured the Confederate myth for their own purposes, although not all of them directly developed the religious implications of the Lost Cause.

27. Wallace, *Religion*, p. 75. For background on the veterans' groups, see William W. White, *The Confederate Veteran* (Tuscaloosa, Ala., 1962). For accounts of local veterans' meetings, see "Worthy Words at Sherman Reunion: W. L. Sanford's Address to the Veterans," *CV* 11 (September, 1903): 400; Charles D. Bulla, "The Success of Defeat," *CV* 11 (October, 1903): 464. The quote was in UCV, *Minutes of the Ninth Reunion*, p. 8.

28. UCV, *Minutes of the Tenth Annual Meeting and Reunion of the UCV . . . 1900* (New Orleans, 1902), p. 70. For examples of this revealing theme in other forums, see *Minutes of the Twelfth Annual Meeting and Reunion of the UCV . . . 1902* (New Orleans, n.d.), p. 10; "The Confederate Dead of Mississippi: Prayer," *SHSP* 18 (January–December, 1890): 297; "The Monument to General Robert E. Lee: The Prayer," *SHSP* 17 (January–December, 1889): 301–2; "Editorial Paragraphs," *SHSP* 11 (January–December, 1883): 143.

29. For hymns at the reunions, see UCV, *Minutes of the Seventh Annual*

Meeting and Reunion of the UCV . . . 1897 (New Orleans, 1898), p. 15; *Minutes of the Tenth Reunion,* p. 40; *Minutes of the Thirteenth Annual Meeting and Reunion of the UCV . . . 1903* (New Orleans, n.d.), p. 50. For the memorial services, see UCV, *Minutes of the Tenth Reunion,* p. 15; *Minutes of the Seventeenth Reunion,* p. 110; *Minutes of the Thirtieth Annual Meeting and Reunion of the UCV . . . 1920* (New Orleans, n.d.), p. 41; and "Reunion of Confederate Veterans," CV 6 (June, 1898): 244.

30. "The Reunion," CV 5 (July, 1897): 339; CV 5 (June, 1897): 243; "Comment on Nashville Reunion," CV 5 (September, 1897): 463; CV 5 (August, 1897): 429.

31. *Ritual of the United Daughters of the Confederacy* (Austin, n.d.); UDC, *Minutes of the Twelfth Annual Meeting of the UDC . . . 1905* (Nashville, 1906), 265–66. Local women's groups in 1900 formed an organization similar to the UDC, the Confederated Memorial Associations of the South. See *History of the Confederated Memorial Associations of the South* (New Orleans, 1904), pp. 32–34.

32. Cornelia Branch Stone, *UDC Catechism for Children* (n.p., 1912); Poppenheim, *History of the UDC,* pp. 1–12; UDC, *Minutes of the Nineteenth Reunion,* p. 398.

33. "Chaplain Jones' Prayer," *Minutes of the Eighteenth Annual Meeting and Reunion of the UCV . . . 1908* (New Orleans, n.d.), pp. 49–50; *Minutes of the Twentieth Annual Meeting and Reunion of the UCV . . . 1910* (New Orleans, n.d.), pp. 53–54, 121. See also "The Confederate Dead in Stonewall Cemetery, Winchester, Va.," SHSP 22 (January–December, 1894): 42; "Unveiling of the Soldiers' and Sailors' Monument: Dr. Hoge's Prayer," SHSP 22 (January–December, 1894): 353; "Confederate Dead of Florida," SHSP 27 (January–December, 1899): 112. The failure to make specifically Christian references in the American civil religion is noted by Robert N. Bellah, "Civil Religion in America," and Martin E. Marty, "Two Kinds of Two Kinds of Civil Religion," both in Richey and Jones, *American Civil Religion,* pp. 23, 28, 148; and Conrad Cherry, *God's New Israel: Religious Interpretations of American Destiny* (Englewood Cliffs, N.J., 1971), pp. 9–10.

34. For examples of the interdenominational character of the Lost Cause, see John Lipscomb Johnson, *Autobiographical Notes* (privately printed, 1958), p. 279; Moses D. Hoge to Peyton Hoge, May 22, 1891, and January 20, 1893, Moses Drury Hoge Papers, Historical Foundation of the Presbyterian and Reformed Churches, Montreat, N.C.; "Gordon Memorial Service at Nashville," CV 12 (June, 1904): 293; J. William Jones, *The Davis Memorial Volume; or, Our Dead President, Jefferson Davis, and the World's Tribute to His Memory* (Waco, Tex., 1890), pp. 590–91, 595, 598. For examples of Catholic and Jewish involvement in the Lost Cause, see "Monument to Father

Ryan in Mobile," *CV* 21 (October, 1913): 489–90; "The Reunion," *CV* 5 (July, 1897): 341; "Address of Rabbi J. K. Gutheim," *SHSP* 10 (June, 1882): 248–50; "Sir Moses Ezekiel," *CV* 25 (May, 1917): 235–36.

35. See Thomas L. Connelly, *The Marble Man: Robert E. Lee and His Image in American Society* (New York, 1977), p. 45; "Appeal to the South," Atlanta *Christian Index*, February 28, 1884, p. 4; *CV* 5 (July, 1897): 359; *CV* 5 (August, 1897): 401, 439; Edward P. Humphrey, "Moses and the Critics," *Southern Bivouac*, n.s. 1 (August, 1885): 134–39; "Bishop John James Tigert," *CV* 15 (January, 1907): 25.

36. Mrs. Sam P. Jones and Walt Holcomb, *The Life and Sayings of Sam P. Jones* (Atlanta, 1907), pp. 142–48, 447–48; George C. Rankin, *The Story of My Life; or More Than a Half Century as I Have Lived It and Seen It Lived* (Nashville, 1912), p. 227; J. William Jones, *Personal Reminiscences, Anecdotes and Letters of Gen. Robert E. Lee* (New York, 1875), p. 333; UCV, *Minutes of the Tenth Reunion*, pp. 102–4, 108.

37. Bearden, "The Episcopal Church in the Confederate States," pp. 269–75; Dunstan, "The Episcopal Church in the Confederacy," p. 10; G. MacLaren Brydon, "Historic Parishes: Saint Paul's Church, Richmond," *Historical Magazine of the Protestant Episcopal Church* 23 (September, 1954): 277–91; Norton, *Rebel Religion*, pp. 34–35; Silver, *Confederate Morale*, p. 77; Edgar L. Pennington, "The Church in the Confederate States," *Historical Magazine of the Protestant Episcopal Church* 17 (December, 1948): 358.

38. Eliade, *Patterns*, pp. 394, 407.

CHAPTER II: CRUSADING CHRISTIAN CONFEDERATES

1. For background on the Lost Cause myth, see Osterweis, *Myth of the Lost Cause*; Daniel Aaron, *The Unwritten War: American Writers and the Civil War* (New York, 1973); Paul M. Gaston, *The New South Creed: A Study in Southern Mythmaking* (New York, 1970); Richard Weaver, *The Southern Tradition at Bay: A History of Postbellum Thought*, ed. George Core and M. E. Bradford (New Rochelle, N.Y., 1968); Richard Barksdale Harwell, "The Confederate Heritage," in Louis D. Rubin, Jr., and James J. Kilpatrick, eds., *The Lasting South: Fourteen Southerners Look at Their Home* (Chicago, 1957), pp. 16–27; William B. Hesseltine, *Confederate Leaders in the New South* (Baton Rouge, 1950); Susan E. Durant, "The Gently Furled Banner: The Development of the Myth of the Lost Cause, 1865–1900" (Ph.D. dissertation, University of North Carolina, 1972); and Sharon E. Hannum, "Confederate Cavaliers: The Myth in War and Defeat" (Ph.D. dissertation, Rice University, 1965).

2. Mark Schorer, "The Necessity of Myth," and Clyde Kluckhohn, "Recurrent Themes in Myth and Mythmaking," in Henry A. Murray, *Myth and*

Mythmaking (New York, 1960), pp. 355, 58; John Greenway in "Introduction" to Melville Jacobs, comp., *The Anthropologist Looks at Myth* (Austin, 1966), p. x, calls myth "sublimated reality."

3. Henry A. Murray, "Definitions of Myth," in Richard M. Ohmann, ed., *The Making of Myth* (New York, 1962), p. 10; Richard Slotkin, *Regeneration through Violence: The Mythology of the American Frontier, 1600–1860* (Middletown, Conn., 1973), pp. 6–8; Ruth Benedict, "Myth," in Edwin R. A. Seligman, ed., *Encyclopedia of the Social Sciences* (New York, 1930), 11: 178–81. See also Joseph Campbell, *The Hero with a Thousand Faces* (Princeton, N.J., 1972 [1949]), pp. 8–9; and Greenway, "Introduction," *Anthropologist Looks at Myth*, p. xi.

4. Eliade, *Myth and Reality*, p. 8.

5. Ibid., p. 5; Benedict, "Myth," p. 178. See also Slotkin, *Regeneration through Violence*, p. 269; Lord Raglan, "Myth and Ritual," in Thomas A. Sebeok, ed., *Myth: A Symposium* (Philadelphia, 1955), pp. 76–77; Richard Chase, *Quest for Myth* (Baton Rouge, 1946), pp. 72–73; and George B. Tindall, "Mythology: A New Frontier in Southern History," in Frank E. Vandiver, ed., *The Idea of the South: Pursuit of a Central Theme* (Chicago, 1964), pp. 1–15.

6. United Confederate Veterans, *Minutes of the Seventeenth Annual Reunion*, pp. 112–13; Randolph McKim, "The Confederate Soldier," CV 13 (March, 1905): 113–21; "Address of Rev. E. C. De La Moriniere," in UCV, *Minutes of the Twentieth Annual Reunion*, p. 124; Robert C. Cave, *The Men in Gray* (Nashville, 1911), pp. 52–53; "Address of Rev. Dr. S. A. Goodwin," in Jones, *Davis Memorial Volume*, p. 655; UCV, *Minutes of the Tenth Reunion*, pp. 29–30, 38; "Address of Rev. H. Melville Jackson," SHSP 16 (January–December, 1888): 195, 203; Albert T. Bledsoe, "Hon. A. H. Stephens on the Late War," *Southern Review* 11 (July, 1872): 145.

7. For the Washington and Lee connection, see Warren A. Candler, *High Living and High Lives* (Nashville, 1912), p. 176; Randolph H. McKim, *The Motives and Aims of the Soldiers of the South in the Civil War* (n.p., n.d.), p. 27; Lucien Lee Kinsolving, "Triennial Missionary Sermon before the General Convention," in O. A. Kinsolving, G. H. Kinsolving, and L. L. Kinsolving, *Memorials: Sermons Preached on Special Occasions by a Father and Two of His Sons* (Austin, 1911), p. 38; "Historical Sketch," CV 11 (April, 1903): 148–49; Cave, *Men in Gray*, p. 111; "Death of General Lee," *Christian Advocate*, October 15, 1870, p. 5; "The Moral Influence of Representative Men," *Religious Herald*, March 1, 1866, p. 2; "The Natal Day of Gen. R. E. Lee," SHSP 28 (January–December, 1900): 241–42. For blood ties between Revolutionaries and Confederates, see William M. Green, *Address Delivered before the Board of Trustees, University of the South, Sewanee, Tenn., Aug. 4th, 1879* (Charles-

ton, S.C., 1879), pp. 9, 15; William Mercer Green, *Memoir of Rt. Rev. James Hervey Otey* (New York, 1885), p. 93; Emerson, *Monuments*, p. 78; Jones, *Davis Memorial Volume*, p. 43; McNeilly, *Memorial to Overton*, pp. 18–19; Robert H. Crozier, *The Confederate Spy; or, Startling Incidents of the War Between the States. A Novel* (Louisville, 1885), p. 174; Joseph P. B. Wilmer, *Gen'l. Robert E. Lee. An Address Delivered before the Students of the University of the South, October 15, 1870* (Nashville, 1872), p. 6. For the similarity in principles, see Candler, *High Lives*, p. 175; "Shooting at the Eagle: Dr. O. P. Fitzgerald's Fourth of July Oration," *Christian Advocate*, July 18, 1889, p. 2; Hoge, *Hoge*, p. 549; Jones, *Davis Memorial Volume*, p. 655; Thomas R. Markham, "Tribute to the Confederate Dead," *SHSP* 10 (April, 1882): 176.

8. "Letter from Bishop Andrew," *Christian Advocate*, July 5, 1866, p. 2; Albert T. Goodloe, *Confederate Echoes: A Voice from the South in the Days of Secession and of the Southern Confederacy* (Nashville, 1907), pp. 228–29; R. A. Alston, "Defense of Mr. Davis," *Christian Advocate*, September 6, 1866, p. 6; Susan Pendleton Lee, *Memoirs of William Nelson Pendleton* (Philadelphia, 1893), p. 414; Walter B. Capers, *The Soldier-Bishop: Ellison Capers* (New York, 1912), pp. 99–101; Charles T. Quintard, *Nellie Peters' Pocket Handkerchief and What It Saw: A Story of the War* (Sewanee, 1907), p. 8; John B. Adger, *My Life and Times 1810–1899* (Richmond, 1899), pp. 335–36; Patrick H. Mell, Jr., *Life of Patrick Hues Mell* (Louisville, 1895), pp. 145–46; John L. Underwood, *The Women of the Confederacy* (New York, 1906), pp. 153–54; "Southern War Poetry," *Southern Review* 1 (April, 1867): 278–79; Rankin, *The Story of My Life*, p. 77; *Christian Advocate*, November 18, 1876, p. 8; J. L. B., "The Temper of Northern Baptists," *Religious Herald*, October 19, 1865, p. 1; "Comment by Rev. James H. McNeilly," *CV* 21 (November, 1913): 556; "Review of *The Negro and the White Man*," *Christian Advocate*, December 22, 1898, p. 5; Joseph Mack, "Work among the Negroes II," in George A. Blackburn, *Life and Letters of John L. Girardeau* (Columbia, S.C., 1916), pp. 66–67; "Witticisms of Bishop Wilmer," *CV* 13 (November, 1905): 518; and "Restitution," *Christian Advocate*, July 26, 1866, p. 2.

9. James H. McNeilly, "What Caused the War," *CV* 17 (August, 1909): 404; McNeilly, "Northern Conscience and the War," *CV* 24 (November, 1916): 286–87; "Alas: A Satire on the Times," *Southern Review* 9 (October, 1871): 948–49; George G. Smith, *The Life and Times of George Foster Pierce* (Sparta, Ga., 1888), pp. 436–37; Donald Frazer, "Modern Infidelity," *Southern Presbyterian Review* 17 (November, 1866): 347–48.

10. W. Dudley Powers, "Memorial Address," *CV* 1 (November, 1893): 323; R. A. Holland, "Eulogy to Robert E. Lee," in Jones, *Personal Reminiscences*, p. 472; D. T. Moore, "Eulogy to Lee," in Jones, *Reminiscences*, p. 474; Hoge, "The Private Soldier: An Address before the Mass-meeting Held in

the Interest of the Monument on Libby Hill, Richmond, Va., Nov. 30, 1892," in Hoge, *Hoge*, pp. 459–60; McKim, "Confederate Soldier," p. 121; Cooke, *Stonewall Jackson*, p. 580; Beverly Dandridge Tucker, *Confederate Memorial Verses* (Norfolk, n.d.), p. 5; "A Monument to Southern Women," CV 2 (October, 1894): 313.

11. Dixon Wector, *The Hero in America: A Chronicle of Hero-Worship* (Ann Arbor, 1963 [1941]), pp. 273–306, 486–87; Marshall Fishwick, *American Heroes: Myth and Reality* (Washington, 1954), pp. 73–84, 229–30.

12. "Inscriptions on Arlington Confederate Monument," CV 28 (April, 1920): 124; Hoge, "The Private Soldier," in Hoge, *Hoge*, p. 457; UCV, *Seventeenth Reunion*, p. 112; Pegram Dargan, "Call It Not a 'Lost Cause,'" CV 4 (June, 1896): 195. See also McKim, *Motives and Aims*, pp. 30–31.

13. Richard H. Wilmer, *The Recent Past from a Southern Standpoint: Reminiscences of a Grandfather* (New York, 1887), pp. 34, 211, 275; Wilmer, *In Memoriam: A Sermon in Commemoration of the Life and Labors of the Rt. Rev. Stephen Elliott* (Mobile, 1867), pp. 12–14, 16–17. See also Walter C. Whitaker, *Richard Hooker Wilmer: A Biography* (Philadelphia, 1907); Gardiner C. Tucker, "Richard Hooker Wilmer, Second Bishop of Alabama," *Historical Magazine of the Protestant Episcopal Church* 7 (June, 1938): 132–53; and "Rt. Rev. Richard H. Wilmer," CV 14 (March, 1906): 106.

14. Goodloe, *Confederate Echoes*, p. 434; William Pinkney, "Ode," in *Burial Ceremonies of Confederate Dead, December 11, 1874* (Washington, 1875), p. 14; Randolph McKim, *The Soul of Lee* (New York, 1918), p. 139; "The Boy Preacher as a Soldier," *Southern Bivouac* 2 (November, 1883): 129–31; John B. McFerrin, "Religion in the Army of Tennessee II," *Home Monthly* 4 (February, 1868): 79–81; Arthur B. Kinsolving, *The Story of a Southern School: The Episcopal High School of Virginia* (Baltimore, 1922), pp. 67, 75; "Address of Rev. H. Melville Jackson," SHSP, p. 203; Joseph B. Cheshire, *The Church in the Confederate States: A History of the Protestant Episcopal Church in the Confederate States* (New York, 1912), pp. 69–70; P. D. Stephenson, "The Men of the Ranks," CV 17 (September, 1909): 436–38; Arthur H. Noll, ed., *Doctor Quintard: Chaplain C.S.A. and Second Bishop of Tennessee. Being His Story of the War* (Sewanee, 1905), pp. 1–2; "Religion in Gray," *Christian Advocate*, March 25, 1876, p. 3; James McNeilly, "Religion in the Confederate Armies," CV 23 (January, 1915): 29; McNeilly, "Religion in the Confederate Armies," CV 21 (May, 1913): 230–31; White, *Southern Presbyterian Leaders*, p. 343. For a rare example of a Christian who was said to have emerged from the war "backslidden," see *Christian Advocate*, March 18, 1876, p. 12.

15. Underwood, *The Women of the Confederacy*, p. 56; G. W. Anderson, "Religion in the Confederate Army," CV 6 (December, 1898): 579; Wilmer,

In Memoriam, pp. 12–13; Randolph H. McKim, *A Soldier's Recollections: Leaves from the Diary of a Young Confederate* (New York, 1910), p. 212.

16. William W. Bennett, *A Narrative of the Great Revival which Prevailed in the Southern Armies* (Philadelphia, 1877), pp. 11, 16, 426–27; Jones, *Christ in the Camp*, pp. 6, 461–64. The Cromwell analogy was also used by Noll, Quintard, p. 2. Jones's study originally appeared serially in *Religious Herald*, beginning with "Jesus in the Camp: or Religion in Lee's Army," *Herald*, July 29, 1886, p. 1; for examples of the memoirs Jones's volume evoked, see "Ex-Chaplain Martin Bibb Tells about His Work Among the Confederates," *Herald*, April 14, 1887, p. 1; and "The Old Confederates and Rev. F. Denison," *Herald*, March 3, 1887, p. 1; Bennett, *Great Revival*, pp. 426–27; Jones, *Christ in the Camp*, pp. 461, 464. J. Leighton Wilson, in the "Fourth Annual Report of the Executive Committee of Domestic Missions," *Minutes of the General Assembly of the Presbyterian Church in the United States, 1865* (Augusta, 1865), p. 390, said, "That our camps should have been made nurseries of piety, is something not only new and unprecedented in warfare, but may be regarded as an encouraging token of God's purpose to favor and bless our future Zion."

17. Campbell, *The Hero with a Thousand Faces*, pp. 58, 91; "Rev. Dr. George C. Harris' Address," in UCV, *Minutes of the Eleventh Annual Meeting and Reunion of the United Confederate Veterans . . . 1901* (New Orleans, n.d.), pp. 56–57. See also Camille Williams, "The South's Great Battle Abbey," *CV* 1 (November, 1893): 361; Candler, *High Living*, p. 51; "Speech of Rev. H. Melville Jackson," *SHSP* 11 (December, 1883): 573; Randolph McKim, "The Confederate Soldier," *CV* 13 (March, 1905): 121; "The Confederate Dead in Stonewall Cemetery, Winchester, Va.," *SHSP* 22 (January–December, 1894): 42.

18. UCV, *Seventeenth Reunion*, p. 114; Henry M. Wharton, *White Blood: A Story of the South* (New York, 1906), p. 117. See also UCV, *Minutes of the Twenty-fifth Annual Meeting and Reunion of the United Confederate Veterans . . . 1915* (New Orleans, n.d.), p. 97; Henry W. Battle, "The Reunion Address," *CV* 23 (July, 1915): 295; "The Confederate Dead of Mississippi: Prayer," *SHSP* 18 (January–December, 1890): 296.

19. "Sermon from a Veteran to Comrades," *CV* 9 (December, 1901): 549–50; "General William N. Pendleton," *Southern Bivouac* 1 (March, 1883): 299; Capers, *The Soldier-Bishop*, p. 129; James Power Smith, "With Stonewall Jackson: Jackson's Religious Character," *SHSP*, n.s. 5 (August, 1920): 67, 69–70; James R. Winchester, "Gen. William Nelson Pendleton," *CV* 4 (August, 1896): 262–63; and "Address of Rev. H. Melville Jackson," *SHSP*, pp. 196–98; T. V. Moore, "Memorial Discourse on the Death of General Robert E. Lee," *Christian Advocate*, November 5, 1870, p. 2. James C.

Bonner's "The Historical Basis of the Southern Military Tradition," *Georgia Review* 9 (Spring, 1955): 74–85, overlooked the role of religion in the South's military cult.

20. "Rev. Dr. George C. Harris' Address," in UCV, *Eleventh Reunion*, pp. 59–60; "Mrs. Sallie Nesbitt Sizemore," CV 21 (July, 1913): 347; "Capt. Sallie Tompkins," CV 24 (November, 1916): 521; "Woman's Monument at Jackson, Miss.," CV 20 (July, 1912): 324–26 (Weddell quote); "Memorial Hour," CV 24 (August, 1916): 375; J. B. Cranfill, *From Memory: Reminiscences, Recitals, and Gleanings from a Bustling and Busy Life* (Nashville, 1937), pp. 23, 93. UCV, *Minutes of the Ninth Annual Reunion*, p. 156; McKim, *Soul of Lee*, p. 149; James B. Gambrell, "The New War for the Life of Civilization," in "Recollections of Confederate Scout Service," MS autobiography on microfilm at the Dargan-Carver Library, Baptist Sunday School Board, Nashville; Robert L. Dabney, "The Matron of Old Virginia," *Central Presbyterian*, November 20, 1867, p. 2; "Southern War Poetry," *Southern Review* 1 (April, 1867): 276. For background, see Campbell, *Hero with a Thousand Faces*, pp. 109, 116; and Anne Firor Scott, *The Southern Lady: From Pedestal to Politics* (Chicago, 1970).

21. Goodloe, *Confederate Echoes*, p. 300; Underwood, *The Women of the Confederacy*, pp. 27, 45–46, 70, 153–54; "The Woman of the South: Sonnets Dedicated Patriotically to the Mothers of the Daughters of the Confederacy," CV 28 (May, 1920): 163; William S. Harrison, *Sam Williams: A Tale of the Old South* (Nashville, 1892), pp. 185, 302; "Address of Rev. G. W. Beale at the Northern Neck Soldiers' Reunion, November 11, 1884," SHSP 16 (January–December, 1888): 109–12; Tilla D. Baskette, "The Soldier's Widow," *Christian Advocate*, July 25, 1867, p. 6; "Tributes to Miss Winnie Davis," CV 6 (October, 1898): 467–69. Bishop Collins Denny, in "Robert E. Lee, The Flower of the South," SHSP, n.s. 3 (September, 1916): 5–6, also described Southern women as madonnas.

22. UCV, *Ninth Reunion*, p. 156; "Address by Miss Elizabeth Lumpkin," CV 13 (July, 1905): 298–99; Henry W. Battle, "Reunion Address," CV 23 (July, 1915): 195; Underwood, *Women*, p. 310; Felton, *Sermon on Lee*, p. 7; Rebecca L. Felton, undated and untitled MS article on Temperance, and "A Party without a Principle," MS article in Political File, both in Rebecca Latimer Felton Papers, University of Georgia Library, Athens.

23. I. W. Grimes, "Manliness," *Southern Churchman*, June 8, 1907, p. 24; Underwood, *Women*, p. 44; *Christian Advocate*, October 25, 1884, p. 8. See also "Address of Rev. H. Melville Jackson," SHSP 16 (January–December, 1888): 202; and "Tribute to Gen. Robert E. Lee," MS sermon on microfilm at Dargan-Carver Library, Southern Baptist Sunday School Board, Nashville.

24. "Address by Rev. E. C. De La Moriniere," in UCV, *Twentieth Re-*

union, pp. 126–27. See also "A Noble Foe," *Christian Advocate*, February 13, 1886, p. 2; Abram J. Ryan, *Poems: Patriotic, Religious, Miscellaneous* (New York, 1896), pp. 24–25; "The Chaplain on Review," CV 14 (October, 1906): 476–77; Emma Francis Lee Smith, "Robert E. Lee," CV 27 (January, 1919): 1; "Robert E. Lee," *Christian Index*, October 20, 1870, p. 162; *Christian Index*, August 20, 1874, p. 2; C. C. Penick and Frank Stringfellow, "The Heroic Element in General R. E. Lee," *Southern Bivouac* 3 (March, 1885): 308–9; James McNeilly, "Robert Edward Lee," CV 26 (April, 1918): 141; Holland, "Eulogy to Lee," in Jones, *Personal Reminiscences*, p. 473; "Sermon by W. T. Brantley," ibid., p. 479; William H. Felton, *Sermon on the Life and Character of Gen. Robt. E. Lee, Preached at Cartersville, Ga., Sunday, Oct. 16, 1870* (Cartersville, 1870), p. 8; "Memorial Services for Gen. Lee," *Christian Advocate*, October 29, 1870, p. 4; Tucker, *Verses*, p. 5; Robert Tuttle, "General Lee and Traveller," CV 3 (March, 1895): 74; "Robert E. Lee," *Southern Churchman*, January 19, 1907; Albert T. Bledsoe, "The Great Virginian," *Southern Review* 9 (July, 1871): 691–92; Marshall W. Fishwick, "Virginians on Olympus: Robert E. Lee: Savior of the Lost Cause," *Virginia Magazine of History and Biography* 58 (April, 1950): 163–80. Thomas L. Connelly, in "The Image and the General: Robert E. Lee in American Historiography," *Civil War History* 19 (March, 1973): 50–64, and in *The Marble Man*, pp. 94–95, discussed Lee as a Christ figure, but he improperly implied Lee's uniqueness in this respect.

25. White, *Southern Presbyterian Leaders*, p. 457; "He Sincerely Honors the Character of Gen. Lee," CV 14 (June, 1906): 273; Felton, *Sermon on Lee*, pp. 19, 21; Collins Denny, "Robert E. Lee, the Flower of the South," *SHSP*, n.s. 3 (January–December, 1916): 12.

26. Randolph H. McKim, *Lee the Christian Hero: A Sermon Delivered in the Lee Memorial Church, Lexington, Virginia, Sunday January 20, 1907* (Washington, 1907), pp. 5–8; McKim, *The Soul of Lee*, pp. 8, 43, 117, 121–22, 128, 187–88, 203. J. William Jones wrote in *Personal Reminiscences*, p. 327, that when Lee died, his soldiers "wept that a loved and loving *father* had passed from their midst."

27. See Mrs. John William Jones, "Our Dead Chief," in Jones, *The Davis Memorial Volume*, pp. 611–12; M. B. Wharton, "The Death of Jefferson Davis," ibid., p. 603; "Prayer by Father Hubert," ibid., p. 532; "Bishop Keener on Jefferson Davis," *Christian Advocate*, December 19, 1889, p. 8; Moses D. Hoge, "Prayer at the Re-interment of President Davis," in Hoge, *Hoge*, p. 497.

28. "Jefferson Davis," *Christian Advocate*, December 12, 1889, p. 8; Jones, *Davis Memorial Volume*, pp. viii, 514; Clement Evans, "Unveiling of Davis Monument," in UCV, *Seventeenth Reunion*, p. 154; *Christian Advocate*, July

5, 1866, p. 4, December 6, 1866, p. 6; "Innocence Vindicated," *Christian Index*, August 23, 1866, p. 135; "Address of De La Moriniere," UCV, *Twentieth Reunion*, pp. 125–26.

29. Jones, *Davis Memorial Volume*, pp. 530, 657; United Daughters of the Confederacy, *Minutes of the Fourth Annual Meeting of the United Daughters of the Confederacy . . . 1897* (Nashville, 1898), p. 20; *Minutes of the Fourteenth Annual Meeting*, pp. 6, 49–50, 223; *Minutes of the Nineteenth Annual Meeting*, p. 395. See also "The Ninety-third Anniversary of the Birth of President Jefferson Davis," *SHSP* 29 (January–December, 1901): 1–33; *CV* 12 (February, 1904): 56; Mildred Rutherford, *Jefferson Davis the President of the Confederate States and Abraham Lincoln the President of the United States, 1861–1865* (Athens, Ga., 1916).

30. "Father Brannon's Poem: 'Confederate Comrades,'" in UCV, *Minutes of the Twenty-first Reunion*, p. 104; John William Jones, "The Career of General Jackson's," *SHSP* 35 (January–December, 1907): 81. See also "Was Stonewall Jackson a Fraud?" *Religious Herald*, February 25, 1886, p. 1; "General T. J. Jackson," *Central Presbyterian*, January 13, 1869, p. 2; Beverly R. Tucker, "Stonewall Jackson," *CV* 28 (February, 1920): 49; Smith, "With Stonewall Jackson," p. 71; James B. Cranfill, *Dr. J. B. Cranfill's Chronicle: A Story of Life in Texas* (New York, 1916), p. 17; and "Stonewall Jackson's Victory at McDowell," *Christian Observer*, August 8, 1917, pp. 20–21.

31. *CV* 25 (March, 1917): 137; White, *Southern Presbyterian Leaders*, pp. 446–50. See also Powers, "Memorial Address," pp. 331–32; and James Power Smith, "Jackson's Religious Character: An Address at Lexington, Va.," *SHSP*, n.s. 43 (September, 1920): 67–75.

32. Robert L. Dabney, *Life and Campaigns of Lieut.-Gen. Thomas J. Jackson* (New York, 1866), pp. 706–26; Cooke, *Jackson*, pp. 445, 507. See also "The Last Hours of Stonewall Jackson," *Christian Advocate*, February 27, 1886, p. 2; "Last Hours of Stonewall Jackson—Narrative by His Medical Attendant," *Christian Index*, May 31, 1866, p. 92; "The House Where Stonewall Jackson Died," *CV* 25 (February, 1917): 51.

33. See, e.g., Ella Wheeler Wilcox, "Sam Davis," *CV* 8 (March, 1900): 139; "Uncrowned Heroes—Sam Davis the Theme," *CV* 10 (June, 1902): 255; S. A. Cunningham, "Sam Davis," *American Historical Magazine* 4 (July, 1899): 195–206; "The Sam Davis Drama," *CV* 4 (December, 1896): 402; *CV* 5 (January, 1897): 16; Edythe J. R. Whitley, *Sam Davis: Hero of the Confederacy* (Nashville, 1971), pp. 210–11.

34. "Honoring Sam Davis in California," *CV* 10 (September, 1902): 389; "Tell the Children All to Be Good," *CV* 8 (November, 1900): 478; Emerson, *Monuments*, p. 329; *CV* 4 (June, July, August, 1896): 189–92, 204–6, 253; *CV* 4 (November, 1896): 374. See also "Sam Davis, an American Hero," *CV*

8 (March, 1900): 99; and Mrs. W. B. Romine, "Sam Davis: His Capture, Death, and Monument at Pulaski," in William Thomas Richardson, *Historic Pulaski: Birthplace of the Ku Klux Klan, Scene of Execution of Sam Davis* ([Nashville?], 1913), pp. 98–99.

35. Robert C. Cave, "Honoring the Private Soldier," CV 2 (June, 1894): 163–64; "The Chaplain General Speaks," UCV, *Twentieth Reunion,* pp. 134–35; "Unveiling of the Soldiers' and Sailors' Monument," *SHSP* 22 (January–December, 1894): 336–80; Thomas Markham, "Tribute to the Confederate Dead," *SHSP* 10 (April, 1882): 175; Hoge, "The Private Soldier," in Hoge, *Hoge,* pp. 456–60; Pinkney, "Ode," pp. 14–15; McKim, *Motives and Aims,* pp. 30–31; H. L.. Piner, "Echoes of the Confederacy," CV 15 (November, 1907): 502–4; Stephenson, "The Men of the Ranks," pp. 436–38; "Dr. Curry's Able Address," *Minutes of the Sixth Annual Meeting and Reunion of the United Confederate Veterans . . . 1896* (New Orleans, 1897), p. 70.

36. E. H. Hutton, "Address of the Prophet of the Day," in *Semi-centennial of the University of the South, 1857–1907: Sermons, Poem, Addresses and Letters* (Sewanee, n.d.), p. 65; H. H. Waters to Sally Blake, April 19, 1894, Charles T. Quintard to William M. Polk, December 10, 1885, both in Leonidas Polk Papers, Southern Historical Collection, University of North Carolina, Chapel Hill; George H. Kinsolving, *An Anniversary Missionary Sermon Preached in Christ Church, Houston, St. David's Church, Austin and Christ Church, Tyler* (n.p., n.d.), pp. 6–7; Kinsolving, *Texas George,* p. 42; Green, *Address Delivered before the Board of Trustees,* pp. 17–19; Sally Blake to Alexander Gregg, October 27, 1879, Polk Papers.

37. William M. Polk, *Leonidas Polk: Bishop and General* (New York, 1915), 1: 357, 362, 365; John Fulton to William M. Polk, January 19, May 9, 1882, Polk Papers; J. P. B. Wilmer to Mrs. Frances A. Polk, August 16, 1864, quoted in Polk, *Polk,* 2: 392; Quintard, *Nellie Peters' Pocket Handkerchief;* Polk, *Polk,* p. 387. See also Charles P. McIlwaine, "Leonidas Polk: The Bishop-General Who Died for the South," *SHSP* 18 (January–December, 1890): 371–80; "General Polk's Death," ibid., pp. 380–81.

38. "Speech of Gen. Ellison Capers at the Unveiling of the Confederate Monument at Chickamauga Battlefield, May 27, 1901," in Capers, *Capers,* pp. 296–97, 348–50. See also "An Address by Rev. Ellison Capers, Memorial Day, May 20, 1890, Greenville, S.C.," ibid., pp. 338, 192; and Ellison Capers, "Captain Francis Huger Harleston," *SHSP* 12 (July, August, September, 1884): 361–66; letter from Ellison Capers, March 22, 1892, Ellison Capers folder, Episcopal Bishops' Biographical Folders, Episcopal Church Historical Society, Austin, Tex.

39. "Excerpts from Press Criticisms on *The Soldier Bishop,*" pamphlet in Capers folder, ibid. See also A. I. Robertson, "Ellison Capers, General and

Bishop," CV 7 (June, 1899): 260–61; and William P. DuBose, "Ellison Capers," *Sewanee Review* 16 (April, 1908): 368–73; Capers, *Capers*, pp. 271, 286–87, 316.

40. For examples of other military men portrayed as religious heroes, see "The Confederate Reunion," *Christian Advocate*, July 28, 1898, p. 2; CV 12 (February, 1904), 53–54; Cranfill, *Cranfill's Chronicle*, p. 415; Teresa Strickland, "Gen. Wade Hampton: A Tribute," CV 12 (May, 1904), 213; Mrs. Eugenia Hall Arnold, "The Christian Character of Our Great Leaders," CV 28 (February, 1920): 53–55; White, *Southern Presbyterian Leaders*, p. 452; "General Clement A. Evans Tells of Stephen D. Lee," in Emerson, *Monuments*, pp. 206–8; "General Gordon and the Baptists," *Christian Index*, January 21, 1904, p. 6; Oscar P. Fitzgerald and Charles B. Galloway, *Eminent Methodists* (Nashville, 1898), p. 138; Dabney, *Jackson*, p. 709; William Preston Johnston, *The Life of Gen. Albert Sidney Johnston* (New York, 1878), pp. 721–27; "The Moral Influence of Representative Men," *Religious Herald*, March 1, 1866, p. 2; "Memorial Meeting: Dr. Goodwin's Address," SHSP 18 (January–December, 1890): 17; "New Orleans, Louisiana: Discourse of Rev. B. M. Palmer, D.D.," SHSP 18 (January–December, 1890): 210–17. For examples of Southern preachers defending those Confederate leaders who had dubious religious commitments, see James H. McNeilly, "Blessing for Gen. Forrest," CV 7 (October, 1899): 446; "Gen. J. E. B. Stuart," CV 11 (September, 1903): 390–92; John B. McFerrin, "Religion in the Army of Tennessee I," *Home Monthly* 4 (January, 1868): 27; "Robert Toombs," *Christian Advocate*, January 2, 1886, p. 8; and W. H. Whitsitt, "A Year with Forrest," CV 25 (August, 1917): 357–62.

41. Marshall Fishwick, *The Hero, American Style* (New York, 1969), p. 10.

CHAPTER III: ABIDING CHILDREN OF PRIDE

1. Charles C. Boldrick, "Father Abram J. Ryan: The Poet-Priest of the Confederacy," *Filson Club History Quarterly* 46 (July, 1972): 201–17; Oscar H. Lipscomb, "Some Unpublished Poems of Abram J. Ryan," *Alabama Review* 25 (July, 1972): 164, 168–72; "When and Where Father Ryan Died," CV 1 (September, 1893): 262; F. V. N. Painter, *Poets of the South: A Series of Biographical and Critical Studies with Typical Poems, Annotated* (New York, 1903), pp. 104–6, 109; Kate White, "Father Ryan—the Poet-Priest of the South," *South Atlantic Quarterly* 18 (January, 1919), 69–74; Young E. Allison, "How Father Ryan Died," *Southern Bivouac*, n.s. 2 (August, 1886): 167–71.

2. Abram J. Ryan, "The South," SHSP, n.s. 3 (September, 1916): 1–2; "The South: Its Ruins," CV 11 (March, 1903): 102.

3. Ryan, "In Memory of My Brother," in *Poems*, pp. 50–53; Ryan, "The Land We Love," *New Eclectic* 3 (December, 1868): 501.

4. "Origin of the Conquered Banner," *CV* 5 (August, 1897): 436–37; Lipscomb, "Unpublished Poems," pp. 167, 170–71; Boldrick, "Father Ryan," p. 210.

5. Elliott, "Forty-fifth Sermon: On the State Fast-day," in *Sermons*, pp. 497, 505, 507. Also condemning Southern pride was Basil Manly, Sr., in a sermon reprinted in *Christian Index*, November 22, 1866, p. 1.

6. "Thanksgiving Day: Its Afterclaps," *Christian Index*, December 16, 1869, p. 2; "Day of Thanksgiving," *Southern Presbyterian*, November 14, 1872, p. 2. See also "The Two Proclamations," *Christian Index*, November 22, 1866, p. 1.

7. "Notes on the Times," *Christian Index*, January 5, 1865, p. 3; Robert Manson Myers, ed., *The Children of Pride: A True Story of Georgia and the Civil War* (New Haven, 1972), p. 1244; Elliott, *Sermons*, p. 500; Robert L. Dabney to his mother, February 15, 1868, in Thomas C. Johnson, *Life and Letters of Robert L. Dabney* (Richmond, 1903), p. 302; George G. Smith, *The Life and Letters of James Osgood Andrew* (Nashville, 1882), pp. 533, 535. See also J. P. B. Wilmer, *Address of the Bishop of La. to the Convention of the Protestant Episcopal Church in New Orleans, February 14, 1868* (New Orleans, 1868), p. 3; John A. Broadus, *Memoir of James Petigru Boyce* (New York, 1893), p. 199; *History of the Baptist Denomination in Georgia* (Atlanta, 1881), pp. 237, 240; "The State of the Country," *Religious Herald*, January 19, 1865, p. 5; and McKim, *A Soldier's Recollections*, p. 273.

8. "Address of the Bishop of Alabama," *Journal of the Proceedings of the Thirty-fourth Annual Council of the Protestant Episcopal Church, in the Diocese of Alabama, held in St. Paul's Church, Greensboro, May 3, 1865* (Mobile, 1865), p. 14. See also Albert T. Bledsoe, "Southern Voices," *Southern Review* 11 (July, 1872): 41; *SHSP* 6 (December, 1878): 243.

9. Lee, *Memoirs of William Nelson Pendleton*, pp. 422–23, 428; Mary Pendleton to sister, June 5, 1865, William N. Pendleton to Rt. Rev. Horatio Potter, June 1, 1868, and Pendleton to wife, May 10, 1870, all in William Nelson Pendleton Papers, Southern Historical Collection, University of North Carolina, Chapel Hill. For assessments of exiles, see Andrew F. Rolle, *The Lost Cause: The Confederate Exodus to Mexico* (Norman, Okla., 1965); Alfred J. and Katherine Abbey Hanna, *Confederate Exiles in Venezuela* (Tuscaloosa, Ala., 1960); William B. Hesseltine and Hazel C. Wolf, *The Blue and the Gray on the Nile* (Chicago, 1961); Lawrence F. Hill, "The Confederate Exodus to South America," *Southwestern Historical Quarterly* 39 (October, 1935; January, April, 1936): 100–134, 161–99, 309–26; Blanche Henry Clark

Weaver, "Confederate Immigrants and Evangelical Churches in Brazil," *Journal of Southern History* 18 (November, 1952): 446–68.

10. "A Revelation from God to the South," *Religious Herald*, February 16, 1865, p. 13; "The Mystical Babylon," *Christian Index*, February 10, 1866, p. 26. For the same viewpoint, see Albert T. Bledsoe, "The M. E. Churches, North and South," *Southern Review* 10 (April, 1872): 401.

11. Hoge, *Hoge*, pp. 238–39. See also Ernest R. Sandeen, *The Roots of Fundamentalism: British and American Millenarianism, 1800–1930* (Chicago, 1970), pp. 82–83, for a discussion of Cumming.

12. J. W. Sandell, *The United States in Scripture. The Union against the States. God in Government* (Jackson, Miss., [1907?]), p. 6. See also "Birthday Visions," CV 20 (November, 1912): 515; and "Rev. J. W. Sandell," CV 21 (September, 1913): 455.

13. Sandell, *United States in Scripture*, pp. 3, 8, 10–14, 16–18, 23, 25, 37, 38, 50, 52, 58.

14. Wharton, *White Blood*, p. 31; John Leland, "The War—God's Design to Abolish Slavery," *Religious Herald*, February 22, 1866, p. 1; George A. Blackburn, ed., *Sermons by John L. Girardeau* (Columbia, S.C., 1907), 254–55; William Preston Johnston to William N. Pendleton, December 6, 1870, in Pendleton Papers; Robert L. Dabney to Rev. A. C. Hopkins, n.d., in Johnson, *Dabney*, p. 301.

15. John Jones to Mrs. Mary Jones, August 21, 1865, in Myers, *Children of Pride*, p. 1292; McKim, *Recollections*, pp. 273–74; Thomas C. Johnson, *Life and Letters of Benjamin Morgan Palmer* (Richmond, 1906), p. 377.

16. "Narrative of the State of Religion," *Minutes of the General Assembly of the Presbyterian Church in the United States. A.D. 1874* (Richmond, 1874), p. 529. See also R. H. Rivers, "Counsels to Young Men," *Christian Advocate*, March 28, 1867, p. 1; "The Skepticism Engendered by the War," *Religious Herald*, December 21, 1865, p. 12; Richard McIlwaine, *Memories of Three Score Years and Ten* (New York, 1908), pp. 211–12; *Christian Education. The University of the South: Papers Relating to Christian Education at the University, and the Necessity of this Institution to the Country, especially to the South and Southwest, etc.* (Sewanee, [1885]), p. 16.

17. "Religious Literature for the South," *Christian Index*, January 13, 1866, p. 3; "Our Day of Trial," *Christian Index*, January 7, 1875, p. 1; W. B. W. Howe, "Sermon XXX," in *Sermons Preached in His Diocese by the Late Rt. Rev. W. B. W. Howe* (New York, 1897), pp. 333, 335.

18. Elliott, "Forty-fifth Sermon," *Sermons*, pp. 501–2. The official Southern Baptist and Methodist annual meetings were quiet on this issue, but for the responses of the Southern Presbyterian General Assembly see "A Pastoral Letter from the General Assembly to the Churches under Their Care" and

"Narrative of the State of Religion," in *Minutes of the General Assembly of the Presbyterian Church in the United States* (Augusta, Ga., 1865), pp. 380–82; and "Narrative of the State of Religion," *Minutes of the General Assembly of the Presbyterian Church in the United States* (Columbia, S.C., 1867), p. 42. For Elliott's importance, see William A. Clebsch, "Baptism of Blood: A Study of Christian Contributions to the Interpretation of the Civil War in American History" (Ph.D. dissertation, Union Theological Seminary, 1957), pp. 139–216; and Edgar L. Pennington, "Bishop Stephen Elliott and the Confederate Episcopal Church," *Georgia Review* 4 (April, 1950): 233–47.

19. "Our Chastizement," *Christian Index*, January 5, 1865, p. 1; "Notes on the Times," *Christian Index*, January 26, 1865, p. 3.

20. Adger, *My Life and Times*, pp. 348–49; Robert L. Dabney to "Chief of the Freedmen's Bureau, Washington," September 12, 1865, in Robert Lewis Dabney Papers, Alderman Library, University of Virginia (published in New York *Daily News*, October 12, 1865).

21. J. William Jones, "The Private Soldier," CV 2 (September, 1894): 275; Jones, "The Morale of the Confederate Armies," in Clement A. Evans, ed., *Confederate Military History* (Atlanta, 1899), pp. xii, 133–34, 169; Goodwin, "Memorial Sermon," SHSP 37 (January–December, 1909): 342–43.

22. John B. Adger, "Northern and Southern Views of the Province of the Church," *Southern Presbyterian Review* 16 (March, 1866), 398–99; "To Southern Women from a Southern Woman," *Religious Herald*, October 19, 1865, p. 4; Robert C. Cave, "Honoring the Private Soldier," CV 2 (June, 1894): 162; "Relations between Southern and Northern Baptists," *Religious Herald*, October 19, 1865, p. 2; "Where Is the Wisdom," *Christian Index*, January 20, 1866, p. 14; "Strength Derived from Trial," *Christian Index*, May 31, 1866, p. 91; Jones, *The Davis Memorial Volume*, p. viii; Hoge, "Address in the Second Presbyterian Church, Richmond, Va., December 11, 1889, the day appointed by the Governor for the Commemoration of the Death of the Hon. Jefferson Davis," in *Hoge*, p. 466; J. D. Blackwell, "The Supreme Aim of Life," in Thomas O. Summers, ed., *Sermons by Southern Methodist Preachers* (Nashville, 1890), p. 151.

23. James H. McNeilly, "The Failure of the Confederacy—Was It a Blessing?" CV 24 (February, 1916): 67; McNeilly, "By Graves of Confederate Dead," CV 2 (September, 1894): 264–65.

24. *Christian Index*, January 12, 1865, p. 4; "Address of the Bishop of Georgia," *Journal of the Fourth Annual Council of the Protestant Episcopal Church in the Diocese of Georgia . . . 1866* (Savannah, 1866), pp. 14–15, 23; MS sermons 18, 48, 59, 104, and 137, in John Beckwith Sermon Collection, University of Georgia Library, Athens.

25. Henry C. Renfro, "The Endurance of Afflictions," in W. H. Parks, *The Texas Baptist Pulpit: A Collection of Sermons from the Baptist Ministry of Texas* (New York, 1873), p. 272; S. G. Hillyer, "To the Baptists of Georgia," *Christian Index*, November 9, 1865, p. 2. See also Moses Drury Hoge to his sister, May 15, 1865, in *Hoge*, p. 235; "Our Chastizement," *Christian Index*, February 10, 1866, p. 26; Girardeau, "The Nature of Prayer," in *Sermons*, p. 261; Fitzgerald and Galloway, *Eminent Methodists*, pp. 372–73; Basil Manly, Sr., "The Purpose of Calamities," *Christian Index*, June 10, 1869, p. 89; and "The Introductory Sermon, Preached before the Southern Baptist Convention, May 11th, 1871, by Rev. Wm. Williams . . . ," *Christian Index*, June 8, 1871, p. 89.

26. Elliott, "Forty-third Sermon," in *Sermons*, pp. 477–79, 483–86. See also "Religious Literature for the South," *Christian Index*, January 13, 1866, p. 3; "Some Time," *CV* 11 (December, 1903): 563; and "Incomprehensible Things," in Joseph B. Stratton, *A Pastor's Valedictory: A Selection of Early Sermons* (Natchez, Miss., 1899), pp. 134, 136–37; MS sermon 9, in Beckwith Sermon Collection; Girardeau, "The Nature of Prayer," in *Sermons*, pp. 260, 263–65. See also the report of C. K. Marshall's sermon, "The Design of Providence in the Events through Which the South Has Just Passed," in New Orleans (Southwestern) *Christian Advocate*, March 10, 1866, p. 1.

27. William Nelson Pendleton to daughter, June 12, 1865, in Lee, *Memoirs of Pendleton*, p. 415; Blackburn, *Girardeau*, p. 129; Edward R. Miles, "Lines for Memorial Day, 1871," in Ladies Memorial Association, Charleston, S.C., *Confederate Memorial Day at Charleston, 1871: Re-interment of the Carolina Dead from Gettysburg. Address of Rev. Dr. Girardeau, odes, etc.* (Charleston, 1871), p. 28.

28. J. L. Gilbert, "The Relation of the Christian Churches of Our Southern States to Christian Civilization," *Home Monthly* 7 (November, 1869): 284–87.

29. Hoge, *Hoge*, p. 466; Candler, *High Living*, p. 177; "Address of Rev. Dr. B. M. Palmer," *SHSP* 10 (June, 1882): 250–54.

30. "Sermons before the Reunion," *CV* 5 (July, 1897): 350–51.

31. "Fourth Annual Report of the Executive Committee of Domestic Missions," *Minutes of the General Assembly of the Presbyterian Church in the United States* (Augusta, Ga., 1865), p. 392; "Fifth Annual Report of the Executive Committee of Domestic Missions," *Minutes of the General Assembly of the Presbyterian Church in the United States* (Augusta, 1866), p. 46; Girardeau, "The Rest of the People of God," *Sermons*, pp. 343–44; "Discourse Delivered by Rev. W. N. Pendleton, D.D. on the Occasion of Removing the Remains of Confederate Soldiers . . . near the Tomb of Stonewall Jackson," pp. 4, 14–15, MS in Pendleton Papers.

32. Howe, "Sermon XXX," in *Sermons*, p. 340; "Sermons before the Reunion," p. 351.

33. Randolph H. McKim, "The Gettysburg Campaign," *SHSP*, n.s. 2 (September, 1915): 294–95; Goodwin, "Memorial Sermon," pp. 338–39, 343–45. See also "The Nineteenth of January: Lee's Birthday," *SHSP* 19 (January, 1891): 392–93.

34. "Unveiling Confederate Monument at Montgomery, Ala.," *SHSP* 26 (January–December, 1898): 183–84; Elliott, "Watch Ye Therefore," in *Sermons*, p. 562.

CHAPTER IV: A SOUTHERN JEREMIAD

1. Perry Miller, *The New England Mind: From Colony to Province* (Cambridge, Mass., 1953), pp. 27–39; Miller, *Errand into the Wilderness* (Cambridge, Mass., 1956), pp. 3–15; Sacvan Bercovitch, *The Puritan Origins of the American Self* (New Haven, 1975), pp. 114–225.

2. Gaston, *New South Creed*, p. 156; C. Vann Woodward, *Origins of the New South, 1877–1913* (Baton Rouge, 1951), pp. 172–73; Robert D. Little, "The Ideology of the New South: A Study in the Development of Ideas, 1865–1910" (Ph.D. dissertation, University of Chicago, 1950), p. 142.

3. "Oration at the Dedication of the New Capitol of Mississippi, June 3, 1903," in Charles B. Galloway, *Great Men and Great Movements: A Volume of Addresses* (Nashville, 1914), p. 136; "Pensions, and so Forth," *Christian Advocate*, April 25, 1889, p. 1; "A Word More from a Limping Confederate," *Religious Herald*, July 7, 1887, p. 1; "A Dance in a Graveyard," *CV* 5 (March, 1897): 130; "Reunion Suggestions and Comments," *CV* 9 (July, 1901): 293.

4. Joseph B. Stratton, *Address Delivered July 23d, 1875, before the Trustees, Professors and Students of Jefferson College, Washington, Adams County, Mississippi* (Natchez, 1875), p. 9; J. P. B. Wilmer, *Annual Address of the Bishop of Louisiana to the Council of the Diocese* (New Orleans, 1874), p. 3; Johnson, *Life and Letters of Palmer*, p. 437.

5. Richard M. Weaver, "Albert Taylor Bledsoe," *Sewanee Review* 52 (Winter, 1944): 34–45; Bledsoe, *Is Davis a Traitor; or Was Secession a Constitutional Right Previous to the War of 1861?* (Baltimore, 1866); Bledsoe, "Chivalrous Southrons," *Southern Review* 6 (July, 1869): 109, 117; Bledsoe, "The Origin of the Late War," *Southern Review* 1 (April, 1867), 257–74.

6. Gaston, *New South Creed*, pp. 7, 190.

7. Miller, *Errand*, p. 7; *Christian Advocate*, May 14, 1887, p. 2.

8. Robert L. Dabney, *The New South: A Discourse Delivered at the Annual Commencement of Hampden Sidney* [sic] *College, June 15, 1882* (Raleigh, N.C., 1883), pp. 2, 6–7, 12.

9. Ibid., pp. 13, 16; Dabney, "Autobiography," p. 109, MS in Robert Lewis Dabney Papers.

10. "Bishop Wilmer's Address," *Journal of the Forty-Ninth Annual Convention of the Protestant Episcopal Church in the Diocese of Alabama* (Mobile, 1880), p. 39; Wilmer, *The Recent Past*, p. 136; John C. Calhoun Newton, *The New South and the Methodist Episcopal Church, South* (Baltimore, 1887), pp. 24–28; Oscar P. Fitzgerald, *Fifty Years: Observations—Opinions—Experiences* (Nashville, 1903), p. 206; *Christian Advocate*, March 26, 1887, p. 3.

11. Henry A. Scomp, *King Alcohol in the Realm of King Cotton* (Chicago, 1888), p. 562; Charles C. Pearson and J. Edwin Hendricks, *Liquor and Anti-Liquor in Virginia, 1619–1919* (Durham, N.C., 1967), pp. 152–53, 157–58; William M. Robinson, "Prohibition in the Confederacy," *American Historical Review* 37 (October, 1931): 50–58; Hunter D. Farish, *The Circuit Rider Dismounts: A Social History of Southern Methodism, 1865–1900* (Richmond, 1938), pp. 312–17; *Christian Advocate*, July 5, 1866, p. 1; "Stonewall Jackson's 'Most Dreaded Foe,'" *SHSP* 23 (January–December, 1895): 333–34; W. A. Jarrel, "Stonewall Jackson's Experience," *Texas Baptist Herald*, October 19, 1876, p. 1; "A Letter of Stonewall Jackson," *Southern Presbyterian*, June 27, 1872, p. 3; "The Jackson Generals," *Central Presbyterian*, May 1, 1878, p. 4; Jones, *Personal Reminiscences*, p. 171; Felton, *Sermon on Lee*, pp. 8, 13; "Reviews and Notices," *Christian Index*, March 7, 1872, p. 38; Herbert Asbury, *The Great Illusion: An Informal History of Prohibition* (Garden City, N.Y., 1950), p. 99.

12. Andrew Sinclair, *Prohibition: The Era of Excess* (Boston, 1962), p. 30; Scomp, *King Alcohol*, pp. 5, 558, 560, 563, 660.

13. Garnie W. McGinty, *Louisiana Redeemed: The Overthrow of Carpetbag Rule, 1876–1880* (New Orleans, 1941), p. 181; Berthold C. Alwes, "The History of the Louisiana State Lottery Company," *Louisiana Historical Quarterly* 27 (Fall, 1944): 972–94; William Ivy Hair, *Bourbonism and Agrarian Protest: Louisiana Politics, 1877–1900* (Baton Rouge, 1969), p. 26; "Gift Enterprises and Lotteries," *Southern Presbyterian*, July 13, 1871, pp. 1–2; Thomas J. Bailey, *Prohibition in Mississippi, or Anti-Liquor Legislation from Territorial Days, with Its Results in the Counties* (Jackson, 1917), pp. 214–15.

14. "The Lottery Evil," *Texas Baptist Herald*, January 9, 1879, p. 2; "The Lottery," *Southern Presbyterian*, October 12, 1871, p. 1; "Gift Enterprises and Lotteries," *Southern Presbyterian*, July 13, 1871, p. 2; T. Harry Williams, *Pierre Gustave Toutant Beauregard: Napoleon in Gray* (Baton Rouge, 1955), pp. 274–90; McGinty, *Louisiana Redeemed*, p. 184.

15. Thomas F. Gailor, *Some Memories* (Kingsport, Tenn., 1937), pp. 91–92, 129; Oscar P. Fitzgerald, *Sunset Views in Three Parts* (Nashville, 1900),

pp. 204–5; *Christian Advocate*, August 16, 1884, p. 1, January 23, 1886, p. 8; Joy J. Jackson, *New Orleans in the Gilded Age: Politics and Urban Progress, 1880–1896* (Baton Rouge, 1969), p. 126; McGinty, *Louisiana Redeemed*, pp. 36–37, 185, 190.

16. Howard M. Hamill, *The Old South: A Monograph* (Nashville, 1904), pp. 20–21, 23–24, 27; Hamill, "From One Who Loved Him," CV 22 (February, 1914): 54; James H. McNeilly, "The Failure of the Confederacy—Was It a Blessing?" CV 24 (April, 1916): 160–63.

17. Oscar P. Fitzgerald, "Fourth-of-July Sermon," *Christian Advocate*, July 17, 1886, pp. 7, 14; James B. Gambrell, "The Southern Outlook," *Baptist Standard*, March 28, 1895, p. 1; Gambrell, "A Call to the Universal Conquest of the World," *Baptist Standard*, May 26, 1892, p. 3. See also Eighmy, *Churches in Cultural Captivity*, p. 46; Richard Carroll, "Movement of the Negroes from the Southern Cities to the North and West Is Becoming Serious," *Christian Advocate*, August 2, 1917, p. 1; William L. Duren, *Charles Betts Galloway: Orator, Preacher, and "Prince of Christian Chivalry"* (Atlanta, Ga., 1932), pp. 226–27; and Rowland T. Berthoff, "Southern Attitudes Toward Immigration, 1865–1914," *Journal of Southern History* 17 (August, 1951): 328–60.

18. Fitzgerald, *Fifty Years*, p. 206; "Bishop O. P. Fitzgerald on the Old South," CV 15 (May, 1907): 209–10. For religion's role in Populism, see Robert C. McMath, Jr., *Populist Vanguard: A History of the Southern Farmers' Alliance* (Chapel Hill, 1975), pp. 62, 133; and Frederick A. Bode, "Religion and Class Hegemony: A Populist Critique in North Carolina," *Journal of Southern History* 38 (August, 1971): 417–38.

19. *Christian Advocate*, February 10, 1898, p. 1; Underwood, *Women of the Confederacy*, p. 53; "Presidential Elections," *Christian Index*, November 25, 1880, p. 1; "The South," *Christian Advocate*, April 24, 1880, p. 1; Eugene C. Routh, *The Life Story of Dr. J. B. Gambrell* (Oklahoma City, 1929), p. 119; McNeilly, "Failure of the Confederacy," pp. 162–63; Hamill, *Old South*, pp. 12, 60–61, 63, 65; Robert L. Dabney, "Ecclesiastical Equality of Negroes," in Clement R. Vaughan, ed., *Discussions of Robert Lewis Dabney* (Richmond, Va., and Mexico, Mo., 1891–96), 2: 206; Robert L. Dabney to Charles Dabney, March 24, 1893, and Robert L. Dabney, "Politics and Parties in the United States, Again," p. 41, MS article, both in Robert Lewis Dabney Papers.

20. Dabney to D. H. Hill, January 8, 1886, Charles Dabney Papers, Southern Historical Collection, University of North Carolina, Chapel Hill; "A. H. Colquitt—the Christian Statesman," in Candler, *High Living*, pp. 151, 154–56; *Memorial Addresses on the Life and Character of Alfred Holt Col-*

quitt (Washington, 1895), pp. 102–3; *Christian Index*, January 28, 1875, p. 6; Woodward, *Origins of the New South*, pp. 17, 67.

21. Hamill, *The Old South*, pp. 45–47, 67–68, 70; "Memorial Day at Nashville," CV 22 (August, 1914): 367; "The Religious Aspect of Patriotism," CV 25 (June, 1917): 261–63.

22. Newton, *New South*, pp. 24–28; Gambrell, "A Call to the Universal Conquest of the World," p. 3; McNeilly, "Failure of the Confederacy," p. 163. See also Hamill, *Old South*, pp. 67–68, 70.

23. Miller, *Errand*, pp. 8–9, 11–15.

24. "Rev. James McNeilly," CV 30 (November, 1922): 403–4; McNeilly, *Religion and Slavery: A Vindication of the Southern Churches* (Nashville, 1911), pp. 24–25; McNeilly, "By Graves of Confederate Dead," CV 2 (September, 1894): 264–66; McNeilly, "Ideals of the Old South," CV 25 (April, 1917): 147–48; McNeilly, "The Failure of the Confederacy," p. 160.

25. *Baptist Standard*, May 26, 1892, p. 3, August 4, 1892, p. 2; "Recollections of Confederate Scout Service," MS on microfilm at Dargan-Carver Library, Baptist Sunday School Board, Nashville; Alfred M. Pierce, *Giant against the Sky: The Life of Bishop Warren Akin Candler* (Nashville, 1948), pp. 18–19, 21–22, 25, 59–60, 86, 195–97; Eighmy, *Churches in Cultural Captivity*, pp. 43–46.

26. Gambrell, "Call to the Universal Conquest," p. 3; *Baptist Standard*, August 4, 1892, p. 2; Candler, *High Living*, pp. 21, 37–38, 180–82, 199–200; Candler, "Concerning American Commerce," CV 16 (December, 1908): xx.

27. Vaughan, *Discussions*, 2: 591; "Twenty-fifth Annual Report of the Foreign Mission Board of the Southern Baptist Convention," *Proceedings of the Fifteenth Meeting of the Southern Baptist Convention . . . 1870* (Baltimore, 1870), p. 1; *Proceedings of the Twenty-fourth Session of the Southern Baptist Convention . . . 1879* (Atlanta, 1879), pp. 29, 35; *Christian Index*, June 17, 1880, p. 1; Archibald T. Robertson, *Life and Letters of John Albert Broadus* (Philadelphia, 1909), p. 295; *Journal of the General Conference of the Methodist Episcopal Church, South . . . 1866* (Nashville, 1866), p. 21.

28. Victor I. Masters, *The Call of the South* (Atlanta, 1918), pp. 30, 108, 119–20.

CHAPTER V: MORALITY AND MYSTICISM

1. For background on Southern racial attitudes, see George M. Frederickson, *The Black Image in the White Mind: The Debate on Afro-American Character and Destiny, 1817–1914* (New York, 1971), esp. chs. 6–10; C. Vann Woodward, *The Strange Career of Jim Crow* (New York, 1966); Thomas T.

Gossett, *Race: The History of an Idea* (Dallas, 1963), esp. chs. 7, 11, 13; Claude H. Nolen, *The Negro's Image in the South: The Anatomy of White Supremacy* (Lexington, Ky., 1967); and David M. Reimers, *White Protestantism and the Negro* (New York, 1965), esp. ch. 2. For the importance of the paternalistic approach to the New South movement, see Gaston, *New South Creed*, ch. 4.

2. The framework of this chapter owes much to the interpretations of Frederickson, *Black Image in the White Mind*, pp. 216–22; and Guion Griffis Johnson's "The Ideology of White Supremacy, 1876–1910," in Fletcher Melvin Green, ed., *Essays in Southern History* (Chapel Hill, 1949), pp. 139–43. See also H. Shelton Smith, *In His Image, But: Racism in Southern Religion, 1780–1910* (Durham, N.C., 1972), esp. chs. 5 and 6; Reimers, *White Protestantism*, pp. 25–50; Nolen, *Negro's Image*, pp. 201–2; Ernest Trice Thompson, *Presbyterians in the South* (Richmond, 1973), 2: 198–202; Rufus B. Spain, *At Ease in Zion: A Social History of Southern Baptists, 1865–1900* (Nashville, 1967), pp. 45–46, 56, 126; Farish, *The Circuit Rider Dismounts*, pp. 167–76, 209, 217–23, 232–33.

3. Albert T. Bledsoe, "The African in the United States," *Southern Review* 29 (January, 1874): 137–38, 143, 151–52, 159–62, 174; Jeremiah B. Jeter, "Our Relations to the Freedmen," *Religious Herald*, October 19, 1865, p. 2; *Religious Herald*, January 25, 1866, p. 2; *Religious Herald*, June 28, 1866, p. 2; *Religious Herald*, December 25, 1873, p. 2; *Religious Herald*, March 19, 1868, p. 2; John B. Adger, "Northern and Southern Views of the Province of the Church," *Southern Presbyterian Review* 16 (March, 1866): 390; Adger, "The Presbyterian Union, North," *Southern Presbyterian Review* 22 (July, 1871): 398–99.

4. Goodloe, *Confederate Echoes*, pp. 66–67; Howe, "Sermon XXX," in *Sermons Preached in His Diocese*, p. 342; Harrison, *Sam Williams*, p. 283; George G. Smith, *The Boy in Gray: A Story of the War* (Macon, Ga., 1894), p. 15. See also Thomas M. Hanckel, "A Memoir," in *Sermons by Stephen Elliott*, pp. viii–xiv; Harrison, *Gospel Among the Slaves*, p. 19; Cave, *The Men in Gray*, p. 67; Hamill, *The Old South*, p. 20; Wilmer, *Recent Past*, pp. 44, 49, 221–23.

5. "Pastoral Letter from the General Assembly to the Churches under Their Care," *Minutes of the General Assembly of the Presbyterian Church in the United States* (Augusta, Ga., 1865), p. 385; "Report on the Nature and Functions of the Church," *Minutes of the General Assembly of the Presbyterian Church in the United States* (Richmond, 1876), p. 295; "Forty-Seventh Annual Report of the Home Mission Board," *Proceedings of the Southern Baptist Convention, Held with the Churches of Atlanta, Georgia, May 6–10, 1892* (At-

lanta, 1892), pp. iv–v; James B. Gambrell, "An Open Letter," *Christian Index*, April 5, 1894, p. 1; "Dr. Gambrell Responds," *Religious Herald*, April 19, 1894, p. 68.

6. "North and South," *Christian Index*, December 2, 1880, p. 4; Richard Carroll, "Movement of the Negroes from the Southern Cities to the North and West Is Becoming Serious," *Christian Index*, August 2, 1917, p. 2; Albert T. Bledsoe, "Chivalrous Southrons," *Southern Review* 6 (July, 1869): 123; "Address," *Journal of the Fourth Annual Council of the Protestant Episcopal Church in the Diocese of Georgia . . . 1866* (Savannah, 1866), p. 26. See also Capers, *The Soldier-Bishop*, pp. 77–78; Cave, *Men in Gray*, p. 60; Harrison, *Gospel*, p. 328; Duren, *Charles Betts Galloway*, p. 264; Hamill, *The Old South*, p. 36.

7. Rebecca Felton, "Southern Womanhood in War Times," MS in Rebecca Latimer Felton Papers, University of Georgia Library, Athens; Harrison, *Sam Williams*, p. 35. See also White, *Southern Presbyterian Leaders*, p. 307.

8. The McKeethen material in "In Memoriam," newspaper clipping dated October 2, 1874, in Leonidas Polk Papers. See also Sumner A. Cunningham, "Give the Old Slave a Home," *CV* 1 (March, 1893): 80; G. L. Tucker, "Faithful to the 'Old Mammy,'" *CV* 20 (December, 1912): 582; Howard Weedon, "Me and Mammy," *CV* 24 (June, 1916): 256; "Letter from a Colored Pastor," *Religious Herald*, July 6, 1876, p. 3; "Aunt Dinah," *Christian Advocate*, March 15, 1884, p. 2; "Southern Womanhood in War Times," MS in Felton Papers; Rankin, *Story of My Life*, pp. 26–28; Randolph Preston, Sr., "Recollections of Lexington and Washington and Lee University in 1900," p. 14f, typescript dated 1955 in McCormick Library, Washington and Lee Archives, Lexington, Va.; H. E. Wallace, "Mammy," *Southern Churchman*, June 4, 1896, p. 3; Bessie Clarke, "Mammy Charlotte," *Southern Churchman*, May 28, 1896, p. 2; William S. White, "One of the Old Mammies in the Gilmer Family," *Southern Churchman*, December 31, 1896, p. 3.

9. A. H. Gilmer, "Our Mammy," *Southern Churchman*, June 25, 1896, p. 4; Hamill, *The Old South*, p. 18; "Monument to Faithful Slaves," *CV* 13 (March, 1905): 123–24; "Slave Monument Question," *CV* 12 (November, 1904): 525; "Pensions for Faithful Negroes," *CV* 29 (August, 1921): 284.

10. Poppenheim, *History of the UDC*, pp. 77–79.

11. "Southern Womanhood in War Times," Felton Papers. See also *Central Presbyterian*, February 13, 1867, p. 1, March 3, 1869; *Religious Herald*, September 20, 1900, p. 3; Hamill, *The Old South*, pp. 34–35.

12. "Around the World," *Christian Advocate*, July 20, 1893, p. 2; John D. Paris, "The Moral and Religious Status of the African Race in the Southern

States," MS in Southern Historical Collection, University of North Carolina, Chapel Hill; Hamill, *The Old South*, p. 31. See also Warren A. Candler, "The Wisest Educational Policy for the South," *Christian Advocate*, January 6, 1898, p. 2.

13. Robert L. Dabney, "Ecclesiastical Equality of Negroes," in Vaughan, ed., *Discussions*, 2: 206; Dabney to Moses D. Hoge, May 16, 1896, Robert Lewis Dabney Papers.

14. Kenneth K. Bailey, "The Post–Civil War Racial Separations in Southern Protestantism: Another Look," *Church History* 46 (December, 1977): 453–73.

15. J. M. Rittenhouse, "The Freedmen," *Central Presbyterian*, April 30, 1884, p. 1; Wilmer's comments were quoted in Whitaker, *Wilmer: A Biography*, p. 240; Paris, "Moral and Religious Influence," pp. 8–10; *Minutes of the General Assembly of the Presbyterian Church in the United States* (Richmond, 1874), p. 596; "The Church Work for the Negro," *Southern Churchman*, March 18, 1911, p. 3. See also "Report of the Committee on Duty to the Colored Race," *Proceedings of the Twenty-third Session of the Southern Baptist Convention . . . 1878* (Nashville, 1878), pp. 24–26.

16. Thomas U. Dudley, "How Shall We Help the Negro?" *Century Magazine* 30 (June, 1885): 273–78; UCV, *Minutes of the Tenth Annual Reunion*, p. 41; "Bishop Dudley's Lecture on Lee," *CV* 11 (May, 1903): 201; "Bishop Thomas U. Dudley," *CV* 13 (May, 1905): iv; William P. DuBose, "Thomas Underwood Dudley: An Appreciation," *Sewanee Review* 13 (January, 1905): 102–8.

17. Charles B. Galloway, "Some Thoughts on Lynching," *South Atlantic Quarterly* 5 (October, 1906): 351–53; William L. Duren, *Galloway*, pp. 231–32, 261, 266–72; Galloway, "Our Brother in Black," *Christian Advocate*, March 29, 1883, p. 2; Warren A. Candler, *Bishop Charles Betts Galloway: A Prince of Preachers and a Christian Statesman* (Nashville, 1927), pp. 275–79; Galloway, "Oration at the Dedication of the New Capitol of Mississippi," in *Great Men and Great Movements*, p. 136.

18. Brattan, "The Christian South and Negro Education," *Sewanee Review* 16 (April, 1908), 290–95; Brattan, *Wanted—Leaders! A Study of Negro Development* (New York, 1922), pp. 35, 52, 93.

19. Brattan, "The Christian South and Negro Education," pp. 290–97; Paris, "Moral and Spiritual Status," Southern Historical Collection, University of North Carolina, Chapel Hill, pp. 8, 15.

20. James B. Gambrell, "The New War for the Life of Civilization," a chapter in "Recollections of Confederate Scout Service," MS on microfilm in the Dargan-Carver Library, Baptist Sunday School Board, Nashville; Eyre

Damer, *When the Ku Klux Rode* (New York, 1912), p. 88; Paris, "Moral and Religious Status," p. 4; James B. McNeilly, "Reconstruction in Tennessee," *CV* 28 (October, 1920): 370; McNeilly, "The Mission of the Veteran," *CV* 25 (November, 1917): 502–3.

21. William P. DuBose, "Reminiscences," p. 140, typescript in Southern Historical Collection, University of North Carolina, Chapel Hill; "Let Us Be Done with Empiricisms," *Christian Advocate*, January 5, 1889, p. 1; W. T. Tardy, *Trials and Triumphs: An Autobiography* (Marshall, Tex., 1919), p. 7; Underwood, *Women*, p. 271. See also *Religious Herald*, May 18, 1871, p. 1; Johnson, *Autobiographical Notes*, pp. 251–54; James B. Gambrell, "The Beginning of the Rehabilitation of the Country," in "Recollections," Dargan-Carver Library; James B. McNeilly, "Reconstruction and the Ku Klux," *CV* 30 (March, 1922): 97.

22. Allen W. Trelease, *White Terror: The Ku Klux Klan Conspiracy and Southern Reconstruction* (New York, 1971), pp. xi, xlvii, 3, 4, 10, 14–19, 27, 45–46; William G. Brown, *The Lower South in American History* (New York, 1969 [1902]), pp. 200–209, 219–21.

23. Trelease, *White Terror*, pp. 19–20, 50–51; Robert L. Preston, "A Vindication of the Ku-Klux Klan," *CV* 21 (February, 1913): 75; Zella H. Gaither, *Arkansas Confederate Homes* (Little Rock, [1920]), pp. 35, 42, 46; Susan P. Jones to William M. Polk, December 25, 1910, Leonidas Polk Papers; Richardson, *Historic Pulaski*, pp. 22–23.

24. Trelease, *White Terror*, pp. 53, 55; *Testimony Taken by the Joint Select Committee to Inquire into the Condition of Affairs in the Late Insurrectionary States* (Washington, 1872), 2: 104, 137; Capers, *Soldier-Bishop*, p. 126; McNeilly, "The Mission of the Veteran," pp. 502–3; Susan P. Jones recalled the mysterious mood of the Klan in a letter to William M. Polk, December 25, 1910, Polk Papers; Mrs. Grace Meredith Newbill, "Birthplace of the Ku Klux Klan," *CV* 25 (July, 1917): 336.

25. Maxwell Bloomfield, "Dixon's *The Leopard's Spots*: A Study in Popular Racism," *American Quarterly* 16 (Fall, 1964): 387–89; Thomas Dixon, Jr., "American Backgrounds for Fiction, North Carolina," *Bookman* 38 (January, 1914), 513.

26. Bloomfield, "Dixon's *Leopard's Spots*," pp. 390–93.

27. Thomas Dixon, Jr., *The Clansman: An Historical Romance of the Ku Klux Klan* (New York, 1905), pp. 292–93; Dixon, *The Leopard's Spots: A Romance of the White Man's Burden, 1865–1900* (New York, 1902), pp. 150–51.

28. Dixon, *Clansman*, p. 319.

29. A. J. Emerson, "*The Birth of a Nation*," *CV* 24 (April, 1916): 141; Mrs. S. E. F. Rose, "The Ku Klux Klan and 'The Birth of a Nation,'" *CV* 24

(April, 1916): 158–59. Wilson's words were quoted in David M. Chalmers, *Hooded Americanism: The History of the Ku Klux Klan* (New York, 1965), pp. 26–27.

30. Chalmers, *Hooded Americanism*, pp. 28–30; William P. Randel, *The Ku Klux Klan: A Century of Infamy* (Radner, Pa., 1965), p. 183; Trelease, *White Terror*, p. 55.

31. Chalmers, *Hooded Americanism*, pp. 30–35, 115, 117; Randel, *Ku Klux Klan*, pp. 184–85.

32. Chalmers, *Hooded Americanism*, pp. 33–35, 40–41, 83, 111–14.

CHAPTER VI: J. WILLIAM JONES

1. George Braxton Taylor, *Virginia Baptist Ministers*, 5th ser. (Lynchburg, Va., 1915), pp. 218–20; Armistead C. Gordon, Jr., "John William Jones," in Dumas Malone, ed., *Dictionary of American Biography* (New York, 1932), 5: 191; CV 17 (May, 1909): 239; Sadie Bell, *The Church, the State and Education in Virginia* (Philadelphia, 1930), p. 609.

2. Taylor, *Virginia Ministers*, pp. 220–25; Jones, "Reminiscences of the Army of Northern Virginia, or the Boys in Gray, as I Saw Them from Harper's Ferry in 1861 to Appomattox Courthouse in 1865," *SHSP* 9 (February, 1881): 90–93; Jones, *Christ in the Camp*, pp. 17–18, 353–55, 379, 383; Gordon, "Jones," p. 191; Jones, "The Morale of the Confederate Armies," in Evans, *Confederate Military History*, 12: 154–55; Jones, "A Reminiscence of an Official Interview with General R. E. Lee," *SHSP* 10 (January–February, 1882): 91–92.

3. Jones, *Christ in the Camp*, pp. 353–54; Taylor, *Virginia Ministers*, p. 225; John G. Barrett and John S. Moore, *The History of Manly Memorial Baptist Church, Lexington, Virginia* (Lexington, 1966), pp. 12–13; Pearson and Hendricks, *Liquor and Anti-Liquor in Virginia*, pp. 157–58; "Twenty-first Annual Report: Domestic and Indian Mission Board," *Proceedings of the Southern Baptist Convention . . . 1866* (Richmond, 1866), p. 46.

4. Taylor, *Virginia Ministers*, p. 225; Barrett and Moore, *Manly Church*, pp. 12–13; Jones, "The Inner Life of Robert Edward Lee," *Chautauquan* 31 (May, 1900): 188.

5. Taylor, *Virginia Ministers*, p. 226; Barrett and Moore, *Manly Church*, pp. 12–13.

6. Martin E. Marty, "Two Kinds of Two Kinds of Civil Religion," in Richey and Jones, *American Civil Religion*, p. 146.

7. "The Southern Historical Society," *SHSP* 18 (January–December, 1890): 356–57, 363–64; Editor's Note, *SHSP* 5 (May, 1878): 222; Editor's

Note, *SHSP* 4 (December, 1877): 303; "Editorial Paragraphs," *SHSP* 1 (February, 1876): 109; *Christian Index*, October 17, 1878, p. 5.

8. Jones, "Reminiscences . . . to 1865," p. 90.

9. "Lee's Birthday," *SHSP* 19 (January, 1891): 405–6; Jones, *Davis Memorial Volume*, pp. 253–55; Connelly, "The Image and the General," *Civil War History*, pp. 52–55.

10. Jones, "Editorial Paragraphs," *SHSP* 7 (May, 1879): 254; Jones, "Reminiscences of the Army of Northern Virginia: Paper No. 2. First Manassas and Its Sequel," *SHSP* 9 (March, 1881): 133; Jones, *Virginia's Next Governor, Gen. Fitzhugh Lee* (New York, 1885), p. 24.

11. "George W. Cable in the *Century* Magazine," *SHSP* 13 (January–December, 1885): 148; "Opposed to the Name Rebellion," CV 2 (June, 1894): 199; UCV, *Minutes of the Fifth Annual Meeting and Reunion of the UCV . . . 1895* (n.p., n.d.), pp. 33–34; Jones, "Nullification and Secession," CV 5 (February, 1897): 63. The Gettysburg letters appeared in vols. 4 and 5 of *SHSP*. Jones, "The Longstreet–Gettysburg Controversy," *SHSP* 23 (January–December, 1895): 342–48; Jones, "The Treatment of Prisoners during the War between the States," *SHSP* 1 (March, 1876): 113–221; Jones, "Editorial Paragraphs," *SHSP* 1 (February, May, 1876): 109, 399.

12. "Letter of Rev. J. William Jones, Giving Some of the Objections to *Barnes's Brief History of the United States*," in R. E. Lee Camp, United Confederate Veterans, Richmond, *Action of R. E. Lee Camp* (Richmond, 1895), p. 14; Jones, "Is the 'Eclectic History of the United States,' a Fit Book to be Used in Our Schools?" *SHSP* 12 (June, 1884): 283–87; *SHSP* 12 (July, August, September, 1884): 421–26; Jones, "The Private Soldier," CV 2 (September, 1894): 275; UCV, *Minutes of the Fifteenth Annual Meeting and Reunion of the UCV . . . 1905* (n.p., n.d.), pp. 34–35. See also "The 'Barbara Frietchie' Myth," CV 8 (March, 1900): 113–14; and Jones, *Davis Memorial Volume*, p. 251.

13. Jones, "Books about General R. E. Lee," *Christian Index*, April 20, 1871, p. 57; Jones, "Notes and Queries," *SHSP* 10 (January–February, 1882): 92.

14. Jones, *School History of the United States* (New Orleans, 1898), pp. 3–4, 148, 247; Jones, "Reminiscences of the Army of Northern Virginia: Paper No. 5. How Fremont and Shields 'Caught' Stonewall Jackson," *SHSP* 9 (June, 1881): 278–79; Jones, "Reminiscences of the Army of Northern Virginia: Paper No. 2. First Manassas and Its Sequel," *SHSP* 9 (March, 1881): 130–32; Jones, "Reminiscences of the Army of Northern Virginia: Paper No. 3. Down the Valley after Stonewall's Quartermaster," *SHSP* 9 (March, 1881): 188; "Dr. J. William Jones at the University," *Religious Herald*, March 4,

1886, p. 3; "Jesus in the Camp; or, Religion in Lee's Army," *Religious Herald*, July 29, 1886, p. 1; Jones, "Soldiers of '61 and '65," *Southern Bivouac* 1 (March, 1883): 308; Jones, "General Lee to the Rear," *SHSP* 8 (January, 1880): 32.

15. Jones, "Reminiscences of Stonewall Jackson," *CV* 1 (April, 1893): 108–10; Jones, "His Christian Character," in Cooke, *Stonewall Jackson*, p. 507; Jones, "Reminiscences of the Army of Northern Virginia," *SHSP* 9 (February, 1891): 94–95; Jones, *Christ in the Camp*, pp. 88, 90, 96–97; Jones, "Stonewall Jackson," *SHSP* 19 (January, 1891): 164; Jones, "Worked His Way Through: How a Poor Orphan Boy Becomes One of the Immortals," *CV* 9 (December, 1901): 535–37; Jones, "The Inner Life of 'Stonewall' Jackson," *Chautauquan* 30 (October, 1899): 83–88.

16. Jones, "The Inner Life of Robert Edward Lee," *Chautauquan* 31 (May, 1900): 187–88; Jones, *Personal Reminiscences*, p. 442; Jones, "General R. E. Lee's Religious Character," *Christian Index*, November 17, 1870, p. 177; Jones, "A Brief Sketch of Gen. R. E. Lee," *CV* 1 (December, 1893): 357; Jones, *Life and Letters of Robert Edward Lee: Soldier and Man* (New York, 1906), p. 476.

17. Jones, "A Visit to Beauvoir—President Davis and Family at Home," *SHSP* 14 (January–December, 1886): 447–54; Jones, *Davis Memorial Volume*, pp. 441, 462–63, 468; Jones, *Christ in the Camp*, pp. 42, 48, 56–60, 66.

18. Jones, *Christ in the Camp*, p. 8.

19. Ibid., pp. 7, 14, 242–45.

20. Ibid., pp. 243, 249, 261.

21. Ibid., pp. 242–43, 263, 267, 272, 353–54, 384, 390–92, 396. See also Jones, "Morale of the Confederate Armies," pp. 163–65, 167.

22. Jones, *Christ in the Camp*, pp. 223, 225, 396; Jones, *General Isaac Munroe St. John* (New York, 1881), pp. 7, 11; Jones, "Rev. T. D. Witherspoon," *CV* 7 (April, 1899): 178; Norton, *Rebel Religion*, p. 110.

23. "The Monument to General Robert E. Lee," *SHSP* 17 (January–December, 1889): 298; UCV, *Minutes of the Fourth Annual Meeting and Reunion of the UCV . . . 1894* (n.p., n.d.), p. 8; *Minutes of the Sixth Annual Reunion*, p. 127; *Minutes of the Fourteenth Annual Meeting and Reunion of the UCV . . . 1904* (n.p., n.d.), p. 37; *Minutes of the Seventeenth Annual Reunion*, p. 90; *Minutes of the Fifth Annual Reunion*, p. 35.

24. UCV, *Minutes of the Seventh Annual Reunion*, p. 15; *Minutes of the Thirteenth Annual Reunion*, p. 8; *Fourteenth Reunion*, pp. 14–15; "Houston Re-Union of United Confederate Veterans," *CV* 3 (June, 1895): 163; "Memorable Reunion at Owensboro," *CV* 10 (August, 1902): 342; UCV, *Minutes of the Eleventh Annual Meeting and Reunion of the UCV . . . 1901* (New Orleans,

n.d.), p. 9; the last prayer was quoted in Thad Stem, Jr., and Alan Butler, *Senator Sam Ervin's Best Stories* (Durham, N.C., 1973), p. 86.

25. UCV, *Minutes of the Twelfth Annual Reunion*, pp. 42–47. This address was reprinted in CV 10 (August, 1902): 360–61.

26. UCV, *Minutes of the Tenth Annual Reunion*, pp. 102–4, 108.

27. Ibid., p. 108.

28. Southern Baptist Convention, *Proceedings of the Southern Baptist Convention . . . 1866* (Richmond, 1866), pp. 16–18; *Proceedings of the Fourteenth Meeting of the Southern Baptist Convention . . . 1869* (Baltimore, 1869), p. 18; *Proceedings of the . . . Southern Baptist Convention . . . 1883* (Atlanta, 1883), pp. 7, 28–29; *Proceedings of the Southern Baptist Convention . . . 1887* (Atlanta, 1887), p. 6; *Proceedings . . . of the Southern Baptist Convention . . . 1888* (Atlanta, 1888), pp. 6, 40; *Proceedings of the Southern Baptist Convention . . . 1892* (Atlanta, 1892), p. 44; *Proceedings . . . of the Southern Baptist Convention . . . 1893* (Atlanta, 1893), p. 5; *Proceedings . . . of the Southern Baptist Convention . . . 1895* (Atlanta, 1895), p. 29; *Proceedings . . . of the Southern Baptist Convention . . . 1878* (Nashville, 1878), p. 10; Pearson and Hendricks, *Liquor and Anti-Liquor in Virginia*, p. 205. See also "Jones Reminiscences of Lee, Again," *Texas Baptist Herald*, April 22, 1875, p. 1; and Jones, "General Lee's Letter to His Son," *Southern Presbyterian*, April 4, 1872, p. 60.

29. Gordon, "Jones," p. 191; Taylor, *Virginia Ministers*, pp. 226–28; Jones, "'Patriotism and the Sections': Massachusetts and Virginia," CV 5 (January, 1897): 7–9; Jones, "The Career of General Jackson," SHSP 35 (January–December, 1907): 79–98; George L. Christian, *Sketch of the Origin and Erection of the Confederate Memorial Institute at Richmond, Virginia* (Richmond, [1931?]), pp. 5, 12–13; "From Chapel Hill, S.C. [sic]," *Religious Herald*, February 19, 1903, p. 5; David M. R. Culbreth, *The University of Virginia: Memories of Her Student Life and Professors* (New York, 1908), pp. 247, 291.

30. Taylor, *Virginia Ministers*, pp. 227–28. For the examples of the poems of Judith Jones, see CV 2 (September, 1894): 275; CV 5 (August, 1897): 437.

31. "Proceedings of the Virginia Historical Society," *Virginia Magazine of History and Biography* 18 (1910): vii–xviii; "Report of Confederate Memorial Association," UCV, *Minutes of the Nineteenth Annual Reunion*, pp. 52–53; Taylor, *Virginia Ministers*, p. 228.

CHAPTER VII: SCHOOLED IN TRADITION

1. In their varying approaches to the Lost Cause, Rollin Osterweis, William White, Susan Durant, Richard Weaver, Clement Eaton, and Shirley Hannum all fail to discuss the role of Lost Cause colleges.

2. Robert A. Brock, "The Southern Historical Society: Its Origin and History," *SHSP* 18 (1890): 349; Durant, "The Gently Furled Banner," pp. 40–50; UCV, *Minutes of the Third Annual Meeting and Reunion of the UCV . . . 1892* (New Orleans, 1892), pp. 3–5, 8, 99; *Minutes of the Ninth Annual Reunion*, p. 147; White, *Confederate Veteran*, pp. 42–43; Herman Hattaway, "Clio's Southern Soldiers: The United Confederate Veterans and History," *Louisiana History* 12 (Summer, 1971): 213–42; UDC, *Minutes of the Nineteenth Convention*, p. 398; Stone, *UDC Catechism for Children*; UDC, *Minutes of the Eighth Annual Convention, UDC . . . 1901* (Nashville, 1902), pp. 127–28.

3. Jeremiah B. Jeter, "Sunday School Literature—An Important Question," *Religious Herald*, April 12, 1866, p. 2; "Report of the Sunday School and Publication Board," *Proceedings of the Southern Baptist Convention . . . 1866* (Richmond, 1866), p. 31; "Exchange of Prisoners," *Central Presbyterian*, September 9, 1868, p. 2; James H. McNeilly, "The Mission of the Veteran," *CV* 25 (June, 1917): 249; McNeilly, *Religion and Slavery*, pp. 25–26. See also "The Ninth Annual Report of the Sunday School Board," *Proceedings of the Seventeenth Meeting of the Southern Baptist Convention . . . 1872* (Baltimore, 1872), p. 76; "Northern Periodicals," *Christian Index*, January 28, 1869, p. 13; James B. Gambrell, "The South," *Baptist Standard*, January 10, 1895, p. 1.

4. Jones, *School History*; Susan Pendleton Lee, *A School History of the United States* (Richmond, 1895).

5. Hamill, *The Old South*; Wharton, *War Songs and Poems of the Southern Confederacy, 1861–1865* ([Philadelphia?, 1904]); Bledsoe, *Is Davis a Traitor?*; Robert L. Dabney, *A Defence of Virginia; and through Her of the South* (New York, 1867); Dabney, *Life of Jackson*; John R. Deering, *Lee and His Cause; or The Why and the How of the War between the States* (New York, 1907). See also Douglas Southall Freeman, *The South to Posterity: An Introduction to the Writing of Confederate History* (New York, 1939), pp. 34, 38–40.

6. Thomas M. Spaulding, "Clement Anselm Evans," *Dictionary of American Biography*, ed. Allen Johnson and Dumas Malone (New York, 1931), 6: 196–97; Evans, *Contributions of the South to the Greatness of the American Union: An Address by General Clement A. Evans . . .* (Richmond, 1895), pp. 6–7, 263, 298; Evans, "The Civil History of the Confederate States," *Confederate Military History*, 2: 563; Jessie P. Rice, *J. L. M. Curry: Southerner, Statesman and Educator* (New York, 1949); Edwin A. Alderman and Armistead C. Gordon, *J. L. M. Curry: A Biography* (New York, 1911); Curry, *Address of Hon. J. L. M. Curry, LL.D., Delivered before the Association of Confederate Veterans, Richmond, Va., 1896* (Richmond, 1896), pp. 1–4, 25, 27; Curry, "Legal Justification of the South in Secession," in Evans, *Confederate Military History*, 1: 3–4.

7. White, *Confederate Veteran*, pp. 59–60; Mrs. Eugenia H. Arnold, "The Christian Character of Our Great Leaders," *Confederate Veteran* 28 (February, 1920): 55. For the role of the daughters of the Old South in education, see A. D. Mayo, "The Woman's Movement in the South," *New England Magazine*, n.s. 5 (October, 1891): 257.

8. Candler, *Galloway*, pp. 14, 16; "Commencement of the Southern University," *Christian Advocate*, July 19, 1866, p. 2. Kinsolving, *The Story of a Southern School*, pp. 79–80, 102, 132.

9. CV 11 (August, 1903): 379; "General M. P. Lowery: An Autobiography," *SHSP* 16 (January–December, 1888): 365–76; P. W. Shearer, "Gen. Mark Perrin Lowery," CV 15 (January, 1907): 13; "A Living Monument," CV 8 (July, 1900): 334; advertisement for Stonewall Jackson Institute, CV 12 (July, 1904): back cover; CV 25 (May, 1917): 238; CV 25 (June, 1917): inside front cover; CV 25 (July, 1917): back cover; UDC, *Minutes of the Twenty-second Convention*, p. 142; Thompson, *Presbyterians in the South*, 3: 173.

10. Farish, *Circuit Rider Dismounts*, p. 262; Smith, *George Foster Pierce*, p. 496; Candler, "The Value of Public Libraries," in *High Living*, p. 213; Robertson, *John Albert Broadus*, pp. 187–88, 190, 197–98, 211, 224, 233–34; Broadus, *James Petigru Boyce*, pp. 166, 182, 188–89, 195–98, 209–10; Jones, "Morale," p. 132; McIlwaine, *Memories*, pp. 337–38, 340–42.

11. Arthur Ben Chitty, "Heir of Hopes: Historical Summary of the University of the South," *Historical Magazine of the Protestant Episcopal Church* 23 (September, 1954): 258–60; Chitty, *Reconstruction at Sewanee: The Founding of the University of the South and Its First Administration, 1857–72* (Sewanee, 1954), pp. 45, 54–55; George R. Fairbanks, *History of the University of the South at Sewanee, Tennessee* (Jacksonville, Fla., 1905), pp. 38–59, 70, 394; Thomas F. Gailor, *The High Adventure. "Haec olim meminisse juvabit"* (Sewanee, n.d.), p. 3; "A Joke on Andrew Lang," in Lily Baker, Charlotte Gailor, Rose Duncan Lowell, and Sarah Hodgson Torian, eds., *Sewanee* (Sewanee, 1932), p. 126; John Fulton to William M. Polk, May 9, 1882, Polk Papers; Chitty, *Reconstruction at Sewanee*, p. 73; James B. Craighead to George R. Fairbanks, March 9, 1868, George Rainsford Fairbanks Collection, DuPont Library, University of the South, Sewanee, Tenn.; Thomas F. Gailor, *Bishop Quintard and the University of the South: A Memorial Address* (Sewanee, n.d.), p. 9; Richard Wilmer, *In Memoriam*, pp. 13, 14.

12. Habersham Elliott, "The First Settlement at Sewanee," in Baker, *Sewanee*, pp. 20–21; Mrs. W. S. Lovell, "The First Confederate Flag," in Baker, *Sewanee*, p. 23; William S. Slack, "A Fragment of the Cornerstone," in Baker, *Sewanee*, pp. 29–30; Chitty, *Reconstruction*, p. 83; Fairbanks,

Sewanee, p. 69; David Pise to Mrs. Leonidas Polk, February 5, 1867, Polk Papers; Noll, *Doctor Quintard*, pp. 4–6, 148.

13. Charles T. Quintard to William M. Polk, December 10, 1885, Polk Papers; Chitty, *Reconstruction*, pp. 86, 91; Noll, *Quintard*, p. 166.

14. Noll, *Quintard*, pp. 7, 155–56, 158–63, 174–75; *Christian Education*, p. 3; Gailor, *Bishop Quintard*, pp. 11, 13–14; Wilson Gregg and Arthur H. Noll, *Alexander Gregg: First Bishop of Texas* (Sewanee, 1912), p. 108; Sarah Barnwell Elliott, *Sewanee: Past and Present* (Sewanee, 1909), p. 11; Chitty, *Reconstruction*, p. 133, 170, 174–80; Charles T. Quintard to "Robert," June 14, 1870, in Quintard folder, Episcopal Bishops' Biographical Folders, Church Historical Society Archives; Chitty, "Heir of Hopes," 261–62.

15. Sarah Barnwell Elliott, *An Appeal for Southern Books and Relics for the Library of the University of the South: The Reason Why You Soldiers of the Great Civil War Should Care for the University of the South at Sewanee* (Sewanee, 1921); Chitty, *Reconstruction*, pp. 117, 125–26, 130, 142; Moultrie Guerry, *Men Who Made Sewanee* (Sewanee, 1932), pp. 49–71, 73–89, 92; William P. DuBose, *Turning Points in My Life* (New York, 1912), pp. 1–12, 33–53, 113–23; for Ahlstrom's evaluation of DuBose, see *A Religious History*, pp. 727–28; Fairbanks, *History of Sewanee*, pp. 71, 77, 298; Frank Vandiver, *Ploughshares into Swords* (Austin, 1952), pp. 293–97, 302–4.

16. Arthur H. Noll, *General Kirby-Smith* (Sewanee, 1907), pp. 1–3, 257–58, 261, 273–74, 279–86; Joseph H. Parks, *General Edmund Kirby Smith, C.S.A.* (Baton Rouge, 1954), pp. 483–90, 495–509; William N. Guthrie, "Lines in Honor of General Edmund Kirby-Smith," in Baker, *Sewanee*, pp. 81–82; William S. Slack, "General Kirby-Smith," in Baker, *Sewanee*, pp. 66–67.

17. Queenie Woods Washington, "Memories," in Baker, *Sewanee*, pp. 61–63; Louise Finley, "Magnolia Hall," in Baker, *Sewanee*, pp. 100–101; Guerry, *Men Who Made Sewanee*, pp. 80, 94–95; Monte Cooper, "Miss Sada," in Baker, *Sewanee*, pp. 142–43; Chitty, *Reconstruction*, p. 180.

18. DuBose, "Reminiscences," pp. 154–55; Harry Easter, "Early Days," in Baker, *Sewanee*, pp. 43–44; the quoted letter appeared in Chitty, *Reconstruction*, p. 124; "A Glimpse at Fairmont," in Baker, *Sewanee*, p. 65.

19. Wilmer, *Gen.'l. Robert E. Lee*, pp. 5, 9–12. This address was reprinted in the *SHSP* 14 (January–December, 1886): 245–50.

20. "Funeral of Gen. E. Kirby-Smith," *CV* 1 (April, 1893): 100–101; "Monument to Gen. F. A. Shoup," *CV* 11 (July, 1903): 311–12.

21. William P. DuBose, "The Romance and Genius of a University," *Sewanee Review* 13 (October, 1905): 500–502; Elliott, *Sewanee: Past and Present*, p. 10; *Semi-centennial of the University of the South*, pp. 12, 16, 37, 49, 60,

86. For examples of articles expressing this same educational outlook, see H. E. Shepherd, "Higher Education in the South," *Sewanee Review* 1 (November, 1892): 283–89; and St. George L. Sioussat, "Should Idealism Perish in the Industrial South?" *Sewanee Review* 13 (October, 1905): 401–8.

22. Elliott, "An Appeal."

23. Henry A. White, *The Scotch-Irish University of the South: Washington and Lee* ([Lexington, Virginia], n.d.), pp. 21–22; W. G. Bean, *The Liberty Hall Volunteers: Stonewall's College Boys* (Charlottesville, 1964); Walter C. Preston, *Lee: West Point and Lexington* (Yellow Springs, O., 1934), pp. 48–51, 53, 57.

24. Ollinger Crenshaw, *General Lee's College: The Rise and Growth of Washington and Lee University* (New York, 1969), pp. 152–54, 166–70; Preston, *Lee*, pp. 74–75; Paul H. Buck, *The Road to Reunion, 1865–1900* (Boston, 1937), pp. 14–15. See also "Reply of Cyrus H. McCormick to Dr. Lord," *Central Presbyterian*, February 24, 1869, p. 4.

25. Preston, "Recollections of Lexington and Washington and Lee University in 1900," p. 23; the Winkler quotation was in J. William Jones, *Personal Reminiscences*, pp. 130–31; Crenshaw, *Lee's College*, pp. 149, 157; William N. Pendleton to Horatio Potter, June 1, 1868, Pendleton Papers.

26. C. A. Graves, "General Lee at Lexington," in Franklin L. Riley, ed., *General Robert E. Lee After Appomattox* (New York, 1922), pp. 22–23; McIlwaine, *Three Score Years and Ten*, p. 258; Hesseltine, *Confederate Leaders*, pp. 85–88; Preston, "Recollections," pp. 4, 14a; Francis H. Smith, *The Virginia Military Institute: Its Building and Rebuilding* (Lynchburg, Va., 1912); biographical details in Lee, *Memoirs of Pendleton*, pp. 422–28.

27. Marshall W. Fishwick, "Robert E. Lee Churchman," *Historical Magazine of the Protestant Episcopal Church* 30 (December, 1961): 251–53, 255, 257–58; Gamaliel Bradford, Jr., "Lee after the War," *South Atlantic Quarterly* 10 (October, 1911): 303–6; William E. Hassler, "Robert E. Lee: The Educator," *Georgia Review* 21 (Winter, 1967): 503; Littell McClung, "Lexington, Virginia: A Shrine of Southern Memories," p. 5, article in McCormick Library, Washington and Lee University, Lexington, Va.

28. Fishwick, "Lee," pp. 260–63; Edward S. Joynes, "General Robert E. Lee as College President," and Richard W. Rogers, "Reminiscences of General Lee and Washington College," both in Riley, *Lee*, pp. 19–20, 62; Robertson, *Broadus*, pp. 224–26; D. B. Strouse, "Gen. R. E. Lee to a Careless Student," CV 16 (September, 1908): 455–56; Fred Volck to William N. Pendleton, March 29, 1870, in Pendleton Papers; J. William Jones, "The Christian Character of Robert E. Lee," in Riley, *Lee*, pp. 191–94; Thompson, *Presbyterians*, 2: 360.

29. Crenshaw, *Lee's College*, pp. 172, 178–81; Walter E. Harris, "The

Alumni, Great and Otherwise," *Washington and Lee Calyx* 11 (1906): 33; Riley, *Lee*, p. 138.

30. "Dedications," *Washington and Lee Calyx* 1 (1895); "Editorials," *Washington and Lee Calyx* 12 (1907): 208; Margaret J. Preston, untitled poem in *Washington and Lee Calyx* 11 (1906): 38; Preston, "Recollections," p. 18; *Minutes of the Twenty-third Annual Convention of the UDC . . . 1916* (Raleigh, N.C., 1917), p. 193. See also a fable about crusading Washington and Lee knights, in "The Legend of the Castle Les Deux Heros and the Sacred Spear," *Washington and Lee Calyx* 11 (1906): 40–46.

31. Crenshaw, *Lee's College*, p. 184; Thompson, *Presbyterians*, 2: 360; *Ceremonies Connected with the Inauguration of the Mausoleum and the Unveiling of the Recumbent Figure of General Robert Edward Lee at Washington and Lee University, Lexington, Va., June 28, 1883* (Richmond, 1883), p. 3, 5–10; William N. Pendleton to his wife Anzolette, October 31, November 3, December 6, 1870, Joseph E. Johnston to Pendleton, February 13, 1873, Pendleton to the Prince of Wales, February 13, 1874, Pendleton to Rutherford B. Hayes, November 30, 1877, Pendleton to A. B. Beresford Hope, June 5, 1879, all in Pendleton Papers.

32. *Ceremonies at Washington and Lee*, pp. 5–23. The details of the Lee Memorial Association and the dedication day were also in *SHSP* 11 (August–September, 1883): 337–417.

33. Dabney, *Life of Jackson*, pp. 74–79; "The Old Virginia Town, Lexington," *CV* 1 (April, 1893): 108; McClung, "Lexington, Virginia," p. 2.

34. Johnson, *Palmer*, pp. 354–62; Thomas Nelson Page, "The Old South," in his *The Old South: Essays Social and Political* (New York, 1894), pp. 3, 51–54.

35. Crenshaw, *Lee's College*, pp. 282–89; *Lee's Centennial: An Address by Charles Francis Adams, delivered at . . . Washington and Lee University* (Boston, 1907), pp. 2, 6–8, 14, 57.

36. "Washington and Lee University," *CV* 28 (January, 1920): 8–10.

37. Wendell H. Stephenson, *Southern History in the Making: Pioneer Historians of the South* (Baton Rouge, 1964), pp. 71–92; Joseph J. Mathews, "The Study of History in the South," *Journal of Southern History* 21 (February, 1965): 9; UDC, *Minutes of the Fourth Meeting*, p. 37.

CHAPTER VIII: A HARVEST OF HEROES

1. Ella Lonn, "Reconciliation between the North and the South," *Journal of Southern History* 13 (February, 1947): 3; Buck, *Road to Reunion*; Osterweis, *Myth of the Lost Cause*, pp. viii–ix, chs. 3–6.

2. "Dr. Curry's Able Addresses," UCV, *Minutes of the Sixth Reunion*,

p. 71; Candler, "Heroism is Never in Vain," in *High Living*, pp. 181–82.

3. Jackson, "Southern Loyalty," *Christian Advocate*, October 13, 1898, p. 3.

4. "The Good Effects of the War," *Christian Advocate*, July 21, 1898, p. 2; B. F. Riley, "On the Wing," *Christian Index*, July 7, 1898, p. 5; UCV, *Minutes of the Thirtieth Reunion*, p. 39. See also "The War," *Christian Index*, April 21, 1898, p. 6; Galloway, *Men and Movements*, pp. 141–43; "Editorial," CV 6 (November, 1898): 512; "Bishop Gailor's Address," CV 7 (November, 1899): 497.

5. CV 6 (August, 1898): 360; "Editorial," CV 6 (July, 1898): 304; Mc-Neilly, "The Failure of the Confederacy—Was It a Blessing?" CV 24 (February, 1916): 65–68.

6. H. D. C. Maclachlin, "The Religious Aspect of Patriotism," CV 25 (June, 1917): 261; McKim, *Motives and Aims*, pp. vii, 33–34; McKim, *A Soldier's Recollections*, p. 280. See also Charles B. Galloway, "Jefferson Davis," in *Men and Movements*, p. 168.

7. P. D. Stephenson, "The Men of the Ranks," CV 17 (September, 1909): 437–38.

8. "Memorial Sermon," SHSP 37 (January–December, 1909): 339–40, 344–45. See also "Gen. Robert E. Lee," CV 28 (November, 1920): 416.

9. Masters, *Call of the South*, p. 18; Candler, "Heroism Is Never in Vain" and "The Value of Public Libraries," in *High Living*, pp. 178–79, 214.

10. Theodore D. Brattan, "The Christian South and Negro Education," *Sewanee Review* 16 (July, 1908): 292; Masters, *Call of the South*, p. 52; CV 4 (November, 1896): 364; "Report on Home Missions," *Minutes of the Fifty-eighth General Assembly of the Presbyterian Church in the United States* (Richmond, 1918), p. 105. See also McKim, *The Soul of Lee*, p. 141; and "Missions to Foreign Populations, Including Indians and Cubans," *Proceedings . . . of the Southern Baptist Convention . . . 1890* (Atlanta, 1890), pp. 16–17.

11. Masters, *Call of the South*, p. 52; Brattan, "The Christian South," p. 292; McNeilly, Review of *Southern Presbyterian Leaders*, in CV 20 (March, 1912): 134. For the importance of church and home in nurturing morality see Galloway, "Mississippi's Welcome," in *Men and Movements*, p. 246; Candler, "The South the Home of Americanism," in *High Living*, p. 58.

12. UCV, *Minutes of the Thirtieth Reunion*, pp. 36–38, 40–41; *Minutes of the Seventeenth Reunion*, pp. 113–14.

13. Gailor, *Some Memories*, pp. 5–7, 11, 17; *In Memoriam: Major Frank M. Gailor* (n.p., n.d.); interview with Nancy Gailor Cortner, July 23, 1975, Sewanee; interview with and story about Gailor in Memphis *Commercial Appeal*, April 5, 12, 1931, in Newspaper Clipping File, Thomas Frank Gailor

Personal Collection, Jessie Ball duPont Library, University of the South, Sewanee.

14. Gailor, *Some Memories*, p. 16; interviews with Robert Daniel, Nancy Gailor Cortner, Cynthia Ware, Ann Cleveland Robertson, and Bolling Robertson, July 23, 1975, Sewanee; "United Sons of Confederate Veterans," *CV* 5 (July, 1897): 385; USCV, *Yearbook and Minutes of the Twenty-first Annual Convention of the Sons of Confederate Veterans . . . 1926* (Richmond, n.d.), p. 113; *Minutes of the Sixth Annual Reunion of the USCV . . . 1901* (Louisville, n.d.), p. 16; Gailor, "General Forrest," *Sewanee Review* 9 (January, 1901): 1–12; Mrs. Horace Van Deventer to Gailor, September 24, 1935; letter from Kirby-Smith Chapter, UDC, to Gailor family, n.d.; editorial, *Southern Churchman*, October 12, 1935; all in Gailor Collection.

15. For biographical details, see Gailor, *Some Memories*. See also James Elliott Walmsley, "A Churchman," *Washington Post*, May 4, 1938, and clippings from Memphis *Commercial Appeal*, April 19, 1931, and October 31, 1935, Gailor Collection; "Annual Address," *Journal of the Eightieth Annual Convention in the Diocese of Tennessee* (Sewanee, 1912), p. 55.

16. USCV, *Sixth Reunion*, pp. 12–13.

17. Gailor address, May 17, 1917, in *CV* 25 (June, 1917): 252; "National Self-Consciousness and National Responsibility," *CV* 11 (May, 1903): 210–12.

18. "Bishop Gailor's Address," *CV* 7 (November, 1899): 497–98.

19. "Religious Work among the Soldier Boys," *Baptist Standard*, September 27, 1917, p. 5; "What the War Will Do," *Baptist Standard*, April 19, 1917, pp. 10–11; J. F. Love, "The War and Foreign Missions," *Baptist Standard*, May 10, 1917, p. 8; "Is the Church Prepared?" *Southern Churchman*, June 23, 1917, p. 4; "Compensation of War," *Baptist Standard*, October 25, 1917, p. 1; James B. Gambrell, "The Moral Foundations of Society," *Baptist Standard*, March 14, 1918, p. 11; Carroll L. Bates, "The War's Vindication of Christianity," *Southern Churchman*, March 30, 1918, pp. 7–8; "The Spiritual Side of the War," *Southern Churchman*, June 29, 1918, pp. 4–5; John M. Vander Meulen, "The Girdle of Loyalty," *Christian Observer*, November 7, 1917, pp. 3–4.

20. McKim, "America Summoned to a Holy War," in *For God and Country; or The Christian Pulpit in War-Time* (New York, 1918), pp. 81–83.

21. "America Summoned to a Holy War," "The Duty of the Hour," and "The National Crisis," ibid., pp. 8, 81–83, 90–92, 102–3, 116.

22. Joseph Packard, "The Manly and Christian Attitude toward War," *Southern Churchman*, March 31, 1917, p. 5; McKim, *Soul of Lee*, p. vii; Gailor's remarks in *CV* 25 (June, 1917): 252; Gambrell, "Evangelizing the Soldiers—An Interview with General Grebel," *Baptist Standard*, September

6, 1917, p. 10. See also James McNeilly, "A New Book on General Lee," CV 26 (May, 1918): 229–30; "Book Notices: 'The Soul of Lee,'" *Southern Churchman*, February 23, 1918, p. 5; James B. Gambrell, "General Lee's Great Word," *Baptist Standard*, April 25, 1918, p. 10; Gambrell, "Our Best for Our Best," *Baptist Standard*, September 27, 1917, p. 6.

23. D. G. Bickers, "I Am My Father's Son," CV 26 (February, 1918): 52; Littell McClung, "Old Virginia, Once Again," CV 26 (June, 1918): 237. See also UCV, *Reunion of the UCV . . . 1917* (Washington, 1918), p. 51; "To Fight for Southern Principles," CV 25 (August, 1917): 344; Mrs. Virginia F. Boyle, "The Tribute of the South," CV 25 (July, 1917): 356.

24. George W. McDaniel, "The Men Who Fell in the World War," in *A Memorial Wreath* (Dallas, 1921), p. 8; J. W. Bachman, "Heroes of the World War," CV 28 (February, 1920): 44. See also "Historical Department, UDC," CV 26 (January, 1918): 40.

25. "Our Two-Fold Responsibility," *Baptist Standard*, April 12, 1917, p. 6; "A Message from the Southern Baptist Convention on the World Crisis," *Baptist Standard*, May 31, 1917, p. 9; James Gambrell, "The Denominations and the War," *Baptist Standard*, May 16, 1918, p. 10; *Journal of the Eighteenth General Conference of the Methodist Episcopal Church, South . . . 1918* (Nashville, n.d.), pp. 341–42; *Minutes of the Fifty-ninth General Assembly of the Presbyterian Church in the United States . . . 1919* (Richmond, 1919), pp. 38, 87.

26. "The Cause Triumphant," CV 26 (March, 1918): 131.

27. McDaniel, "Lee's Veterans," in *Memorial Wreath*, pp. 23, 26–27, 31–32.

28. McKim, "Injustice to the South," in *The Gray Book* ([Richmond?], n.d.), pp. 35–39. See also Matthew P. Arnold, "Fighting for the Same Principle," CV 26 (June, 1918): 240; Henry E. Sheperd, "Historic Ironies—Sherman and German," CV 26 (January, 1918): 17–18; Will T. Hale, "Historic Exposures Commended," CV 26 (February, 1918): 91; and Leon G. Tyler, "The South and Germany," CV 25 (November, 1917): 506–12.

29. "The American's Creed," CV 26 (May, 1918): 185; UCV, *Thirtieth Reunion*, p. 11; "America's Prayer," *Baptist Standard*, July 4, 1918, p. 3; *Baptist Standard*, February 28, 1918, pp. 3, 12, 32; *Baptist Standard*, July 11, 1918, p. 7; Southern Methodist General Conference, *1918 Journal*, pp. 411–12; *Annual of the Southern Baptist Convention 1917* (Nashville, n.d.), pp. 15, 17; *Annual of the Southern Baptist Convention 1918* (Nashville, n.d.), p. 52; *Annual of the Southern Baptist Convention 1915* (Nashville, n.d.), p. 13; "President Wilson's Prayer," *Christian Observer*, September 12, 1917, p. 2; "President Wilson Asks Congress to Wage Warfare for Humanity," *Christian Observer*,

April 11, 1917, p. 22. For hymns, see "Sons of the South in Khaki," *CV* 26 (April, 1918): 140; "America to France," *CV* 26 (May, 1918): 229; "After the Years," *CV* 26 (June, 1918): 238; "God Save Our Men," *CV* 26 (April, 1918): 160.

30. "Editorial Notes," *Christian Observer*, November 13, 1918, p. 1; "Editorial Notes," *Christian Observer*, July 10, 1918, p. 1; "President Wilson's 'Independence Day' Address," ibid., p. 24; *Minutes of the Fifty-seventh General Assembly of the Presbyterian Church in the United States . . . 1917* (Richmond, 1917), p. 70; Southern Presbyterian Assembly, *1918 Minutes*, p. 41; *Journal of the Eighteenth General Conference of the Methodist Episcopal Church, South . . . 1890* (Nashville, n.d.), p. 298; McKim's sermons are in *For God and Country*; "Memorial Day in New Orleans," *CV* 25 (November, 1917): 523; "Memorial Day at Arlington," *CV* 25 (September, 1917): 397; "Vicksburg National Memorial Celebration," *CV* 25 (November, 1917): 489; "Dedication of Virginia Memorial at Gettysburg: Invocation," *SHSP*, n.s. 4 (September, 1917): 88–89. For the material on the flag, see "Flag Raising on Historic Anniversary," *CV* 25 (December, 1917): 572; Eugene P. Mickel, "Our Flag Shall Float Forever," *Christian Observer*, October 10, 1917, p. 7; McKim, *Recollections*, p. 279; W. H. T. Squires, "The Confederate Flag: Victorious Banner of an Hundred Bloody Battlefields," *Christian Observer*, April 25, 1917, p. 20; UCV, *Thirtieth Reunion*, p. 39.

31. See Arthur Walworth, *Woodrow Wilson: American Prophet* (New York, 1958), 2: 1–17.

32. Southern Methodist General Conference, *1918 Journal*, p. 298; Southern Baptist Convention, *1917 Annual*, p. 101; Southern Presbyterian General Assembly, *1917 Minutes*, p. 23, *1918 Minutes*, pp. 13–14.

33. Peyton H. Hoge, "The Fathers and the Children," *Christian Observer*, May 16, 1917, pp. 3–4; W. J. McGlothlin, "Christianize the South," *Baptist Standard*, June 14, 1917, p. 22.

34. "Reunion Plans," *CV* 25 (May, 1917): 194–95; "The Reunion in Washington," *CV* 25 (July, 1917): 297.

35. "The Reunion in Washington," pp. 297–98; "Address of President Woodrow Wilson," in UCV, *1917 Reunion*, pp. 22–24.

36. "Address of Bishop Collins Denny," in UCV, *1917 Reunion*, p. 49.

37. Ibid., pp. 50–51.

38. "Reunion Plans," *CV* 25 (May, 1917): 195.

39. "The Reunion in Washington," *CV* 25 (July, 1917): 299–300.

BIBLIOGRAPHY

I. PRIMARY SOURCES

A. Manuscripts

Beckwith, John. Sermon Collection. University of Georgia, Athens.

Dabney, Charles. Papers. Southern Historical Collection, University of North Carolina, Chapel Hill.

Dabney, Robert Lewis. Papers. Alderman Library, University of Virginia, Charlottesville.

DuBose, William P. "Reminiscences." Typescript, Southern Historical Collection, University of North Carolina, Chapel Hill.

Episcopal Bishops' Biographical Folders. Church Historical Society Archives, Episcopal Seminary of the Southwest, Austin, Tex.

Fairbanks, George Rainsford. Collection. DuPont Library, University of the South, Sewanee, Tenn.

Felton, Rebecca Latimer. Papers. University of Georgia, Athens.

Gailor, Thomas F. Personal Collection. Jessie Ball DuPont Library, University of the South, Sewanee, Tenn.

Gambrell, James B. "Recollections of Confederate Scout Service." Microfilm copy in Dargan-Carver Library, Sunday School Board, Southern Baptist Convention, Nashville, Tenn.

Hoge, Moses Drury. Papers. Historical Foundation of the Presbyterian and Reformed Churches, Montreat, N.C.

McClung, Littell. "Lexington, Virginia—a Shrine of Southern Memories." Article in McCormick Library, Washington and Lee University, Lexington, Va.

Paris, John D. "The Moral and Religious Status of the African Race in the Southern States." Southern Historical Collection, University of North Carolina, Chapel Hill.

Pendleton, William Nelson. Papers. Southern Historical Collection, University of North Carolina, Chapel Hill.

Polk, Leonidas. Papers. Southern Historical Collection, University of North Carolina, Chapel Hill.

Preston, Randolph, Sr. "Recollections of Lexington and Washington and Lee
    University in 1900." Typescript dated 1955, McCormick Library, Wash-
    ington and Lee University, Lexington, Va.
"Tribute to Gen. Robert E. Lee." Sermon on microfilm, Dargan-Carver Li-
    brary, Sunday School Board, Southern Baptist Convention, Nashville,
    Tenn.

B. Periodicals

Baptist Standard. Dallas and Waco, Tex. 1892–1920.
Central Presbyterian. Richmond, Va. 1865–1900.
Christian Advocate. Nashville, Tenn. 1865–1900.
Christian Index. Macon and Atlanta, Ga. 1865–1900.
Christian Observer. Louisville, Ky. 1917–19.
Confederate Veteran. Nashville, Tenn. Vols. 1–28. 1893–1920.
Home Monthly. Nashville, Tenn. Vols. 4–6, 8. 1868–70.
Religious Herald. Richmond, Va. 1865–1900.
Sewanee Review. Sewanee, Tenn. Vols. 1–28. 1892–1920.
South Atlantic Quarterly. Durham, N.C. Vols. 1–19. 1902–20.
Southern Bivouac. Louisville, Ky. Vols. new series 1–2. 1885–87.
Southern Churchman. Richmond, Va. 1898–1919.
Southern Collegian. Lexington, Va. 1869.
Southern Historical Society Papers. Richmond, Va. Vols. 1–31, new series 1–5.
    1876–1903, 1916–20.
Southern Presbyterian. Columbia, S.C. 1870–90.
Southern Review. Baltimore, Md. Vols. 1–24. 1867–78.
Texas Baptist and Herald. Dallas, Austin, and San Antonio. 1886–91.

C. Organizational Publications

Confederate Monumental Association. Tennessee Confederate Memorial.
    Nashville, n.d.
Confederated Memorial Associations of the South. History of the Con-
    federated Memorial Associations of the South. New Orleans, 1904.
Episcopal Diocese of Alabama. Council Proceedings. Mobile, 1865, 1880.
Episcopal Diocese of Georgia. Council Proceedings. Savannah, 1866.
Episcopal Diocese of Tennessee. Convention Journal. Sewanee, 1912.
Ladies Memorial Association, Charleston, S.C. Address Delivered before the
    Ladies Memorial Association and Citizens of Charleston on Memorial Day,
    May 10, 1893. Charleston, 1893.
———. Confederate Memorial Day at Charleston, 1871: Re-interment of the
    Carolina Dead from Gettysburg. Charleston, 1871.

Methodist Episcopal Church, South. *Journal*. Nashville, 1866–1918.

Presbyterian Church in the United States. *Minutes*. Augusta, Ga., Columbia, S.C., Richmond, Va., and Wilmington, N.C., 1865–1920.

R. E. Lee Camp, United Confederate Veterans, Richmond. *Action of R. E. Lee Camp*. Richmond, 1895.

Southern Baptist Convention. *Proceedings*. Richmond, Va., Baltimore, Md., Nashville, Tenn., Atlanta, Ga., and Cincinnati, O., 1865–1920.

United Confederate Veterans. *Fourth Annual Report of the Monumental Committee*. N.p., 1911.

———. *Minutes of the Annual Meeting and Reunion*. New Orleans, 1891–1920.

———. *Report of the Historical Committee, which was unanimously adopted at the Fourth Annual Reunion . . . 1894*. New Orleans, n.d.

———. *Report of the Historical Committee, which was unanimously adopted at the Twenty-first Annual Reunion . . . 1911*. N.p., n.d.

———. *Texas Division, Jas. J. A. Barker Camp, no. 1555. Burial Ritual*. N.p., n.d.

United Daughters of the Confederacy. *Minutes of the Annual Meeting*. Nashville, Tenn., Opelika, Ala., Jackson, Tenn., Raleigh, N.C., Charlotte, N.C., 1897–1920.

———. *Ritual of the United Daughters of the Confederacy*. Austin, Tex., n.d.

———. Lizzie Rutherford Chapter. *A History of the Origin of Memorial Day as adopted by the Ladies Memorial Association of Columbus, Georgia, and presented to the Lizzie Rutherford Chapter of the Daughters of the Confederacy, under whose direction it is now published*. Columbus, Ga., 1898.

United Sons of Confederate Veterans. *The Gray Book*. N.p., n.d.

———. *Minutes of the Annual Reunion*. Louisville, Ky., Richmond, Va., 1900, 1901, 1926.

D. Books and Articles

"Address of Rev. H. Melville Jackson." *Southern Historical Society Papers* 16 (January–December, 1888): 195–203.

Adger, John B. *My Life and Times, 1810–1899*. Richmond: Presbyterian Committee of Publication, 1899.

———. "Northern and Southern Views of the Province of the Church." *Southern Presbyterian Review* 16 (March, 1866): 390.

———. "The Presbyterian Union, North." *Southern Presbyterian Review* 22 (July, 1871): 398–99.

Baker, Lily, Charlotte Gailor, Rose Duncan Lowell, and Sarah Hodgson Torian, eds. *Sewanee*. Sewanee, Tenn.: Published for the benefit of the University Library Collection of Sewaneeana, 1932.

Bennett, William W. *A Narrative of the Great Revival Which Prevailed in the Southern Armies*. Philadelphia: Claxton, Remsen and Haffelfinger, 1877.

Blackburn, George A., ed. *Sermons by John L. Girardeau*. Columbia, S.C.: State, 1907.

Bledsoe, Albert T. "The African in the United States." *Southern Review* 29 (January, 1874): 137–74.

———. "The Great Virginian." *Southern Review* 9 (July, 1871): 685–99.

———. "Hon. A. H. Stephens on the Late War." *Southern Review* 11 (July, 1872): 120–56.

———. *Is Davis a Traitor; or Was Secession a Constitutional Right Previous to the War of 1861?* Baltimore: Printed for the author by Innes and Company, 1866.

———. "The M. E. Churches, North and South." *Southern Review* 10 (April, 1872): 382–421.

———. "Southern Voices." *Southern Review* 11 (July, 1872): 39–52.

Brattan, Theodore D. "The Christian South and Negro Education." *Sewanee Review* 16 (April, 1908): 290–95.

———. *Wanted—Leaders! A Study of Negro Development*. New York: Episcopal Council, 1922.

Broadus, John A. *Memoir of James Petigru Boyce*. New York: A. C. Armstrong and Son, 1893.

Burial Ceremonies of Confederate Dead, December 11, 1874. Washington: S. and R. O. Polkinhorn, 1875.

Candler, Warren A. *High Living and High Lives*. Nashville: Publishing House of the Methodist Episcopal Church, South, 1912.

Capers, Ellison. *Southern Carolina*. Atlanta: Confederate Publishing, 1899.

Cave, Robert C. *The Men in Gray*. Nashville: Confederate Veteran, 1911.

Ceremonies Connected with the Inauguration of the Mausoleum and the Unveiling of the Recumbent Figure of General Robert Edward Lee at Washington and Lee University, Lexington, Va., June 28, 1883. Richmond: West, Johnston, 1883.

Cheshire, Joseph B. *The Church in the Confederate States: A History of the Protestant Episcopal Church in the Confederate States*. New York: Longmans, Green, 1912.

Christian Education. The University of the South: Papers Relating to Christian Education at the University, and the Necessity of this Institution to the Country, especially to the South and Southwest, etc. Sewanee: James Pott, [1885].

Confederate Memorial Addresses: Monday, May 11, 1885, New Bern, North Carolina. Richmond: Whittet and Shepperson, 1886.

Contributions of the South to the Greatness of the American Union: An Address by General Clement A. Evans, of Atlanta, Georgia, Delivered before the Association of the Army of Northern Virginia, October 10th, 1895, at Richmond, Virginia. Richmond: William E. Jones, 1895.

Cooke, John E. Stonewall Jackson: A Military Biography; with an Appendix by J. William Jones, containing Personal Reminiscences, and a Full Account of the Ceremonies Attending the Unveiling of Foley's Statue, Including the Oration by Moses D. Hoge. New York: D. Appleton, 1876.

Cranfill, James B. Dr. J. A. Cranfill's Chronicle: A Story of Life in Texas. New York: Fleming H. Revell, 1916.

———. From Memory: Reminiscences, Recitals, and Gleanings from a Bustling and Busy Life. Nashville: Publishing House of the Methodist Episcopal Church, South, 1937.

Crozier, Robert H. The Confederate Spy: or, Startling Incidents of the War Between the States. A Novel. 5th ed. Louisville: J. P. Morton and Company, 1885.

Cunningham, Sumner A. "Sam Davis." American Historical Magazine 4 (July, 1899): 195–206.

Curry, J. L. M. Address of Hon. J. L. M. Curry LL.D., Delivered before the Association of Confederate Veterans, Richmond, Va., 1896. Richmond: Johnson Publishing, 1896.

Dabney, Robert L. A Defence of Virginia, and through Her of the South. New York: E. J. Hale and Son, 1867.

———. Life and Campaigns of Lt.-Gen. Thomas J. Jackson. New York: Blelock, 1866.

———. The New South: A Discourse Delivered at the Annual Commencement of Hampden-Sidney [sic] College, June 5, 1882. Raleigh, N.C. Edwards, Broughton, 1883.

Deering, John R. Lee and His Cause; or The Why and the How of the War Between the States. New York: Neale Publishing, 1907.

Dixon, Thomas, Jr. "American Backgrounds for Fiction: North Carolina." Bookman 38 (January, 1914): 511–14.

———. The Clansman: An Historical Romance of the Ku Klux Klan. New York: Doubleday, Page, 1905.

———. The Leopard's Spots: A Romance of the White Man's Burden, 1865–1900. New York: Doubleday, Page, 1902.

DuBose, William P. Turning Points in My Life. New York: Longmans, Green, 1912.

Dudley, Thomas U., Jr. "How Shall We Help the Negro?" Century Illustrated Magazine 30 (June, 1885): 273–80.

Elliott, Sarah Barnwell. An Appeal for Southern Books and Relics for the Library *of the University of the South: The Reason Why You Soldiers of the Great Civil War Should Care for the University of the South at Sewanee.* Sewanee: University Press, 1921.

―――. *Sewanee: Past and Present.* Sewanee: University Press, 1909.

Elliott, Stephen. *Sermons by Stephen Elliott.* New York: Pott and Amery, 1867.

Emerson, Mrs. B. A. C., comp. *Historic Southern Monuments: Representative Memorials of the Heroic Dead of the Southern Confederacy.* New York: Neale Publishing, 1911.

Evans, Clement A., ed. *Confederate Military History.* 12 vols. Atlanta: Confederate Publishing, 1899.

Felton, William H. *Sermon on the Life and Character of Gen. Robert E. Lee, Preached at Cartersville, Ga., Sunday, Oct. 16th, 1870.* Cartersville: Printed at the Semi-Weekly Express Office, 1870.

Fitzgerald, Oscar P., and Charles B. Galloway. *Eminent Methodists.* Nashville: Publishing House, Methodist Episcopal Church, South, 1898.

―――. *Fifty Years: Observations—Opinions—Experiences.* Nashville: Publishing House of the Methodist Episcopal Church, South, 1903.

―――. *Sunset Views in Three Parts.* Nashville: Publishing House of the Methodist Episcopal Church, South, 1900.

Gailor, Thomas F. *Bishop Quintard and the University of the South: A Memorial Address.* Sewanee: University of the South, n.d.

―――. "General Forrest." *Sewanee Review* 9 (January, 1901): 1–12.

―――. *The High Adventure: "Haec olim meminisse juvabit."* Sewanee: University Press, n.d.

―――. *Some Memories.* Kingsport, Tenn.: Southern Publishers, 1937.

Gaither, Zella H. *Arkansas Confederate Homes.* Little Rock: New Era Press, [1920].

Galloway, Charles B. *Great Men and Great Movements: A Volume of Addresses.* Nashville: Publishing House of the Methodist Episcopal Church, South, 1914.

―――. "Some Thoughts on Lynching." *South Atlantic Quarterly* 5 (October, 1906): 351–53.

Gambrell, James B. "A Call to the Universal Conquest of the World." *Baptist Standard*, May 26, 1892, p. 3.

Girardeau, John L. *Sermons by John L. Girardeau.* Ed. George A. Blackburn. Columbia, S.C.: State, 1907.

Goodloe, Albert T. *Confederate Echoes: A Voice from the South in the Days of Secession and of the South Confederacy.* Nashville: Methodist Episcopal Church, South, 1907.

Goodwin, S. A. "Memorial Sermon." *Southern Historical Society Papers* 37 (January–December, 1909): 338–45.

Green, William M. *Address Delivered before the Board of Trustees, University of the South, Sewanee, Tenn., August 4th, 1879.* Charleston, S.C.: Walker, Evans and Cogswell, 1879.

——. *Memoir of Rt. Rev. James Hervey Otey.* New York: James Pott, 1885.

Hamill, Howard M. *The Old South: A Monograph.* Nashville: Publishing House of the Methodist Episcopal Church, South, 1904.

Harrison, William P. *The Gospel among the Slaves.* Nashville: Publishing House of the Methodist Episcopal Church, South, 1893.

Harrison, William S. *Sam Williams: A Tale of the Old South.* Nashville: Publishing House of the Methodist Episcopal Church, South, 1892.

History of the Baptist Denomination in Georgia, with Biographical Compendium and Portrait Gallery of Baptist Ministers and Other Georgia Baptists. Atlanta: J. P. Harrison, 1881.

Hoge, Peyton H. *Moses Drury Hoge: Life and Letters.* Richmond: Presbyterian Committee of Publication, 1899.

Howe, W. B. W. *Sermons Preached in His Diocese by the Late Rt. Rev. W. B. W. Howe.* New York: James Pott, 1897.

In Memoriam: Major Frank M. Gailor. N.p., n.d.

Johnson, John Lipscomb. *Autobiographical Notes.* N.p.: privately printed, 1958.

Johnson, Thomas Cary. *Life and Letters of Benjamin Morgan Palmer.* Richmond: Presbyterian Committee of Publication, 1906.

——. *Life and Letters of Robert Lewis Dabney.* Richmond: Presbyterian Committee of Publication, 1903.

Johnston, William Preston. *The Life of Albert Sidney Johnston.* New York: D. Appleton, 1878.

Jones, John William. *Christ in the Camp; or, Religion in Lee's Army.* Richmond: B. F. Johnson, 1887.

——. *The Davis Memorial Volume; or, Our Dead President, Jefferson Davis, and the World's Tribute to His Memory.* Waco, Tex.: Yeager Publishing, 1890.

——. *General Isaac Munroe St. John.* New York: Cheap Publishing, 1881.

——. "The Inner Life of Robert Edward Lee." *Chautauquan* 31 (May, 1900): 187–90.

——. "The Inner Life of 'Stonewall' Jackson." *Chautauquan* 30 (October, 1899): 84–88.

——. *Life and Letters of Robert Edward Lee: Soldier and Man.* New York: Neale Publishing, 1906.

————. *Personal Reminiscences, Anecdotes and Letters of Gen. Robert E. Lee.* New York: D. Appleton, 1875.

————. *School History of the United States.* 2nd ed. New Orleans: University Publishing Company, 1898.

————. *Virginia's Next Governor, Gen. Fitzhugh Lee.* New York: Cheap Publishing, 1885.

Jones, Mrs. Sam P., and Walt Holcomb. *The Life and Sayings of Sam P. Jones, by His Wife Assisted by Rev. Walt Holcomb, a Co-worker of Mr. Jones.* Atlanta: Franklin-Turner, 1907.

Kidwell, James R. *Childhood Stories.* [Stockdale, Tex., 1959]

Kinsolving, George H. *An Anniversary Missionary Sermon Preached in Christ Church, Houston, St. David's Church, Austin and Christ Church, Tyler.* N.p., n.d.

Kinsolving, O. A., et al. *Memorials: Sermons Preached on Special Occasions by a Father and Two of His Sons.* Austin, Tex.: Von Boeckmann-Jones, 1911.

Lee, Susan Pendleton. *Memoirs of William Nelson Pendleton.* Philadelphia: J. B. Lippincott, 1893.

————. *A School History of the United States.* Richmond: B. F. Johnson Publishing, 1895.

Lee's Centennial: An Address by Charles Francis Adams, delivered at Lexington, Virginia, Saturday, January 19, 1907, on the Invitation of the President and Faculty of Washington and Lee University. Boston: Houghton, Mifflin, 1907.

McDaniel, George W. *A Memorial Wreath.* Dallas: Baptist Standard Publishing, 1921.

McIlwaine, Richard. *Memories of Three Score Years and Ten.* New York: Neale Publishing, 1908.

McKim, Randolph H. *For God and Country; or, The Christian Pulpit in War-Time.* New York: E. P. Dutton, 1918.

————. "Injustice to the South." *The Gray Book.* [Richmond]: n.d., pp. 35–39.

————. *Lee the Christian Hero: A Sermon Delivered in the Lee Memorial Church, Lexington, Virginia, Sunday January 20, 1907.* Washington: Brentano's, 1907.

————. *The Motives and Aims of the Soldiers of the South in the Civil War. Oration Delivered before the United Confederate Veterans at their Fourteenth Annual Reunion at Nashville, Tenn., June 14, 1904.* N.p.: United Confederate Veterans, n.d.

————. *A Soldier's Recollections: Leaves from the Diary of a Young Confederate.* New York: Longmans, Green, 1910.

————. *The Soul of Lee.* New York: Longmans, Green, 1918.

McNeilly, James H. "Failure of the Confederacy: Was It a Blessing." *Confederate Veteran* 24 (April, 1916): 160–63.

————, comp. *Memorial: Colonel John Overton and Mrs. Harriet Overton.* N.p., [1899].

————. *Religion and Slavery: A Vindication of the Southern Churches.* Nashville: Publishing House of the Methodist Episcopal Church, South, 1911.

Masters, Victor I. *The Call of the South.* Atlanta: Home Mission Board, Southern Baptist Convention, 1918.

Mayo, A. D. "The Woman's Movement in the South." *New England Magazine* n.s. 5 (October, 1891): 249–60.

Memorial Addresses on the Life and Character of Alfred Holt Colquitt. Washington: Government Printing Office, 1895.

Newton, John C. *Calhoun. The New South and the Methodist Episcopal Church, South.* Baltimore: King Brothers, 1887.

Page, Thomas Nelson. *The Old South: Essays Social and Political.* New York: Charles Scribner's Sons, 1894.

Parks, W. H. *The Texas Baptist Pulpit: A Collection of Sermons from the Baptist Ministry of Texas.* New York: Printed for the author by Lange, Little and Hillman, 1873.

Pinkney, William. "Ode." *Burial Ceremonies of Confederate Dead, December 11, 1874.* Washington: S. and R. O. Polkinhorn, 1875, pp. 14–16.

Pollard, Edward A. *The Lost Cause: A New Southern History of the War of the Confederates.* New York: E. B. Treat, 1866.

Quintard, Charles Todd. *Nellie Peters' Pocket Handkerchief and What It Saw: A Story of the War.* Sewanee: University Press, 1907.

Rankin, George C. *The Story of My Life; or More than a Half Century as I Have Lived It and Seen It Lived.* Nashville: Smith and Lamar, 1912.

Richardson, William Thomas. *Historic Pulaski: Birthplace of the Ku Klux Klan, Scene of Execution of Sam Davis.* [Nashville]: Methodist Publishing House, 1913.

Rutherford, Mildred. *Jefferson Davis the President of the Confederate States and Abraham Lincoln the President of the United States, 1861–1865.* Athens, Ga.: no imprint, 1916.

Ryan, Abram J. *Poems: Patriotic, Religious, Miscellaneous.* New York: P. J. Kenedy and Sons, 1896.

Sandell, J. W. *The United States in Scripture. The Union Against the States. God in Government.* Jackson, Miss.: Tucker Printing House, [1907].

Scomp, H. A. *King Alcohol in the Realm of King Cotton.* [Chicago]: Blakely Printing, 1888.

Semi-centennial of the University of the South, 1857–1907: Sermon, Poem,

Addresses and Letters. Sewanee: University of the South Press, n.d.

Smith, George G. *The Boy in Gray: A Story of the War.* Macon, Ga.: Macon Publishing, 1894.

———. *The Life and Letters of James Osgood Andrews.* Nashville: Publishing House of the Methodist Episcopal Church, South, 1882.

———. *The Life and Times of George Foster Pierce.* Sparta, Ga.: Hancock Publishing, 1888.

Stone, Cornelia Branch. *UDC Catechism for Children.* No imprint, 1912.

Stratton, Joseph B. *Address Delivered July 23d, 1875, before the Trustees, Professors and Students of Jefferson College, Washington, Adams County, Mississippi.* Natchez, Miss.: Democrat Book and Job Printing for Board of Trustees, 1875.

———. *A Pastor's Valedictory: A Selection of Early Sermons.* Natchez, Miss.: Natchez Printing, 1899.

Summers, Thomas O., ed. *Sermons by Southern Methodist Preachers.* Nashville: Publishing House of the Methodist Episcopal Church, South, 1890.

Tardy, W. T. *Trials and Triumphs: An Autobiography.* Marshall, Tex.: published by Mrs. W. T. Tardy, 1919.

Tucker, Beverly Dandridge. *Confederate Memorial Verses.* Norfolk: Pickett-Buchanan Chapter United Daughters of the Confederacy, n.d.

Underwood, John L. *The Women of the Confederacy.* New York: Neale Publishing, 1906.

Vaughan, Clement R., ed. *Discussions of Robert Lewis Dabney.* 4 vols. Richmond, Va., and Mexico, Mo.: Presbyterian Committee of Publication, 1891–96.

Wharton, Henry M. *War Songs and Poems of the Southern Confederacy, 1861–1865.* [Philadelphia, 1904].

———. *White Blood: A Story of the South.* New York: Neale Publishing, 1906.

Wharton, M. B. "A New Version of Dixie." *Confederate Veteran* 12 (September, 1904): 431–32.

White, Henry Alexander. *The Scotch-Irish University of the South: Washington and Lee.* [Lexington, Va.], n.d.

———. *Southern Presbyterian Leaders.* New York: Neale Publishing, 1911.

Wilmer, J. P. B. *Address of the Bishop of Louisiana to the Convention of the Protestant Episcopal Church in New Orleans, February 14, 1868.* New Orleans: L. Graham, 1868.

———. *A Defense of Louisiana.* N.p., n.d.

———. *Annual Address of the Bishop of Louisiana to the Council of the Diocese.* New Orleans: L. Graham, 1874.

Wilmer, J. P. B. Gen.'l. Robert E. Lee. An Address Delivered before the Students of the University of the South, October 15, 1870. Nashville: Paul and Tavel, 1872.

Wilmer, Richard H. In Memoriam: A Sermon in Commemoration of the Life and Labors of the Rt. Rev. Stephen Elliott. Mobile: Episcopal Church Council, 1867.

―――. The Recent Past From a Southern Standpoint: Reminiscences of a Grandfather. New York: Thomas Whittaker, 1887.

E. Government Document

Testimony Taken by the Joint Select Committee to Inquire into the Condition of Affairs in the Late Insurrectionary States. 13 vols. Washington: Government Printing Office, 1872.

F. Interviews

Robert Daniel, Nancy Gailor Cortner, Cynthia Ware, Ann Cleveland Robertson, and Bolling Robertson. July 23, 1975. Sewanee, Tenn.

II. SECONDARY SOURCES

Aaron, Daniel. The Unwritten War: American Writers and the Civil War. New York: Alfred A. Knopf, 1973.

Ahlstrom, Sydney. A Religious History of the American People. New Haven: Yale University Press, 1972.

Albanese, Catherine L. "Requiem for Memorial Day: Dissent in the Redeemer Nation." American Quarterly 26 (October, 1974): 386–98.

―――. Sons of the Fathers: The Civil Religion and the American Revolution. Philadelphia: Temple University Press, 1976.

Alderman, Edwin A., and Armistead C. Gordon. J. L. M. Curry: A Biography. New York: Macmillan, 1911.

Alston, Wallace M., Jr., and Wayne Flynt. "Religion in the Land of Cotton." H. Brandt Ayers and Thomas N. Naylor, eds. You Can't Eat Magnolias. New York: McGraw Hill, 1972, pp. 99–123.

Alwes, Berthold C. "The History of the Louisiana State Lottery Company." Louisiana Historical Quarterly 27 (Fall, 1944): 964–1118.

Asbury, Herbert. The Great Illusion: An Informal History of Prohibition. Garden City, N.Y.: Doubleday, 1950.

Ayers, H. Brandt, and Thomas H. Naylor, eds. You Can't Eat Magolias. New York: McGraw-Hill, 1972.

Bailey, Kenneth K. "The Post–Civil War Racial Separations in Southern

Protestantism: Another Look." *Church History* 46 (December, 1977): 453–73.

———. *Southern White Protestantism in the Twentieth Century.* New York: Harper and Row, 1964.

Bailey, Thomas J. *Prohibition in Mississippi, or Anti-Liquor Legislation from Territorial Days, with Its Results in the Counties.* Jackson: Printed for the author by Hederman Brothers, 1917.

Banton, Michael, ed. *Anthropological Approaches to the Study of Religion.* New York: F. A. Praeger, 1966.

Barrett, John G., and John S. Moore. *The History of Manly Memorial Baptist Church, Lexington, Virginia.* Lexington: no imprint, 1966.

Bean, W. G. *The Liberty Hall Volunteers: Stonewall's College Boys.* Charlottesville: University of Virginia Press, 1964.

Bearden, Robert E. L., Jr. "The Episcopal Church in the Confederate States." *Arkansas Historical Quarterly* 4 (Winter, 1945): 269–75.

Bell, Sadie. *The Church, the State, and Education in Virginia.* Philadelphia: Science Press, 1930.

Bellah, Robert N. *The Broken Covenant: American Civil Religion in Time of Trial.* New York: Seabury Press, 1975.

———. "Civil Religion in America." Russell E. Richey and Donald G. Jones, eds. *American Civil Religion.* New York: Harper and Row, 1974, pp. 21–44.

Benedict, Ruth. "Myth." Edwin R. A. Seligman, ed. *Encyclopedia of the Social Sciences.* New York: Macmillan, 1930, 11: 178–81.

Bercovitch, Sacvan. *The Puritan Origins of the American Self.* New Haven: Yale University Press, 1975.

Berthoff, Rowland T. "Southern Attitudes toward Immigration, 1865–1914." *Journal of Southern History* 17 (August, 1951): 328–60.

Blackburn, George A. *The Life Work of John Girardeau.* Columbia, S.C.: State, 1916.

Bloomfield, Maxwell. "Dixon's *The Leopard's Spots*: A Study in Popular Racism." *American Quarterly* 16 (Fall, 1964): 387–401.

Bode, Frederick A. "Religion and Class Hegemony: A Populist Critique in North Carolina." *Journal of Southern History* 38 (August, 1971): 417–38.

Boldrick, Charles C. "Father Abram J. Ryan: The Poet-Priest of the Confederacy." *Filson Club Historical Quarterly* 46 (July, 1972): 201–17.

Boles, John. *The Great Revival, 1787–1805: The Origins of the Southern Evangelical Mind.* Lexington: University Press of Kentucky, 1972.

———. *Religion in Antebellum Kentucky.* Lexington: University Press of Kentucky, 1976.

Bonner, James C. "The Historical Basis of the Southern Military Tradition." *Georgia Review* 9 (Spring, 1955): 74–85.

Boswell, E. M. "Rebel Religion." *Civil War Times Illustrated* 11 (October, 1972): 26–33.

Bradford, Gamaliel, Jr. "Lee after the War." *South Atlantic Quarterly* 10 (October, 1911): 303–6.

Brown, William G. *The Lower South in American History.* New York: Greenwood Press, 1969. (Reprint of 1902 edition.)

Bruce, Dickson D., Jr. "Religion, Society and Culture in the Old South: A Comparative View." *American Quarterly* 26 (October, 1974): 399–416.

Bryan, T. Conn. "The Churches in Georgia during the Civil War." *Georgia Historical Quarterly* 33 (December, 1949): 283–302.

Brydon, G. MacLaren. "The Diocese of Virginia in the Southern Confederacy." *Historical Magazine of the Protestant Episcopal Church* 17 (December, 1948): 384–440.

———. "Historic Parishes: Saint Paul's Church, Richmond." *Historical Magazine of the Protestant Episcopal Church* 23 (September, 1954): 277–91.

Buck, Paul H. *The Road to Reunion, 1865–1900.* Boston: Little, Brown, 1937.

Campbell, Joseph. *The Hero with a Thousand Faces.* Princeton, N.J.: Princeton University Press, 1972. (Originally 1949.)

Candler, Warren A. *Bishop Charles Betts Galloway: A Prince of Preachers and a Christian Statesman.* Nashville: Cokesbury Press, 1927.

Capers, Walter B. *The Soldier-Bishop: Ellison Capers.* New York: Neale Publishing, 1912.

Chalmers, David M. *Hooded Americanism: The History of the Ku Klux Klan.* New York: Doubleday, 1965.

Chase, Richard. *Quest for Myth.* Baton Rouge: Louisiana State University Press, 1946.

Cherry, Conrad. *God's New Israel: Religious Interpretations of American Destiny.* Englewood Cliffs, N.J.: Prentice-Hall, 1971.

———. "Two American Sacred Ceremonies: Their Implications for the Study of Religion in America." *American Quarterly* 21 (Winter, 1969): 739–54.

Chitty, Arthur Ben. "Heir of Hopes: Historical Summary of the University of the South." *Historical Magazine of the Protestant Episcopal Church* 23 (September, 1954): 258–65.

Chitty, Arthur Ben. *Reconstruction at Sewanee: The Founding of the University of the South and Its First Administration, 1857–1872.* Sewanee: University of the South Press, 1954.

Christian, George L. *Sketch of the Origin and Erection of the Confederate Me-*

morial Institute at Richmond, Virginia. Richmond: Whittet and Shepperson, [1931].

Christian, W. Asbury. *Richmond: Her Past and Present.* Richmond: L. H. Jenkins, 1912.

Clebsch, William A. "Baptism of Blood: A Study of Christian Contributions to the Interpretation of the Civil War in American History." Ph.D. dissertation, Union Theological Seminary, 1957.

Connelly, Thomas L. "The Image and the General: Robert E. Lee in American Historiography." *Civil War History* 19 (March, 1973): 50–64.

———. *The Marble Man: Robert E. Lee and His Image in American Society.* New York: Alfred A. Knopf, 1977.

Crenshaw, Ollinger. *General Lee's College: The Rise and Growth of Washington and Lee University.* New York: Random House, 1969.

Culbreth, David M. R. *The University of Virginia: Memories of Her Student Life and Professors.* New York: Neale Publishing, 1908.

Cummings, A. D. "The Southern Ministry and Secession." Master's thesis, University of Texas, 1938.

Cushman, Joseph D., Jr. "The Episcopal Church in Florida during the Civil War." *Florida Historical Quarterly* 38 (April, 1960): 294–301.

Damer, Eyre. *When the Ku Klux Rode.* New York: Neale Publishing, 1912.

Daniel, W. Harrison. "An Aspect of Church and State Relations in the Confederacy: Southern Protestantism and the Office of Army Chaplain." *North Carolina Historical Review* 36 (January, 1959): 47–71.

———. "Bible Publication and Procurement in the Confederacy." *Journal of Southern History* 24 (May, 1958): 191–202.

———. "The Effects of the Civil War on Southern Protestantism." *Maryland Historical Magazine* 69 (Spring, 1974): 44–63.

———. "Southern Baptists in the Confederacy." *Civil War History* 6 (December, 1960): 389–401.

Davis, Hugh C. "Edwin T. Winkler, Baptist Bayard." *Alabama Review* 17 (January, 1965): 33–44.

Donegan, Kate Coles. "Personal Reminiscences of Father Ryan." *Alabama Historical Quarterly* 7 (Fall, 1945): 449–50.

DuBose, William P. "Ellison Capers." *Sewanee Review* 16 (April, 1908): 368–73.

———. "The Romance and Genius of a University." *Sewanee Review* 13 (October, 1905): 500–502.

———. "Thomas Underwood Dudley: An Appreciation." *Sewanee Review* 13 (January, 1905): 102–8.

Dunstan, William Edward III. "The Episcopal Church in the Confederacy."
    Virginia Cavalcade 19 (Spring, 1970): 5–15.
Durant, Susan E. "The Gently Furled Banner: The Development of the Myth
    of the Lost Cause, 1865–1900." Ph.D. dissertation, University of North
    Carolina, 1972.
Duren, William Larkin. *Charles Betts Galloway: Orator, Preacher, and "Prince
    of Christian Chivalry."* Atlanta, Ga.: Banner Press, 1932.
Durkheim, Emile. *The Elementary Forms of the Religious Life.* New York: Free
    Press, 1965.
Eaton, Clement A. "The Ebb of the Great Revival." *North Carolina Historical
    Review* 23 (January, 1946): 1–12.
———. *The Growth of Southern Civilization, 1790–1860.* New York: Harper
    and Row, 1961.
Eighmy, John Lee. *Churches in Cultural Captivity: A History of the Social Atti-
    tudes of Southern Baptists.* Knoxville: University of Tennessee Press, 1972.
Eliade, Mircea. *Myth and Reality.* New York: Harper and Row, 1963.
———. *Patterns in Comparative Religion.* New York: Sheed and Ward, 1958.
———. *The Sacred and the Profane: The Nature of Religion.* New York: Har-
    court, Brace, 1959.
Fairbanks, George R. *History of the University of the South at Sewanee, Ten-
    nessee.* Jacksonville, Fla.: H. and W. B. Drew, 1905.
Farish, Hunter D. *The Circuit-Rider Dismounts: A Social History of Southern
    Methodism, 1865–1900.* Richmond: Dietz Press, 1938.
Faulkner, William. *Go Down, Moses and Other Stories.* New York: Random
    House, 1942.
Fishwick, Marshall W. *American Heroes: Myth and Reality.* Washington: Pub-
    lic Affairs Press, 1954.
———. *The Hero, American Style.* New York: David McKay, 1969.
———. "Robert E. Lee Churchman." *Historical Magazine of the Protestant
    Episcopal Church* 30 (December, 1961): 251–65.
———. "Virginians on Olympus: Robert E. Lee: Savior of the Lost Cause."
    Virginia Magazine of History and Biography 58 (April, 1950): 163–80.
Frederickson, George M. *The Black Image in the White Mind: The Debate on
    Afro-American Character and Destiny, 1817–1914.* New York: Harper and
    Row, 1971.
Freeman, Douglas Southall. *The South to Posterity: An Introduction to the Writ-
    ing of Confederate History.* New York: Charles Scribner's Sons, 1939.
Gaston, Paul M. *The New South Creed: A Study in Southern Mythmaking.* New
    York: Vintage Books, 1970.

Geertz, Clifford. "Religion as a Cultural System." Michael Banton, ed. *Anthropological Approaches to the Study of Religion*. New York: F. A. Praeger, 1966, pp. 1–28.

Gerster, Patrick, and Nicholas Cords, eds. *Myth and Southern History*. Chicago: Rand McNally, 1974.

Goody, Jack. "Religion and Ritual: The Definitional Problem." *British Journal of Sociology* 12 (June, 1961): 142–64.

Gordon, Armistead C., Jr. "John William Jones." Dumas Malone, ed. *Dictionary of American Biography*. New York: Scribner's Sons, 1932, 5: 191.

Gossett, Thomas T. *Race: The History of an Idea*. Dallas: Southern Methodist University Press, 1963.

Greeley, Andrew M. *The Denominational Society: A Sociological Approach to Religion in America*. Glenview, Ill.: Scott Foresman, 1972.

Green, Fletcher Melvin, ed. *Essays in Southern History*. Chapel Hill: University of North Carolina Press, 1949.

Greenway, John. Introduction to *The Anthropologist Looks at Myth*. Melville Jacobs, comp. Austin: University of Texas Press, 1966, pp. 9–13.

Gregg, Wilson, and Arthur H. Noll. *Alexander Gregg: First Bishop of Texas*. Sewanee: University of the South Press, 1912.

Guerry, Moultrie. *Men Who Made Sewanee*. Sewanee: University of the South Press, 1932.

Hair, William Ivy. *Bourbonism and Agrarian Protest: Louisiana Politics, 1877–1900*. Baton Rouge: Louisiana State University Press, 1969.

Hanna, Alfred J., and Kathryn A. Hanna. *Confederate Exiles in Venezuela*. Tuscaloosa, Ala.: Confederate Publishing, 1960.

Hannum, Sharon E. "Confederate Cavaliers: The Myth in War and Defeat." Ph.D. dissertation, Rice University, 1965.

Harris, Malcolm H. *History of Louisa County, Virginia*. Richmond: Dietz Press, 1936.

Harwell, Richard Barkdale. "The Confederate Heritage." Louis D. Rubin, Jr. and James J. Kilpatrick, eds. *The Lasting South: Fourteen Southerners Look at Their Home*. Chicago: University of Chicago Press, 1957, pp. 16–27.

Hassler, William E. "Robert E. Lee: The Educator." *Georgia Review* 21 (Winter, 1967): 503–7.

Hattaway, Herman. "Clio's Southern Soldiers: The United Confederate Veterans and History." *Louisiana History* 12 (Summer, 1971): 213–42.

Herberg, Will. "America's Civil Religion: What It Is and Whence It Comes." Russell E. Richey and Donald G. Jones, eds. *American Civil Religion*. New York: Harper and Row, 1974, pp. 76–88.

Herberg, Will. *Protestant, Catholic, Jew: An Essay in American Religious Sociology*. Rev. ed. Garden City, N.Y.: Doubleday, 1960.

Hesseltine, William B. *Confederate Leaders in the New South.* Baton Rouge: Louisiana State University Press, 1950.

———, and Hazel C. Wolf. *The Blue and the Gray on the Nile.* Chicago: University of Chicago Press, 1961.

Hill, Lawrence F. "The Confederate Exodus to South America." *Southwestern Historical Quarterly* 39 (October, 1935, January, April, 1936): 100–134, 161–99, 309–26.

Hill, Samuel S., Jr., et al. *Religion and the Solid South.* Nashville: Abingdon Press, 1972.

———. "South's Two Cultures." Hill, ed. *Religion and the Solid South.* Nashville: Abingdon Press, 1972, pp. 24–56.

———. *Southern Churches in Crisis.* New York: Holt, Rinehart and Winston, 1966.

Hunter, Lloyd A. "The Sacred South: Postwar Confederates and the Sacralization of Southern Culture." Ph.D. dissertation, St. Louis University, 1978.

Jackson, Joy J. *New Orleans in the Gilded Age: Politics and Urban Progress, 1880–1896.* Baton Rouge: Louisiana State University Press, 1969.

Jacobs, Melville, comp. *The Anthropologist Looks at Myth.* Austin: University of Texas Press, 1966.

Johnson, Allen, and Dumas Malone, eds. *Dictionary of American Biography.* 12 vols. New York: Charles Scribner's Sons, 1928–32.

Johnson, Guion Griffis. "The Ideology of White Supremacy, 1876–1910." Fletcher M. Green, ed. *Essays in Southern History.* Chapel Hill: University of North Carolina, 1949, pp. 139–43.

Katz, Herbert and Marjorie. *Museums, U.S.A.: A History and Guide.* Garden City, N.Y.: Doubleday, 1965.

Kinsolving, Arthur B. *The Story of a Southern School: The Episcopal High School of Virginia.* Baltimore: Norman Remington, 1922.

———. *Texas George: The Life of George Herbert Kinsolving.* Milwaukee: Morehouse Publishing, 1932.

Kluckhohn, Clyde. "Recurrent Themes in Myth and Mythmaking." Henry A. Murray, ed. *Myth and Mythmaking.* New York: Beacon, 1960, pp. 46–60.

Lévi-Strauss, Claude. *The Savage Mind.* Chicago: University of Chicago Press, 1962.

Lipscomb, Oscar H. "Some Unpublished Poems of Abram J. Ryan." *Alabama Review* 25 (July, 1972): 163–77.

Little, Robert D. "The Ideology of the New South: A Study in the Development of Ideas, 1865–1910." Ph.D. dissertation, University of Chicago, 1950.

Lonn, Ella. "Reconciliation between the North and the South." *Journal of Southern History* 13 (February, 1947): 3–26.

McGinty, Garnie W. *Louisiana Redeemed: The Overthrow of Carpetbag Rule, 1876–1880*. New Orleans: Pelican, 1941.

McMath, Robert C., Jr. *Populist Vanguard: A History of the Southern Farmers' Alliance*. Chapel Hill: University of North Carolina Press, 1975.

Marty, Martin E. "Two Kinds of Two Kinds of Civil Religion." Russell E. Richey and Donald G. Jones, eds. *American Civil Religion*. New York: Harper and Row, 1974, pp. 139–57.

Mathews, Donald. *Religion in the Old South*. Chicago: University of Chicago Press, 1977.

Mathews, Joseph J. "The Study of History in the South." *Journal of Southern History* 21 (February, 1965): 3–20.

Mead, Sidney E. "The 'Nation with the Soul of a Church.'" Russell E. Richey and Donald G. Jones, eds. *American Civil Religion*. New York: Harper and Row, 1974, pp. 45–75.

Mell, Patrick H., Jr. *Life of Patrick Hues Mell*. Louisville: Baptist Book Concern, 1895.

Miller, Perry. *Errand into the Wilderness*. Cambridge, Mass.: Harvard University Press, 1956.

————. *The New England Mind: From Colony to Province*. Cambridge, Mass.: Harvard University Press, 1953.

Mohler, Mark. "The Episcopal Church and Reconciliation." *Political Science Quarterly* 16 (1926): 571–82.

Monroe, Haskell. "Southern Presbyterians and the Secession Crisis." *Civil War History* 6 (December, 1960): 351–60.

Moorhead, James H. *American Apocalypse: Yankee Protestants and the Civil War, 1860–1869*. New Haven: Yale University Press, 1978.

Murray, Henry A. *Myth and Mythmaking*. New York: Beacon Press, 1960.

Myers, Robert Manson, ed. *The Children of Pride: A True Story of Georgia and the Civil War*. New Haven: Yale University Press, 1972.

Nolen, Claude H. *The Negro's Image in the South: The Anatomy of White Supremacy*. Lexington: University Press of Kentucky, 1967.

Noll, Arthur H., ed. *Doctor Quintard: Chaplain C.S.A. and Second Bishop of Tennessee. Being His Story of the War*. Sewanee: University of the South Press, 1905.

————. *General Kirby-Smith*. Sewanee: University Press at the University of the South, 1907.

Norton, Herman. *Rebel Religion: The Story of the Confederate Chaplains*. St. Louis: Bethany Press, 1961.

———. "Revivalism in the Confederate Armies." *Civil War History* 6 (December, 1960): 410–24.

Ohmann, Richard M., ed. *The Making of Myth*. New York: Putnam, 1962.

Osterweis, Rollin G. *The Myth of the Lost Cause, 1865–1900*. Hamden, Conn.: Archon Books, 1973.

———. *Romanticism and Nationalism in the Old South*. New Haven: Yale University Press, 1949.

Painter, F. V. N. *Poets of the South: A Series of Biographical and Critical Studies with Typical Poems, Annotated*. New York: American Book Company, 1903.

Parks, Joseph H. *General Edmund Kirby Smith, C.S.A.* Baton Rouge: Louisiana State University Press, 1954.

Pearson, Charles C., and J. Edwin Hendricks. *Liquor and Anti-Liquor in Virginia, 1619–1919*. Durham, N.C.: Duke University Press, 1967.

Pennington, Edgar L. "Bishop Stephen Elliott and the Confederate Episcopal Church." *Georgia Review* 4 (April, 1950): 233–47.

———. "The Church in the Confederate States." *Historical Magazine of the Protestant Episcopal Church* 17 (December, 1948): 308–448.

Pierce, Alfred M. *Giant against the Sky: The Life of Bishop Warren Akin Candler*. Nashville: Abingdon-Cokesbury Press, 1948.

Pitts, Charles F. *Chaplains in Gray: The Confederate Chaplains' Story*. Nashville: Broadman Press, 1957.

Polk, William M. *Leonidas Polk: Bishop and General*. 2nd ed. New York: Longmans Green, 1915.

Poppenheim, Mary B., et al. *The History of the United Daughters of the Confederacy*. Richmond: Garrett and Massie, 1938.

Posey, Walter B. "The Protestant Episcopal Church: An American Adaptation." George B. Tindall, ed. *The Pursuit of Southern History: Presidential Addresses of the Southern Historical Association 1935–1963*. Baton Rouge: Louisiana State University Press, 1964, pp. 377–97.

Posey, Walter B. "The Protestant Episcopal Church: An American Adaptation." *Journal of Southern History* 25 (February, 1959): 3–30.

Poteat, Edwin M., Jr. "Religion in the South." W. T. Couch, ed. *Culture in the South*. Chapel Hill: University of North Carolina Press, 1935, pp. 248–69.

Preston, Walter C. *Lee: West Point and Lexington*. Yellow Springs, O.: Antioch Press, 1934.

Raglan, Lord. "Myth and Ritual." Thomas A. Sebeok, ed. *Myth: A Symposium*. Philadelphia: American Philosophical Society, 1955, pp. 122–35.

Randel, William P. *The Ku Klux Klan: A Century of Infamy*. Radnor, Pa.: Chilton, 1965.

Reimers, David. *White Protestantism and the Negro*. New York: Oxford University Press, 1965.

Rice, Jessie P. J. *L. M. Curry: Southerner, Statesman and Educator*. New York: Columbia University Press, 1949.

Richey, Russell E., and Donald Jones, eds. *American Civil Religion*. New York: Harper and Row, 1974.

Riley, Franklin L., ed. *General Robert E. Lee after Appomattox*. New York: Macmillan, 1922.

Rister, Carl C. "Carlota, A Confederate Colony in Mexico." *Journal of Southern History* 11 (February, 1945): 33–50.

Robertson, Archibald T. *Life and Letters of John Albert Broadus*. Philadelphia: American Baptist Publication Society, 1909.

Robinson, William M. "Prohibition in the Confederacy." *American Historical Review* 37 (October, 1931): 50–58.

Rolle, Andrew F. *The Lost Cause: The Confederate Exodus to Mexico*. Norman: University of Oklahoma Press, 1965.

Romero, Sidney J. "The Confederate Chaplain." *Civil War History* 1 (June, 1955): 127–40.

Routh, Eugene C. *The Life Story of Dr. J. B. Gambrell*. Oklahoma City: published by the author, 1929.

Rubin, Louis D., Jr., and James J. Kilpatrick, eds. *The Lasting South: Fourteen Southerners Look at Their Home*. Chicago: H. Regnery, 1957.

Sandeen, Ernest R. *The Roots of Fundamentalism: British and American Millenarianism, 1800–1930*. Chicago: University of Chicago Press, 1970.

Schorer, Mark. "The Necessity of Myth." Henry A. Murray, ed. *Myth and Mythmaking*. New York: George Braziller, 1960, pp. 354–57.

Scott, Anne Firor. *The Southern Lady: From Pedestal to Politics*. Chicago: University of Chicago Press, 1970.

Sebeok, Thomas A., ed. *Myth: A Symposium*. Philadelphia: American Folklore Society, 1955.

Seligman, Edwin R. A., ed. *Encyclopedia of the Social Sciences*. 15 vols. New York: Macmillan, 1930–35.

Shepard, John, Jr. "Religion in the Army of Northern Virginia." *North Carolina Historical Review* 25 (July, 1948): 341–76.

Shepherd, H. E. "Higher Education in the South." *Sewanee Review* 1 (November, 1892): 283–89.

Silver, James W. *Confederate Morale and Church Propaganda*. Tuscaloosa, Ala.: Confederate Publishing, 1957.

———. "The Confederate Preacher Goes to War." *North Carolina Historical Review* 33 (October, 1956): 499–509.

Simpson, Harold B. *Hood's Texas Brigade in Reunion and Memory*. Hillsboro, Tex.: Hill Jr. College Press, 1974.

Sinclair, Andrew. *Prohibition: The Era of Excess*. Boston: Little, Brown, 1962.

Sioussat, St. George L. "Should Idealism Perish in the Industrial South?" *Sewanee Review* 13 (October, 1905): 401–8.

Slotkin, Richard. *Regeneration through Violence: The Mythology of the American Frontier, 1600–1860*. Middletown, Conn.: Wesleyan University Press, 1973.

Smith, Francis H. *The Virginia Military Institute: Its Building and Rebuilding*. Lynchburg, Va.: J. P. Bell, 1912.

Smith, H. Shelton. *In His Image, But: Racism in Southern Religion, 1780–1910*. Durham, N.C.: Duke University Press, 1972.

Spain, Rufus B. *At Ease in Zion: A Social History of Southern Baptists, 1865–1900*. Nashville: Vanderbilt University Press, 1967.

Stem, Thad, Jr., and Alan Butler. *Senator Sam Ervin's Best Stories*. Durham, N.C.: Duke University Press, 1973.

Stephenson, Wendell H. *Southern History in the Making: Pioneer Historians of the South*. Baton Rouge: Louisiana State University Press, 1964.

Taylor, George Braxton. *Virginia Baptist Ministers*. Lynchburg, Va.: J. P. Bell, 1915.

Taylor, William R. *Cavalier and Yankee: The Old South and American National Character*. New York: Harper and Row, 1961.

Thompson, Ernest Trice. *Presbyterians in the South*. 3 vols. Richmond: John Knox Press, 1963–74.

Tindall, George B. "Mythology: A New Frontier in Southern History." Frank E. Vandiver, ed. *The Idea of the South: Pursuit of a Central Theme*. Chicago: University of Chicago Press, 1964, pp. 1–15.

Tindall, George B., ed. *The Pursuit of Southern History: Presidential Addresses of the Southern Historical Association 1935–1963*. Baton Rouge: Louisiana State University Press, 1964.

Trelease, Allen W. *White Terror: The Ku Klux Klan Conspiracy and Southern Reconstruction*. New York: Harper and Row, 1971.

Tucker, Gardiner C. "Richard Hooker Wilmer, Second Bishop of Alabama." *Historical Magazine of the Protestant Episcopal Church* 7 (June, 1938): 132–53.

Vandiver, Frank E., ed. *The Idea of the South: Pursuit of a Central Theme*. Chicago: University of Chicago Press, 1964.

———. *Ploughshares into Swords: Josiah Gorgas and Confederate Ordnance*. Austin: University of Texas Press, 1952.

Walker, Arthur L., Jr. "Three Alabama Baptist Chaplains, 1861–1865." *Alabama Review* 16 (July, 1963): 174–84.

Wallace, Anthony F. C. *Religion: An Anthropological View*. New York: Random House, 1966.

Walworth, Arthur. *Woodrow Wilson: American Prophet*. New York: Longmans Green, 1958.

Warner, W. Lloyd. "An American Sacred Ceremony." Russell E. Richey and Donald G. Jones, eds. *American Civil Religion*. (New York: Harper and Row, 1974), pp. 89–111.

———. *The Living and the Dead: A Study of the Symbolic Life of Americans*. New Haven: Yale University Press, 1959.

Warren, Robert Penn. *The Legacy of the Civil War: Meditations on the Centennial*. New York:Vintage Books, 1961.

Weaver, Blanche Henry Clark. "Confederate Immigrants and Evangelical Churches in Brazil." *Journal of Southern History* 18 (November, 1952): 446–68.

Weaver, Richard M. "Albert Taylor Bledsoe." *Sewanee Review* 52 (Winter, 1944): 34–45.

———. "The Older Religiousness in the South." *Sewanee Review*, 51 (Spring, 1943): 237–49.

———. *The Southern Tradition at Bay: A History of Postbellum Thought*. George Core and M. E. Bradford, eds. New Rochelle, N.Y.: Arlington House, 1968.

Wector, Dixon. *The Hero in America: A Chronicle of Hero-Worship*. Ann Arbor: University of Michigan Press, 1963. (Originally 1941.)

Weddell, Elizabeth W. *St. Paul's Church, Richmond, Virginia: Its Historic Years and Memorials*. 2 vols. Richmond: William Byrd Press, 1931.

Whitaker, Walter C. *Richard Hooker Wilmer: A Biography*. Philadelphia: George W. Jacobs, 1907.

White, Kate. "Father Ryan—the Poet-Priest of the South." *South Atlantic Quarterly* 18 (January, 1919): 69–74.

White, William W. *The Confederate Veteran*. Tuscaloosa, Ala.: Confederate Publishing, 1962.

Whitley, Edythe J. R. *Sam Davis: Hero of the Confederacy*. Nashville: Blue and Gray Press, 1971.

Wight, Willard E. "The Churches and the Confederate Cause." *Civil War History* 6 (December, 1960): 361–73.

Williams, T. Harry. *Pierre Gustavus Toutant Beauregard: Napoleon in Gray*. Baton Rouge: Louisiana State University Press, 1955.

Wilson, John F. *Public Religion in American Culture.* Philadelphia: Temple University Press, 1979.

Wilson, Richard L. "Sam Jones: An Apostle of the New South." *Georgia Historical Quarterly* 57 (Winter, 1973): 459–74.

Woodward, C. Vann. *Origins of the New South, 1877–1913.* Baton Rouge: Louisiana State University Press, 1951.

———. *The Strange Career of Jim Crow.* 2nd ed. New York: Oxford University Press, 1966.

Wooten, Fred T., Jr. "Religious Activities in Civil War Memphis." *Tennessee Historical Quarterly* 3 (June–September, 1944): 131–49, 248–72.

INDEX

Abolitionists, 4
Adams, Charles Francis, Jr., 158–59
Adams, W. Carleton, 105
Adger, John B., 69–70, 102
Ahlstrom, Sydney, 148
American Revolution, 2; and civil religion, 12–13; heroes of, 22; compared with Confederacy, 40; South's role in, 141
American Way of Life, 12
Anderson, G. W., 43
Andrews, James O., 40, 62
Arlington National Cemetery, 179–81
Army, Confederate, 43–44, 121, 135
Army of Northern Virginia, 6, 120, 124, 127, 131
Army of Tennessee, 6
Arnold, Eugenia Hill, 143
Artifacts, wartime, 26
Association of the Army of Northern Virginia, 19, 132

Bachman, J. W., 173, 181
Bailey, Kenneth K., 9
Baptists, Southern: formation of, 2, 4; post–Civil War growth, 8, 98; fears after the Civil War, 9–10, 140; role in Lost Cause, 35; and immigrants, 91; and slavery, 103; and sectionalism, 161. See also Jones, J. William; Wilson, Woodrow; World War I
Barbee, J. D., 53
Beauregard, P. G. T., 50, 89
Beckwith, John, 72–73

Bellah, Robert N., 12, 14
Benedict, Ruth, 38–39
Bennett, William W., 43–44
Bercovitch, Sacvan, 80
Bible Belt, 8, 15
Bickers, D. G., 173
Bierbower, C. G., 174
Blacks: and Confederate heroes, 26; white fear of decline, 99, 106–9, 117–18; paternalism toward, 100–101, 108–10; Negrophobia, 101; religion of, 107–8, 120–21. See also Civil War, Monuments, Slavery
Bledsoe, Albert Taylor, 84, 102, 104, 141
Blue Mountain Female Institute, 144
Brattan, Theodore DuBose, 109–10, 167
Brown, C. C., 155
Brownlow, William, 112
Burrows, J. L., 62

Cable, George Washington, 124
Campbell, Joseph, 44
Candler, Warren A., 40, 74; and the New South, 92–93, 96–98; and education, 143, 145; and World War I, 162; and regionalism, 166–67
Capers, Ellison: and Lost Cause ritual, 32, 45; as Lost Cause hero, 55–56
Capers, Walter B., 56, 113
Carr-Burdette College, 144
Carroll, Richard, 103
Catholics, Roman, 34
Cave, R. Lin, 49, 167
Cave, Robert C., 54

Chitty, Arthur Ben, 146
Chosen people, concept of, 1, 39, 71, 77, 80, 97
Churches, Christian: as focus of Lost Cause, 33–35. *See also* Baptists, Southern; Civil War; Episcopalians; Methodists, Southern; Presbyterians, Southern
Church of the Redeemer, Biloxi, Mississippi, 25
Civil religion: Southern, 1, 12–13, 25, 33, 36; American, 12–13, 29, 33, 119, 161, 164, 171, 175; concept of, 12–14, 177
Civil War: effect on religion, 4, 5, 8, 10, 120; and Confederate myth, 24, 37; women in, 46; blacks in, 103–4. *See also* Civil religion, Jeremiad
Colquitt, Alfred H., 92–93
Confederacy: reasons for defeat of, 1, 5, 22–23, 58, 60, 63–78, 166, 168; results of defeat of, 7, 30, 38, 58, 62, 74, 78, 84; sentimentalization of, 38; vindication of, 73–77, 178. *See also* Civil religion, Jeremiad
Confederate chaplains, 6, 36
Confederate Memorial Institute, 136–37, 142
Confederate Veteran, 29, 34, 47, 53
Cooke, John Esten, 52
Cultural nationalism, concept of, 3
Cultural revitalization movements, 11
Cumming, John, 64
Cunningham, Sumner, 53, 83, 105, 163
Curry, J. L. M., 47, 142, 162

Dabney, Robert Lewis, 20, 52, 62; reaction to defeat, 66, 69; and Southern decline, 85–86, 92, 107; and writing of history, 142
Daniel, book of, 64
Daniel, John W., 157
Daniels, Josephus, 175
Davis, Jefferson: during Civil War, 5, 26; and Confederate Memorial Day, 28; becomes Episcopalian, 35, 129; as Christian martyr, 50–51; defense of, 126–29; ceremony honoring, 134

Davis, Sam, 11, 26, 45; as Christ figure, 53–54
Davis, Winnie, 46–47, 51
Deering, John R., 142
De La Moriniere, E. C., 48, 50
Democracy, concept of. *See* Civil religion
Democratic party, 93, 112
Denny, Collins, 180–81
Destiny, Southern, 76–77, 97–98, 165–66
Dixon, Thomas, Jr., 114–16
Doggett, D. S., 20–21
DuBose, William P., 111, 147–49, 151
Dudley, Thomas, 108
Durkheim, Emile, 15

Eager, George B., 77
Early, Jubal, 57, 89, 157
Education, 139–60 *passim*
Eighmy, John L., 9–10
El Dorado, Arkansas, 29
Eliade, Mircea, 25, 39
Elliott, Sarah, 148–51
Elliott, Stephen, 5. *See also* Civil War
Emerson, A. J., 115
Emory University, 96, 145
Enlightenment, 12–13
Episcopal High School, Alexandria, Virginia, 143
Episcopalians: early history of, 2; role in Lost Cause, 35; Prayer for the President by, 42, 63; and sectionalism, 161. *See also* Civil War, Jefferson Davis, University of the South
Evangelism, Southern: in North, 74; in Lost Cause, 119, 133, 138. *See also* Revivalism
Evans, Clement, 50, 142
Existentialism, 15–16
Expatriates, Confederate, 63

Fairbanks, George Rainsford, 148
Farris, Mrs. M. D., 33
Fasting, days of, 5, 27, 61
Faulkner, William, 1
Felton, Rebecca, 47, 104, 106
Felton, William, 47

Fishwick, Marshall, 57, 154
Fitzgerald, Oscar P., 40, 87, 89–91
Fitzhugh, George, 79
Flags: American, 19, 29, 176, 182; Confederate, 20, 28–29, 176, 182
Foley, T. H., 19
Forrest, Nathan Bedford, 57, 112, 169
Fort Sumter, South Carolina, 4
Frazer, Donald, 41
Fulton, John, 145
Funerals, 28, 33, 39, 51

Gailor, Thomas F., 150, 168–72
Galloway, Charles B., 109
Gambrell, James: and New South, 91, 94, 96; defends South, 103, 110. See also World War I
Gardner, William F., 143
Gaston, Paul, 81
Geertz, Clifford, 10–11, 24
Germany, 171–72, 175
Gettysburg, battle of, 125
Gilbert, J. L., 74
Gilmer, A. H., 105
Girardeau, John L., 66, 73–74, 76
Goodloe, Albert T., 46, 102
Goodwin, R. A., 39, 70, 76, 166
Gordon, George B., 112
Gordon, John B., 112
Gorgas, Josiah, 148
Granberry, John C., 130
Grand Army of the Republic, 30
Greeks, ancient, 22, 31–32, 39
Green, William, 54
Griffith, D. W., 115
Grimes, I. W., 47

Hamill, Howard M., 90, 92–93, 105, 106, 141
Hampden Sydney College, 21, 85
Hampton, Wade, 157
Harper's Ferry, 105–6
Harris, George C., 44, 46
Harrison, George P., 180
Harrison, William, 102
Haxton, Llewellyn, 143
Herberg, Will, 12
Hill, Daniel Harvey, 19

Hill, Samuel S., 7–8, 11, 15–16
Hillyer, S. G., 72
History, Christian interpretation of, 73
Hoge, Moses Drury, 40, 42, 64; and Confederate defeat, 70, 74. See also Monuments
Hoge, Peyton, 31, 177
Hollywood Cemetery, 18, 51, 137
Hornady, H. C., 71
Howe, W. B. C., 67, 76, 102
Hymns: Confederate, 26; Lost Cause, 31; World War I, 176

Iconography, of Lost Cause, 25
Interdenominationalism: of Southern churches, 9, 33–34; of Lost Cause, 9, 33–34, 160. See also Revivalism
Israelites: compared to Confederates, 39, 43, 71, 72, 166

Jackson, A. N., 162
Jackson, Julia, 24, 157
Jackson, Stonewall: dying words of, 27; as model, 48, 87; as prophet-warrior, 51–52; relationship with J. William Jones, 120, 127–28; prewar career of, 152
Jefferson, Thomas, 3
Jeremiad, concept of, 79–82, 94–99
Jesus Christ: compared to Confederacy, 24–25, 71–72, 75; compared to Confederates, 31, 44–45, 51, 56; relationship to Lost Cause, 33, 135; compared to postwar Southerners, 63; and Woodrow Wilson, 177–78
Jeter, Jeremiah Bell, 140
Jews, 33–34
Job, book of, 72
Johnston, Joseph E., 6, 156
Johnston, William Preston, 66
Jones, Carter Helm, 42, 45, 134, 137, 168
Jones, J. William, 33, 43–44, 50–52, 119–38 passim, 155. See also Confederacy, Education
Jones, John, 66
Jones, Mary, 62
Jones, Sam, 35

Kemper, James L., 19, 21
Kinsolving, Arthur, 143
Kirby Smith, Edmund, 89, 148–50
Ku Klux Klan, 100–101, 110–18, 182

Lacy, B. T., 5
Latimore, T. B., 45
Lee, George Washington Custis, 155
Lee, Robert E.: as saint, 25, 172; com-
   pared to George Washington, 40;
   compared to Jesus Christ, 45, 123,
   128; as Christian knight, 48–49; and
   jeremiad, 82; postwar career of, 90,
   120–21, 143, 152, 154–55; death of,
   122, 155–56; as national hero, 159
Lee, Susan Pendleton, 141
Lee Memorial Association, 156
Lévi-Strauss, Claude, 29
Lexington, Virginia, 62, 121–22, 152–
   53, 155, 158
Liberty, concept of, 38, 164–66, 173–74
Lincoln, Abraham, 4, 181
Lincoln-Lee Legion, 87
Little, Robert, 81
Louisiana Lottery Company, 88–90, 97

McBryde, R. J., 157
McDaniel, George, 173–74
McGlothlin, W. J., 179
McIlwaine, Richard, 66, 145
McKeethen, Betsy, 104–5
McKim, Randolph, 33, 39, 41, 49, 164–
   65. See also Confederacy, World
   War I
Maclachlin, H. D. C., 93, 165
McNeely, James H., 40–41, 46, 71, 141;
   and New South, 90, 94–95; and Ku
   Klux Klan, 110–13; and Spanish-
   American War, 163; and Southern re-
   ligion, 94, 167
Magnum, A. W., 85
Mahone, William, 92
Marty, Martin E., 122
Masters, Victor I., 98, 166–67
Mead, Sidney E., 12
Memorial Day: Confederate, 28, 33, 36,
   93; American, 176
Methodists, Southern: formation of, 2,

4; postwar growth of, 8, 98; role in
   Lost Cause, 35; and Southern Review,
   84; and sectionalism, 161; and World
   War I, 174–77
Millennialism, 2, 64
Miller, Perry, 79–80, 82, 94, 97
Monument Boulevard, Richmond, Vir-
   ginia, 29
Monuments, Confederate: to Stonewall
   Jackson, 18–24, 128, 157; to Jefferson
   Davis, 19, 29, 133, 137; to Con-
   federacy, 29, 170; to Robert E. Lee,
   34, 156–57; Inscriptions on, 41; to
   Sam Davis, 53; at Chickamauga, 55;
   to blacks, 105; at Stone Mountain,
   116; at Shiloh, 172; at Arlington,
   180–81
Moore, T. V., 45
Mount Olivet Cemetery, 93
Murray, Henry A., 38
Mythology, concept of, 38–39

Nashville, Tennessee, 31–32, 34, 111
Nelson, C. K., 56
New South movement, 38, 79, 84–85;
   critics of, 81–82, 90, 95; and segrega-
   tion, 101
Newspapers, denominational, 34
New Testament, 127
Newton, John C. Calhoun, 86, 94
Nicholls, Francis, 89

Old South, myth of, 13, 37, 84, 87, 92,
   95
Old Testament, 25, 51–52, 71, 79, 127
Owen, B. A., 31, 162, 168

Packard, Joseph, 172
Page, Thomas Nelson, 144, 158
Palmer, Benjamin Morgan, 66, 74, 83,
   158
Paris, John, 106, 108, 110
Patterson, Malcolm, 53
Pendleton, William Nelson, 62–63, 73,
   76, 153, 154, 156
Phillips, Wendell, 152
Polk, Leonidas, 54–55, 104, 141, 145
Polk, William M., 55

Pollard, Edward A., 7, 126
Populism, 91
Prayers, 31
Presbyterians, Southern: sectional division of, 2, 4, 161; and slavery, 103; and blacks, 108; and immigrants, 167; and World War I. *See also* Confederacy, Washington and Lee University
Preston, Randolph, 153, 155
Prohibition, 87–88
Pro-slavery argument, 4, 79, 103–4
Pulaski, Tennessee, 111, 113
Puritanism: New England, 2, 12, 79–82, 85, 94, 97; Southern, 44, 52

Quintard, Charles T., 55, 66, 146–47

Race, concept of, 11–12, 100–101, 114, 116–18, 167
Reconstruction: myth of, 13, 37, 110, 114–15; and postwar problems, 42, 62, 83, 88, 101, 140
Renfro, Henry C., 72
Revelation, book of, 63–65
Revivalism: Great Revival (1787–1805), 2; in Confederacy, 6–7, 121, 130–32; tradition of, 12–13; postwar, 34, 35, 98, 120, 122
Richmond, Virginia, 18–21, 29, 34, 136–37, 174
Richmond College, 20, 156
Rittenhouse, J. M., 108
Romanticism: European, 3; Southern, 38, 51, 59; Christian, 48
Roosevelt, Theodore, 151, 169
Rouse, Charles Broadway, 136
Ryan, Abram, 25, 58–61, 112, 157

St. Paul's Episcopal Church, Richmond, Virginia, 25, 35
Sandell, J. W., 64–65
Schorer, Mark, 38
Scomp, H. A., 87–88
Sessums, David, 151
Sewanee, Tennessee, 145–51
Sewanee Review, 150–51
Shaver, D., 61

Shepherd, Heyward, 105–6
Sherman, William, 40, 168
Shoup, Francis Asbury, 148
Silver, James W., 5
Simmons, William J., 115–16
Slavery, 4, 10, 68–69, 102–4, 106
Slotkin, Richard, 38
Smith, George, 102
Smith, H. Shelton, 101
South Carolina, 3–4
Southern Baptist Theological Seminary, 120, 122
Southern Historical Society, 123–24, 136, 140
Southern Historical Society Papers, 123, 140
Southern identity, 1, 36, 80, 97–99, 118
Southern Methodist Publishing House, 34, 53
Southern Publicity Association, 116
Southern Way of Life, 12, 100, 119, 135, 138–39
Spanish-American War, 38, 161–63
States' rights, principle of, 65, 164–65
Stephenson, P. D., 43, 165
Stickler, G. B., 158
Stone, Cornelia Branch, 32
Stonewall Jackson Institute, 144
Stratton, Joseph B., 83
Swanson, Claude A., 29

Tardy, W. T., 111
Taylor, Hannis, 60–61
Taylor, William, 3
Textbooks, 125–26, 139, 141
Thanksgiving Day, 28, 61, 176
Thornwell, James H., 5
Tichenor, I. T., 6
Trent, William P., 160
Trinity Church, Portsmouth, Virginia, 25

Underwood, John L., 46–47, 111, 136–37
Union Gospel Tabernacle, 31
Unitarianism, 3
United Confederate Choirs, 27, 180, 182

United Confederate Veterans: organized, 30, 162; reunions of, 30–32, 116, 132–33, 179–82; Chaplains' Association of, 31; Memorial Services of, 31, 33, 35, 179–80; Historical Committee of, 140

United Daughters of the Confederacy: and Lost Cause ritual, 25–26, 32–33; and Lost Cause heroes, 51, 149, 169; and black monument, 105; and Confederate history, 140–41, 144; and education, 156; organized, 162

United Sons of Confederate Veterans, 30, 162, 168

University of the South, 89, 145–52, 169

Valentine, Edward C., 156

Vance, James I., 26, 47, 75, 76

Vanderbilt University, 31

Virginia, 2, 13, 124, 141, 152, 174

Virginia Military Institute, 122, 152, 155

Virtue, concept of Southern, 8, 13, 16–17, 28, 37–38, 44, 56, 104, 165, 170; women and, 46; after Civil War, 81–82, 86, 90, 93, 100, 106, 120, 179; attack on, 141; national virtue and, 162; and World War I, 172–74

Waddell, DeB., 46

Wallace, Anthony F. C., 10–11, 24, 30

Waller, C. D., 144

Warner, Charles Dudley, 151

Warner, W. Lloyd, 29

Warren, Robert Penn, 16

Washington, George, 40, 152, 154

Washington and Lee University, 83, 121, 151–60

Weaver, Richard M., 3

Wharton, Henry M., 45, 65, 141

White, Edward, 182

White, Henry A., 49, 52, 152

White House of the Confederacy, 18, 26

White supremacy. See Race

William, Mrs. Charles, 28

Wilmer, J. P. B., 55, 70, 83, 150

Wilmer, Richard, 42, 62, 86, 102–3, 108, 146

Wilson, John, 14

Wilson, Woodrow, 115, 176–80, 182

Winchester, James R., 53

Winkler, Edwin T., 153

Women: and Confederate myth, 46–48; and education, 143, 149

Woodward, C. Vann, 81, 95

World War I, 38, 81, 161, 171–82

Yankee: as symbol of evil, 24–25, 40–41, 47–48, 57, 63–64, 81

Young Men's Christian Association, 120, 122–23, 155